PRENTICE-HALL
FOUNDATIONS OF MODERN SOCIOLOGY SERIES

PRENTICE-HALL
FOUNDATIONS OF MODERN SOCIOLOGY SERIES

Alex Inkeles, Editor

SOCIAL PROBLEMS

AMITAI ETZIONI

*Columbia University
and
the Center for Policy Research*

Prentice-Hall, Inc., Englewood Cliffs, New Jersey

Library of Congress Cataloging in Publication Data

Etzioni, Amitai.
    Social problems.

    (Prentice-Hall foundations of modern sociology
series)
    Includes bibliographical references and index.
    1. United States—Social conditions—1960—
2. Social problems. 3. Sociology—Methodology.
4. Social policy. I. Title.
HN65.E88   309.1′73′092   75-38703
ISBN 0-13-817411-3
ISBN 0-13-817403-2 pbk.

© 1976 by Prentice-Hall, Inc., Englewood Cliffs, New Jersey

Printed in the United States of America

10 9 8 7 6 5 4 3 2 1

Prentice-Hall International, Inc., London
Prentice-Hall of Australia Pty. Limited, Sydney
Prentice-Hall of Canada, Ltd., Toronto
Prentice-Hall of India Private Limited, New Delhi
Prentice-Hall of Japan, Inc., Tokyo
Prentice-Hall of Southeast Asia Pte. Ltd., Singapore

CONTENTS

CHAPTER 4

GOAL SETTING, 79

CHAPTER 5

ORGANIZATION, 102

CHAPTER 6

POWER, 123

CHAPTER 7

CONSENSUS, 148

PREFACE

Most books about social problems focus on their sources, patterns, and consequences. They ask, quite properly, why and how has a particular problem arisen? Does it affect an entire society or merely some segments of it: the poor but not the rich, blacks but not whites, the South but not the North? How detrimental are its consequences for indivduals affected as well as society as a whole? Although we are also concerned with these questions, our primary emphasis is different. We ask what are the basic factors which underlie specific social problems, and, how does our understanding of these factors enable us to analyze the strengths and weaknesses of programs designed to overcome various social problems?

Thus, a given power structure in society, a society's particular mode of planning (or lack of planning), a change in the values members subscribe to, a rise in knowledge, an improvement in administration and other such factors are viewed, first, as forces that can serve to explain the sources of specific social problems from poverty to alcoholism, from pollution to discrimination. Next, an understanding of these factors explains why some problems are likely to be more resistant than others to efforts to overcome them and why some social endeavors and public policies are more effective than others. For social problems to recede, if not to be overcome, it is necessary for the underlying forces to be turned, at least partially, to the service of social change; i.e. that power be mobilized on the side of the corrective efforts, that adequate planning be accomplished, that commitment to the values inspiring the attempts to bring about change be high, and so on. It is our thesis that anyone who will become familiar with these underlying factors will be able to understand better and deal better with social problems of all sorts, whether they are discussed here or not or, indeed, whether they are conditions presently confronting society or yet to appear.

This book is best used in conjunction with one or more books of the more descriptive type or with a variety of smaller monographs and other source material on specific problems. Its aim is to provide an analytic perspective for those who will acquire descriptive details elsewhere. Because it is also intended for use by teachers and students from a variety of backgrounds, the book opens with a review of the perspectives offered by the major contemporary schools of thought, including structural-functionalism, the conflict-alienation approach, ethnomethodology, and the neoconservative orientation. This overview is in turn followed by a presentation of the author's approach, whose development has greatly benefited from the existing volume of work and thought. Although the illustrative references in the volume are to contemporary American problems, the approaches advanced and the forces identified seem relevant to any society.

AMITAI ETZIONI
Professor of Sociology,
Columbia University and
Director, the Center
for Policy Research

CHAPTER 1
THE MAIN
APPROACHES

Most of us would probably agree that drug abuse is a social problem, whereas driving a car hardly qualifies. Yet, in 1968, the most recent year for which official statistics are available, accidental poisoning by drugs (including heroin, barbiturates, opiates, tranquilizers, sleeping pills, and aspirin) caused 1,692 deaths in the United States, whereas in 1970, automobile accidents killed about 55,000 Americans, more than died in 20 years of war in Southeast Asia. Each year, drugs damage the health of thousands of persons, whereas those injured by automobiles number in the millions. Drivers cause personal and property damage totaling billions of dollars each year. Heroin uses up poppies, a not invaluable resource, but automobiles consume billions of dollars worth of scarce natural resources. In addition, automobiles require highways that destroy nature and neighborhoods and pollute cities.

The point of all this is not that automobiles are a social problem or that drug abuse is not, but that the criteria for deciding what is a social problem are not as self-evident as they may at first seem. Actually, an examination of the sociological literature on the subject reveals a great variety of definitions of what constitutes a social problem and rather different lists of society's major current problems. Some sociologists consider strikes to be a social problem because they represent a "dangerous concentration of power in the hands of one group," whereas others view the alienation of powerless workers as a social problem; some see a problem in the rising divorce rate, whereas others are disturbed by society's insistence that an "unnatural" monogamy be legally enforced; some point to the menace of the population explosion, and others to abortion as a decline in morality. Moreover, behind these differences in definition lie diverse perspectives regarding (1) the extent to which social problems may be overcome and society improved and (2) the ways in which this can be done. We shall next introduce the major issues confronted by these differing approaches to social problems and then discuss briefly the way in which each of the main approaches address these issues.

THREE MAJOR ISSUES

The three major issues faced by students of social problems are:

1. What is societal reality made of? Can it be recast?
2. What are the basic qualities of human nature? Is it benign or evil? Is it set early in life or can it be later modified?
3. Where are the levers that must be moved in order to alter existing social conditions?

Societal Reality

What are the qualities of the societal world in which social problems appear and in which efforts to correct them are made? Is the social element pliable or resistant? Is its existence primarily *subjective*; that is, does it exist chiefly "in the mind," as a matter of definitions, thoughts, sentiments, meanings, and values? For example, would marijuana use or homosexuality cease to be social problems if we ceased to view them as problematic? Or are our problems rooted in *objective* conditions, such as the shortage of resources, the overabundance of human beings, or the amassing of goods by the few to the deprivation of the many?

Human Nature

Are people inherently "good" and naturally inclined to live in harmony with one another? Are social problems therefore caused by institutions or social conditions that corrupt people and distort human nature? Or are people inherently "evil" beings who would prey on one another like wolves were it not for the restraining influence of social institutions? Is it the *weakening* of these institutions that gives rise to social problems? Or, taking still another view, can human nature be molded quite freely according to the prevailing social expectations, with problems appearing mainly when these expectations are unclear or mutually conflicting?

Dynamics

What levers can be applied to deal with social problems? Education? Communication? Persuasion? A more egalitarian distribution of resources?

Institutional reform? Revolution? Abolition of taboos? Personal liberation? And how competent are we in analyzing the causes of our social problems, formulating the corrective measures, and then *acting* on this knowledge? The different answers to these questions are the subject not only of sociology but also of social philosophy and ideology. They have been of interest to many an intellectual person and concerned citizen and have been the subject of lengthy deliberation by sociology's founding fathers and by many contemporary social scientists. Needless to say, we cannot explore these issues in depth here; rather our purpose is to sketch them in broad outline. Fuller discussion of these matters can be found in the works cited throughout this chapter.

THE MAIN APPROACHES

For convenience of presentation, the many answers to these questions are divided into four groupings: (1) the consensus and structural-functional approaches; (2) the conflict or alienation approaches; (3) symbolic interactionism and ethnomethodology; and (4) neoconservatism. We cannot stress enough that followers of these approaches are not rigidly united by homogeneity of thought. Each scholar has his or her position, which differs from others who follow the same basic approach, and there are, in addition, significant subgroupings. The main groupings help primarily to organize the discussion and no one who is interested in more than an introduction to the field should use them as a substitute for the study of each individual scholar. Moreover, one must take into account that even individual scholars often change their approach during a lifetime. For instance, quite a few of the contemporary neoconservatives were liberals and functionalists in the 1960s and subscribed to the alienation approach in the 1930s and early 1940s. Similarly, a scholar may change his or her position between publications of the same period. Hence, the classification by approach is meant to serve as an axis around which to organize major contemporary works. As a device for classifying individuals, it should be used with great restraint.

The Consensus and Structural-Functional Approaches

Societal Reality: According to the consensus approach, a significant element of societal reality is largely whatever the persons who constitute it define it to be. An often cited definition of social problems, in this context, is: Social problems are "what people think they are."[1] I.e., "A situation which is perceived by some group as a source of dissatisfaction

1. Richard C. Fuller and Richard R. Myers, "The Natural History of a Social Problem," *American Sociology,* 6 (1941), 320.

for its members and in which preferable alternatives are recognized so that the group, or individuals in the group, are motivated to effect some change."[2] The authors add that the problem is social (rather than, say, geological) because its causes are assumed to be social rather than natural.

Thus, according to this approach, a condition counts as a social problem if many people agree that it is a problem. If just one person or even a few persons perceive something as a problem, it does not qualify; however, if they succeed in convincing others, it eventually might. The exact number of people who must be both troubled by a problem *and* hopeful of solving it before the problem qualifies as "social" has been the subject of considerable discussion. Some assert that those troubled must make up a "sizeable proportion of the population."[3] Others believe that "a significant number of people—or a number of significant people—must agree both that this condition violates an accepted value or standard, and that it should be eliminated, resolved, or remedied."[4]

Arnold Rose makes the point that the "relevant public" varies from society to society, although, historically, an elite group often played a key role in defining a situation as problematic.[5] The elite may have been intellectual (for example, John Steinbeck called attention to the plight of the migrant workers), political (President John F. Kennedy and President Lyndon B. Johnson "rediscovered" poverty), or religious (Reverend Martin Luther King, Jr., focused attention on the problems of the black community). In contemporary society, consensus about a problematic condition can also result from the proselytizing efforts of a social movement (for example, student protestors), and not necessarily an elite.

Although people may differ greatly as to the relative "priority" or saliency they attribute to a problem, they tend—due to the influences of nationwide educational, political, and media factors—to recognize more or less the same set of problems. At any given time, some problems are viewed by many as severe, whereas other problems are considered to be minor.[6]

Although all who subscribe to the consensus approach see great significance in what members of a society define as problematic, they

2. Irving Tallman and Reese McGee, "Definition of a Social Problem," in *Handbook on the Study of Social Problems*, ed. Erwin O. Smigel (Chicago: Rand McNally, 1971), p. 41.

3. Paul B. Horton and Gerald R. Leslie, *The Sociology of Social Problems*, 5th ed. (Englewood Cliffs, N.J.: Prentice-Hall, 1974), p. 4.

4. Joseph Julian, *Social Problems* (Englewood Cliffs, N.J.: Prentice-Hall, 1973), p. 9.

5. Arnold Rose, "History and Sociology of Study of Social Problems," in *Handbook for the Study of Social Problems*, ed. Smigel, p. 4.

6. William Watts and Lloyd A. Free, eds., *State of the Nation, 1974* (Washington, D.C.: Potomac Associates, 1974).

differ in the ultimate degree of subjectivity they attribute to a social problem. On the highly subjective side, the problem is seen as having no other existence apart from people's hopes and fears. Thus, if nobody worried about gambling or prostitution and learned to tolerate or accept these as merely "different" modes of behavior, then they would cease to be social problems. Moreover, technically at least, rampant poverty, either going unnoticed or seen as an "inevitable" part of the way things are, is not a social problem by this approach.

Other members of the consensus school see a mixture of subjective *and* objective forces at work. As Joseph Julian phrases it, "the critical point is that for a social problem to exist, there must be both an 'objective' and a 'subjective' element. The objective part is the condition itself, the subjective part is the belief that the condition should be changed."[7] Thus, according to this variant, alcoholism is a social problem for two reasons: (1) because people see the conduct involved as problematic and as violating their perceptions of what is proper and "normal"; *and* (2) because alcoholics cannot fulfill their social roles effectively and thereby cause social *damage* to their families, to themselves, and to strangers driving on the same road.

According to the structural-functional approach brought to the social problems area by Robert K. Merton and Robert A. Nisbet, a social problem exists wherever there is a significant discrepancy between social standards and societal reality.[8] A social problem manifests itself when one or more of a society's needs, as observed by social scientists, is not met or when its continued fulfillment is threatened. Typically, members of the society are aware of this condition, but they may not be.[9] Thus, problems are not "accidental" or due to ill will; their roots lie in the neglect of one or more basic societal needs.

Moreover, societal definitions of right and wrong, of acceptable versus intolerable, are not arbitrary or random—that is, it is not just that, as in the consensus view, some people "feel like" being troubled by, say, the youth rebellion or inflation. The norms society seeks to uphold are

7. Julian, *Social Problems*, pp. 9–10.

8. See Introduction, "The Study of Social Problems" and Epilogue, "Social Problems and Sociological Theory" in *Contemporary Social Problems*, 3rd ed., ed. Robert K. Merton and Robert A. Nisbet (New York: Harcourt Brace Jovanovich, 1971), pp. 1–28, 793–845.

9. Functionalists differ in opinion on the question of the universality of societal needs. Do all societies have the same functional prerequisites, as Talcott Parsons assumes (*The Social System*. New York: Free Press, 1951) or do they perhaps have varying ones, a possibility Merton raised ("Manifest and Latent Functions," in *Social Theory and Social Structure*. New York: Free Press, 1968)? Estimates differ as well concerning the range and degree of "deviance" (that is, individual violation of norms) and "dysfunction" (that is, structural strain) a society can tolerate. But all use a standard derived from theory to define problems, rather than relying on societal participants' converging perceptions.

its particular answer to the environmental and internal challenges the society must cope with if it is to survive and preserve its particular structure intact. Thus, if the young will not accept their elders' and society's prescribed role specifications, say, of getting married and having children or the necessity of work, then the society will either collapse or its structure will have to be changed radically.

Human Nature: Both consensus theorists and structural-functionalists tend to see human nature as highly pliable. Although persons are viewed as having a set of physiological needs, these needs can be satisfied in a very large variety of ways. And the greater part of human behavior is motivated by socially acquired needs, such as those for money and power, which are inculcated in the young through the socialization process.[10] As Alex Inkeles put it:

> Man's "original nature" is seen largely in neutral terms, as neither good nor bad. It is, rather, a potential for development, and the extent to which the potential is realized depends on the time and society into which a man is born and on his distinctive place in it. If it does not quite treat him as a "tabula rasa," modern sociology nevertheless, regards man as a flexible form which can be given all manner of content.
>
> "Socialization," the process of learning one's culture while growing out of infant and childhood dependency, leads to internalization of society's values and goals. People come to want to do what from the point of view of society they must do. Man is, therefore, seen, in his inner being, as mainly moral, by and large, accepting and fulfilling the demands society makes on him.[11]

According to structural-functional theory, individuals learn from their culture not only what aspirations to have and what needs other than purely physical to experience; they are also taught that certain means of achieving desired goals are legitimate, while others are not. Social problems are generated when, as in contemporary American society, large numbers of lower-class individuals are socialized to the goals and aspirations of the dominant culture (via TV at least), but when inequality of opportunity prevents access to culturally approved means of attaining these goals. These individuals may react by finding illegitimate means to reach these goals (for example, drug pushing) or by giving up their aspirations and "retreating" into alcoholism and drug addiction.[12]

10. Kingsley Davis, *Human Society* (New York: Macmillan, 1949), pp. 195–233.

11. Alex Inkeles, *What is Sociology?* (Englewood Cliffs, N.J.: Prentice-Hall, 1964), p. 50.

12. For examples of structural-functional explanations of juvenile delinquency in terms of adequate socialization to cultural goals but inadequate access to legitimate means, see Albert K. Cohen, *Delinquent Boys* (New York: Free Press, 1955), and Richard A. Cloward and Lloyd E. Ohlin, *Delinquency and Opportunity* (New York: Free Press, 1960). For theoretical base, see Robert K. Merton, "Social Structure and Anomie" in *Social Theory and Social Structure* (New York: Free Press, 1960).

Dynamics: Consensus theorists have no explicit statement about the specific ways in which social problems may be overcome, other than by pointing to factors that enhance consensus building (see Chapter 7). Or they draw their "dynamics" from the structural-functionalists. The structural-functional approach tends to perceive the main source of social problems in technical failures of the social system; that is, in ad hoc aberrations in the social equilibrium, which are expected to occur occasionally in any system of interrelated but heterogeneous parts. In principle, society is expected to be able to generate the vectors that will correct the imbalances, just as the body of a person who is ill mobilizes forces to overcome the illness, usually successfully. Such social "dysfunctions" may cause individual deviant behavior ranging from alcoholism to stealing. And these disturbances in the social order may render problematic the successful attainment of collective goals. The forces of education and policing, broadly conceived ("socialization" and "social control" in the sociological parlance), are the corrective vectors. Only a few structural-functionalists postulate that to maintain a society and resolve its social problems, its entire societal pattern may first need to undergo transformation.[13]

On the level of individual behavior, a well-functioning society is seen as having a relatively clear set of norms and role expectations to which newborn children are "socialized." If there is inadequate or inappropriate socialization, the child is likely to grow up to join a problem population. For example, he may become mentally ill, a juvenile delinquent, a homosexual, a "marginal man," and so forth.

Such a failure in socialization can occur in any of the following ways: (1) the socialization process is incomplete or defective (for example, the parents are not available or neglect the child, or the schools function chiefly to keep the children off the streets and out of the labor market rather than to educate them); (2) socialization is divided against itself (for example, the parents come from different class, ethnic, religious, or racial backgrounds, or immigrant parents have a culture that differs from that of their children's school, or the poor and those discriminated against racially are socialized to middle-class aspirations, but to lower-class behavioral norms and methods of making it); or (3) the individual may be effectively socialized, but into a deviant or deprived subculture (for example, the socialization of the habitual runaway into crime through his detainment with juvenile delinquents in youth shelters).[14]

---

13. Amitai Etzioni, *The Active Society* (New York: Free Press, 1968), pp. 78–83; Francesca Cancian, "Functional Analysis of Change," *American Sociological Review*, 25:6 (1960), 818–826.

14. Among the writings that advance one or another of these arguments are Robert E. Faris, *Social Disorganization* (New York: Ronald Press, 1948); W. I. Thomas and F. Znaniecki, *The Polish Peasant in Europe and America* (New York: Knopf, 1927);

In addition, an effectively socialized person needs to be rewarded for achievements and punished for lack of performance. This is the function of social control. If the flow of these rewards and punishments is interrupted, social problems will arise. For example, if the flow of financial incentives and rewards is disrupted by economic crisis, people may riot. Similarly, failure to punish an offense or insufficient punishment encourages further deviance and eventual social breakdown.

The correctives are seen to lie in strengthening or repairing existing socialization and control processes and in resocializing or rehabilitating deviants. From this stems the interest in finding ways to lessen the divorce rate (broken homes provide poor socialization), in founding settlement houses in slums (for resocialization of deviants), in the Americanization of schools in immigrant neighborhoods (in order to avoid conflicting socialization), in providing psychotherapy for the neurotic and for homosexuals, and in strengthening social control correctives (for example, utilization of peer-group sanctions to advance a program to overcome drug abuse, such as Synanon or Alcoholics Anonymous).

Note that, by and large, the structural-functionalists view, not society, but individual and family pathology, deviant subcultures, or deficient educational institutions as the source of problematic behavior. However, a number of the structural-functionalists (among them Robert K. Merton and Richard A. Cloward) have pointed out that the "opportunity structure" of society may generate a great deal of deviant behavior. For example, when the society stresses economic success, but prevents minorities from being successful by closing legitimate economic avenues by discriminating against minority groups in the area of jobs and credit, deviant behavior may result.

The overall stance toward resolution of social problems conveyed by both consensus theorists and structural-functionalists is one of optimism. The consensus branch is optimistic because it focuses on what seem to be a highly malleable aspects of societal reality—attitudes and values. The structural-functionalists study changes in social structure and values from the viewpoint of their compatability with the society's basic needs. Thus, a society whose members would agree that having children is not "in" obviously would not survive very long. The structural-functional optimism stems from what they perceive to be the great flexibility of individuals to adapt their personalities to their societal environment and from the conviction that society possesses built-in self-correcting tendencies. Structural-functionalists thus believe that social

Marshall Clinard, *Sociology of Deviant Behavior* (New York: Holt, Rinehart & Winston, 1957); Cohen, *Delinquent Boys*; Walter B. Miller, "Lower-Class Culture as a Generating Milieu of Gang Delinquency," *Journal of Social Issues*, 14:3 (1958), 5–19.

problems can often be corrected through adjustment, rather than through complete transformation of the society.

The Conflict or Alienation Approaches

These approaches have long been viewed as the main alternative to the consensus and structural-functionalist approaches in the study of social problems. (Recently, symbolic interactionism, ethnomethodology, and neoconservatism have been gaining in prominence.) The contrast is often phrased in terms of consensus versus conflict sociology, or functional-structural-functionalism versus alienation, although a number of theorists have suggested that the two approaches are not necessarily incompatible, and various combinations of both have been applied to the study of social problems.[15]

Societal Reality: The conflict school locates the source of most social problems in the existence of "illegitimate social control and exploitation."[16] C. Wright Mills distinguished "personal troubles" from "issues of social structure" by attributing the former to individual character and interpersonal relations and the latter—more serious issues—to the institutional arrangements and contradictions.[17] Although the structural-functionalists also point to social structure as an important source of social problems, their concept of "dysfunction" as a failure in the working of the social system tends to focus on specific conditions that affect particular subsections of society—for instance, poor housing, unemployment, race prejudice—rather than on grand distortions of the overall structure. In contrast, the conflict approach tends to see specific problems as the hydra-headed manifestations of a pervasive condition—such as capitalism. And it often views "contradictions" or fundamental strains and conflicts within the social structure, not as temporary dysfunctions subject to remedy by reform, but as evidence of the "inevitable unfolding of self-destructive tendencies," whose consequences will be overcome only after the total situation has been fundamentally changed.

Similarly, although the consensus approach sees *a* society, within which problems arise, the conflict approach stresses that the very concept

15. Merton, *Social Theory and Social Structure*, pp. 91–100; Gerhard E. Lenski, *Power and Privilege: A Theory of Social Stratification* (New York: McGraw-Hill, 1966), pp. 14–22; Herbert J. Gans, *More Equality* (New York: Pantheon, 1973), pp. xi–xix.

16. John Horton, "Order and Conflict Theories of Social Problems," in *Radical Perspectives on Social Problems*, ed. Frank Lindenfeld (New York: Macmillan, 1968), p. 41.

17. C. Wright Mills and Hans Gerth, *Character and Social Structure: The Psychology of Social Institutions* (New York: Harcourt Brace Jovanovich, 1953), *passim*.

of "a society" (implying a community in the name of which all members may be asked to make sacrifices for higher collective goals) has no existence except as a tool for those in power. It is an ideological fig leaf behind which the powerful can conceal the naked self-aggrandizing thrust and pass it off as essential to the good of the whole. To conflict theorists, "class" rather than "society" is the central fact of social life. Conflict theorists recognize no, or only a weak, society-wide *collective conscience* in Emile Durkheim's sense of shared values and a feeling of belonging. Instead, there are the interests and consciousness of classes in strife with each other. That is, similar values and sense of a common fate unite all who stand in the same relation to the bases of power and authority, which may be political as well as economic.[18] This struggle pits the propertyless and powerless against the owners and the mighty. To the extent that there appear to be society-wide values and bonds, such as "national unity," these are seen as a "false consciousness" fostered by the ruling class to deflect workers' attention from their true interests. This school tends to hold that classes in reality cut across "societies," with workers everywhere being members of the same proletariat, while all capitalists belong to a transnational bourgeoisie. The multinational corporations are but a recent expression of this fact.

Conflict theorists assert that contemporary societal reality is created out of the dynamics of class struggle. Classes with unalterably opposed "objective interests" compete for control of scarce resources and the fruits of labor. Under capitalism, the bourgeoisie controls the means of production and the state and hence monopolizes the product of the industrial machinery, doling out some of it to members of other classes.

Hence, conflict theorists such as Norman Birnbaum and Alvin Gouldner perceive social problems as disguised political issues. There is nothing "abnormal" about social problems. They are the natural children of capitalistic economic structure and power relations. In the case of some social problems, this link is quite evident: crime is not caused by the mugger, but by the social, economic, and political structure that deprives him of a decent standard of living; alcoholism is an escape workers resort to instead of facing their true enemies—their exploiter and the social tensions generated by routinized work. In the case of other social problems, the link is not as evident, but the general approach nevertheless applies. Thus, Irving L. Horowitz points out that deviant behavior arises out of political issues whose true nature is veiled by society's treatment of them according to a "therapeutic model". For

18. C. Wright Mills, *The Power Elite* (New York: Oxford University Press, 1956); Gabriel Kolko, *Roots of American Foreign Policy: An Analysis of Power Purpose* (Boston: Beacon Press, 1969); G. William Domhoff, *The Higher Circles: The Governing Classes in America* (New York: Random House, 1971).

instance, society views homosexuals as sick persons to be made to adapt to a socially prescribed heterosexual ("normal") role, instead of taking action to abolish the discriminating laws.[19]

Social problems are the result of a system in which the few exploit the many, amass privileges, and establish a market economy. This competitive "fetishism of commodities" creates an object-dominated world and generates a productive machine that oppresses those it allegedly serves—ultimately even its founders and owners. Thus, according to Marx, in the period of history under capitalism,

> everything, which up to now has been considered as inalienable, is sold as objects of exchange, of chaffering. It is the time in which objects, which earlier have been conveyed, but never exchanged, have been given away, but never offered for sale, have been acquired, but never been bought: virtue, love, conviction, knowledge, consciousness and so on, the time which, in a word, everything has been transformed into a commercial commodity. It is the time of general corruption, of universal bribery or, in the language of economics, it is the time when each object, physical as well as moral, is put on the market as an object of exchange to be taxed at its correct value.[20]

This dehumanization is a root of our social problems. They arise from the transformation of everything previously valued as an end in itself, including man himself, into an instrumentality, an exchange value, a thing to be traded for other things on the market. No satisfying interpersonal relation or acceptance of self is possible in such a world.[21]

Those taking the alienation approach differ greatly in the extent to which they accept the Marxist theoretical framework.. Some may merely borrow one or more of his concepts, whereas others are interested in alienation and conflict without being Marxist at all. Thus, on the question of what shapes society's structures and problems, rigid Marxists tend to stress the "real," objective factors, while many conflicts or alienation theorists hold that subjective factors, such as ideas, sentiments, values, and psychological predispositions, play a somewhat greater role.

Also, many who use, and use productively, the concept of *alienation* —for instance, Melvin Seeman[22]—and correlate it with various personality

19. Irving L. Horowitz, *Professing Sociology* (Chicago: Aldine, 1968), pp. 108–126. For a case study of another social problem from this viewpoint, see Harry D. Krause, *Illegitimacy, Law, and Social Policy* (Indianapolis, Ind.: Bobbs-Merrill, 1971).

20. Karl Marx quoted in Joachim Israel, *Alienation* (Boston: Allyn & Bacon, 1971), p. 44.

21. Karl Marx, "Alienated Labor," in *Man Alone: Alienation in Modern Society*, ed. Eric and Mary Josephson (New York: Dell, 1962), p. 95.

22. Melvin Seeman, "Alienation, Membership and Political Knowledge: A Comparative Study," *Public Opinion Quarterly*, 30 (1966), 353–367.

disorders,[23] do not endorse all or even part of the sociological, philosophical, or ideological implications the term has for Marxists.

Above all, some conflict theorists maintain that conflict often occurs between collectivities that are not necessarily classes—for example, ethnic groups, races, or regional groupings. Even when conflict does occur between classes, these groups may be based on social status or power, not necessarily on economic factors,[24] and the pattern of conflict may well involve a large variety of patterns.

Human Nature: The purists of this approach pay little attention to the innate characteristics of human beings, because they see human nature as "within history." That is, they maintain that human nature is determined by the historical, economic, and social condition in which human beings find themselves. Nevertheless, in brief asides by the young Marx[25] and in later interpretations of Marx's thought,[26] it is suggested that humans have the inherent potential to embrace a Lockian, harmonious, loving coexistence, but that *pre*revolutionary societal regimes block its expression and transform people into Hobbesian beasts. Only after "the" revolution, and the transition from socialism (the early postrevolution era) to communism, during which, it is stated, the residues of bourgeois domination will be overcome, will the positive, true human nature be realized and social problems vanish. The human race is capable of a Utopian existence, but this can occur only after the proper socioeconomic conditions are created and the basis of conflict between society's members is removed through the abolition of private property and the state.

A number of "leftist psychologists" have elaborated major variants of the Marxist view. Of these, the most influential perhaps has been Herbert Marcuse. While accepting Freud's theory of an innate human nature whose most important characteristic is the sex instinct, Marcuse rejects Freud's pessimistic view that the existence of civilization requires sublimation of our urges, a process that exacts an inevitable cost in repression, and hence neurosis. Instead, he envisions a basically unrepressed,

23. Arthur W. Kornhauser, *Mental Health of the Industrial Worker: A Detroit Study* (Huntington, N.Y.: Robert E. Krieger, 1965); A. McLean, *Occupational Stress* (Springfield, Ill.: Charles C Thomas, 1974).

24. Ralf Dahrendorf, *Class and Class Conflict in Industrial Society* (Stanford, Calif.: Stanford University Press, 1959).

25. Karl Marx, *Economic and Philosophical Manuscripts of 1844*, ed. Dirk J. Struik, trans. Martin Milligan (New York: International, 1964).

26. Israel, *Alienation*; Bertell Ollman, *Alienation: Marx's Conception of Man in Capitalist Society* (New York: Cambridge University Press, 1971); Erich Fromm, *Marx's Concept of Man* (New York: Frederick Ungar, 1951).

spontaneously loving person in the "new man" whom Marxists have said would be created by postrevolutionary socialist society.

Whereas Freud held that Eros and Thanatos, the two principles of love and death, of creation and destruction, were inherent in human nature and that social control has to be exercised to sublimate *both*, Marcuse views "civilization as a dialectical struggle between the forces of Love and Death, in which the defeat of Thanatos could be assured only through the liberation of Eros."[27] According to Marcuse, sexual repression is not a condition occasioned by civilization per se viewed ahistorically but merely a prerequisite for the continuance of capitalist civilization, which makes the worker sublimate sex into labor energy to produce the capitalist surplus. Therefore, the postrevolutionary socialist society would need only a minimal residue of repression in order to contain the occasional accidental destructiveness of the impulsive *id*.

A number of other leftist Freudians (Norman O. Brown, Wilhelm Reich) went several steps further than Marcuse. Dropping Freud's notion about the dangerous character of unrestrained Eros and the existence of Thanatos, the death instinct, they found civilization's constraints unnecessary and linked their psychological theories not to Marxism but to anarchism. Because there is no positive purpose to socialization—only frustration of man's freedom and goodness—then not only the political order but society itself, with its commandments and taboos, would be dispensed with in their liberated world. People are "good"; society is problematic.

Dynamics: As far as the prerevolutionary condition is concerned, the typical conflict interpretations of social problems focus on one core explanation, that of alienation. People drink themselves sick, commit suicide, have nervous breakdowns, even exploit their own kind, because their basic existence is distorted, not because of a specific problem arising independently and having a unique social cause.

Purists see the historical process, which will transform the existing societal condition and the problems it generates, as semiautomatic—an unfolding of a scenario that can be accelerated or slowed down a bit, but not basically altered. Sooner or later, the people, led by the workers (who in turn are led by the avant-garde, or politically active cadres, or the Party) will remove the superstructure of oppression and bring societal institutions into harmony with objective reality. Public ownership of the means of production and elimination of classes, the creation of a society without inherent significant differences of interest among groups of members, are seen as the essential "treatment" for social problems.

The more psychological variants stress that persons will also have

---

27. Paul Robinson, *The Freudian Left* (New York: Harper & Row, 1969), p. 213.

to be transformed in order to free them from the ideological and psychic shackles through which the outgoing regimes have exerted their hold on individuals. Thus, for instance, poor blacks will have to realize that they are not inferior and can act politically. Frantz Fanon, a black psychiatrist from the French Antilles, pointed out that imperialist powers had colonized not only countries, but also the minds and hearts of their inhabitants. Applying the Marxist dialectic to the psychology of racism, Fanon concluded that for colonial people to free themselves mentally, they would have to pass through a period of violent rejection of their colonial mentors and their culture.[28]

Again, purists stress that reforms such as those that provide public work to the unemployed, welfare to the poor, psychotherapy to the neurotic, and so on, are worthless so long as the basic alienating condition is not corrected. Once this condition has been rectified, reforms will hardly be needed. Indeed, conflict theorists argue, first, that social problems are not problems simply because everyone recognizes them as such and wants them corrected, but precisely because those in power do *not* really want to solve them.[29] Second, significant segments of the class in power actually benefit quite directly from the continued existence of many social problems. For example, other people's poverty is a prime source of income for slum landlords, ghetto supermarket owners, and large companies who sell their defective merchandise in poor neighborhoods.[30] Finally, investing resources and political energy in bringing about such limited reforms is anathema to the revolutionary because it deflects energy from the major target and gives people the illusion of progress, of coping with social problems, whereas actually nothing significant can be achieved in this manner.[31]

In recent years, though, there has been a growing recognition, especially in the United States, that revolutions are rare and very difficult to come by, that there have been only a handful throughout history, and that revolution itself does not automatically end all problems. At the same time, there has been a growing interest in conceiving alternative institutions to be nurtured within the womb of the "bad" society, until

28. Frantz Fanon, *Black Skins, White Masks*, trans. Charles L. Markman (New York: Grove Press, 1967); Frantz Fanon, *The Wretched of the Earth*, trans. Constance Farrington (New York: Grove Press, 1968).

29. Willard Waller's view reported in Jerome H. Skolnick and Elliot Currie, *Crisis in American Institutions* (Boston: Little, Brown, 1973), p. 3.

30. David Caplovitz, *The Poor Pay More: Consumer Practices of Low-Income Families* (New York: Free Press, 1963).

31. See G. William Domhoff, "How to Commit Revolution in Corporate America," in *Social Conflict*, ed. Philip Brickman (Lexington, Mass.: D. C. Heath, 1974), pp. 432–445.

they are strong enough to take over. These will permit the growth of new, free individuals. Among such alternative institutions are Paul Goodman's and Ivan Illich's notions of education without schooling[32] (somewhat more moderate versions include the "open classroom" and the "free university of the street"); David Cooper's "anti-hospital";[33] the current revival of interest in communes as minisocialist societies capable of overcoming the alienation of labor; and interest in new forms of family relations (for example, open marriage).

Conflict theorists tend to be pessimistic in the short run but optimistic in the longer run. They are pessimistic because they tend to view the existing problem-causing order as resistant to change and assert that most attempts at reform "within the system" are futile.[34] On the other hand, they are optimistic in the long run for two reasons: (1) they expect historical forces to propel the social condition toward a revolutionary ending of the old regime and the introduction of a new world; and (2) they believe the new world could be perfected, and therefore free from problems.

Symbolic Interactionism and Ethnomethodology

The prime focus of symbolic interactionists and ethnomethodologists is the immediate context of the behavior that is considered problematic. (The subtle differences between these two groupings and their different histories need not be explored for present purposes. Briefly, the latter are more interested in *a*social, individual concepts while the former are more interested in the interactions in shaping meaning.) In their daily interactions and communication, people shape each other and their common social world. Inherent difficulties in carrying out these seemingly elementary processes of exchanging words, gestures, and cues of approved and condemned behavior are sources of social problems. Thus, people may be troubled, and may engage in troubling behavior, because they are unable to agree on the meaning of "the world," proper conduct, or even basic concepts, and because of inherent limitations in the human ability to communicate and order communication. In addition, the *way*

32.   Ivan Illich, *De-Schooling Society* (New York: Harper & Row, 1972); Paul Goodman, *Growing Up Absurd* (New York: Random House, 1960).

33.   David Cooper, "The Anti-Hospital: An Experiment in Psychiatry," in *Radical Perspectives on Social Problems*, 2nd ed., ed. Frank Lindenfeld (New York: Macmillan, 1973), pp. 432–442.

34.   Simone de Beauvoir said that "such interim gains as better jobs for women, token positions and apparent sexual integration were counter-productive within the existing political system. The role of feminists in France," she said, "is to sap this regime but not play their game." *The New York Times*, October 5, 1975.

people and acts are "labeled"—for example, whoever and whatever is called "stupid" or "criminal"—deeply affects the social condition.

What joins interactionists (such as Erving Goffman, Howard S. Becker, Edwin Lemert, Kai T. Erikson, Tamotsu Shibutani) and ethnomethodologists (such as Harold Garfinkel, Aaron V. Cicourel, Jack Douglas, Peter McHugh, Alan Blum, Thomas Scheff) is a common perception of social reality as composed of the meanings or "definitions of the Situation" that are communally constructed and reconstructed in an infinite number of daily transactions and encounters among individuals. This approach is an intellectual heir of the "Chicago School," which included such scholars as Herbert Blumer, Ezra Park, W. I. Thomas, Florian Znaniecki, and others who were ethnographers of the urban settings of deviants and marginal people such as prostitutes, dice rollers, and con men. Gerald Suttles' recent work continues this tradition.[35]

Societal Reality: The interactionist-ethnomethodological approach finds it unproductive to conceptualize the social world chiefly in terms of stable social structures, statutes, roles, and institutions, but instead focuses on the more fluid concept of processes:

> Where others might see "things," "givens," or "facts of life," the ethnomethodologist sees (or attempts to see) process: the process through which the perceivedly stable features of socially organized environments are continually created and sustained. . . . Where others have treated "deviance" as a property somehow inhering in the acts so designated, the labeling theorist invites the analyst to conceive of deviance as a communal creation.[36]

The elements out of which societal reality is communally constructed and reconstructed are personal and interpersonal activities and the rules that ascribe meaning to them. These rules are somewhat similar to what the consensus approach refers to as "norms"; however, interactionists and ethnomethodologists focus not on generalized norms or abstract values, but on their concrete, specific, daily manifestations; not on "social injustice," but on being labeled a "nigger"; not on "crime," but on how crime is defined and on the ways in which this definition is applied to some persons and not to others, even though both are acting in a similar way.

The rules used to decide what is or is not considered "deviant" or "problematic" include not only the moral norms embodied in custom, religion, and law, but also "conventions" of language and behavior. They

---

35. Gerald Suttles, *The Social Order of the Slum* (Chicago: University of Chicago Press, 1970).

36. Melvin Polner, "Sociological and Common Sense Models of the Labelling Process," in *Ethnomethodology*, ed. Roy Turner (New York: Penguin Books, 1974), p. 27.

are akin to the rules of a game. They make order out of chaos. They establish conditions of expectancy, predictability, and trust, without which people are unable to orient their action toward each other.[37] Indeed, one indication of insanity and loss of social contact is the use of sounds and signs whose meanings are *not* shared by others. However, quite different rules can be worked out and played by. Each of life's interactions is a kind of poker game. We and other players must agree on, and stick to, a common set of rules, at least for this round. Thus, this approach sees critical problems not only in reaching agreement on the moral, substantive side, but also, on the cognitive side of communication, in establishing conventions regarding the meaning of words and of items of behavior.[38] And problems exist everywhere in the completion of each transaction or sentence, as well as in special events such as mental breakdowns, riots, and so on.[39]

To say that this approach conceives of societal reality as subjective rather than objective does not mean that its proponents see it as whatever each individual may think it is. Rather, it is "intersubjective" in that it is embodied in the rules the members of a group carry in their heads and use to orient their behavior and to interpret the behavior of others. In interpreting one another's actions and responding appropriately, the group "creates" rather than "discovers" reality.[40] To illustrate: Labeling theorists note the different "careers" characteristic of first offenders (such as a youth caught with some marijuana) who are labeled criminals compared with those who are not so labeled. Because of their labels, the former have a hard time getting a job, are assumed to be dangerous ("imputation of auxiliary traits"), and hence may ever more deeply involve themselves in drug abuse and possible crime. The latter, who have committed the same act but were not labeled criminal—perhaps only through the accident of coming before a more lenient judge or being let off by a compassionate cop—may go on to become "normal" citizens.[41] The power of labels is also revealed by a study of migrant workers which shows that the social consequences of an arrest record were the same

37. Harold Garfinkel, "A Conception of, and Experiments with, 'Trust' as a Condition of Stable Concerted Actions," in *Motivation and Social Interaction*, ed. O. J. Harvey (New York: Ronald Press, 1963) and Garfinkel, *Studies in Ethnomethodology* (Englewood Cliffs, N.J.: Prentice-Hall, 1967), p. 276.

38. See Aaron V. Cicourel, *Cognitive Sociology* (New York: Free Press, 1974).

39. Alan F. Blum, "Methods for Recognizing, Formulating, and Describing Social Problems" in *Handbook on the Study of Social Problems*, ed. Smigel, pp. 177–205.

40. Garfinkel, *Studies in Ethnomethodology*, p. vii.

41. Gene Kassenbaum, *Delinquency and Social Policy* (Englewood Cliffs, N.J.: Prentice-Hall, 1974), p. 67.

whether they were convicted or acquitted.[42] Note that unlike the structural-functionalists, who would tend to search for a societal need behind social definitions, here it is assumed that a great deal of arbitrariness is behind what is called "in" (acceptable) or "out" (deviant). As Jack Douglas put it: "Labeling theory argued . . . that the categorization of something or someone is an *independent* variable."[43] Or, as Gene Kassenbaum put it: "The clearest difference between criminal and non-criminal is that the criminal is a person who has been found to have violated the law and has been dealt with as such."[44]

It follows that deviant acts and persons are not objectively deviant; they are so only according to the rules applied to them on the spot, which are not necessarily accepted by the entire society but vary from group to group and from situation to situation. Radically inclined members of the interactionist-ethnomethodological approach stress, however, the role of power and mystification (laws, courts, judges, robes, and so on) in the successful introduction of particular rules, and a definition of the situation. Such a view might turn radical adherents of this approach into Marxists, were it not that the power they perceive is not that of control of economic resources or means of violence, but the ability of individuals or groups to get their perceptions and attributions of meaning accepted as legitimate both in day-to-day encounters and in the management of institutions and society. Some members of this school accordingly take a passionate political stance toward labeling; others take a more detached, ethically neutral view, in which social life is seen as either theater of the absurd or as a kind of great big game.

Human Nature: Human nature is an alien concept to this approach because such a concept implies specific characteristics such as drives, basic human needs, traits that all persons share and that are not manufactured or deeply recast by their interactions. Thus, the following was written about the work of Erving Goffman, an early master of this approach:

42. Richard D. Schwartz and Jerome H. Skolnick, "Two Studies of Legal Stigma," in *The Other Side: Perspectives on Deviance*, ed. Howard S. Becker (New York: Free Press, 1969), pp. 103–118. For a discussion of the official labeling of alcoholism as a crime rather than a disease, see Jack Weiner, "It Is a Crime: No It Isn't," in *Studies in the Sociology of Social Problems*, ed. Paul B. Horton and Gerald R. Leslie (New York: Appleton-Century-Crofts, 1971), pp. 462–464.

43. Jack D. Douglas, ed., *Deviance and Respectability* (New York: Basic Books, 1970), p. 12. See also John P. Hewitt and Randall Stokes, "Disclaimers," *American Sociological Review*, 40 (1975), 1–11; John P. Hewitt and Peter M. Hall, "Social Problems, Problematic Situations, and Quasi-Theories," *American Sociological Review*, 38 (1973), 367–374; Marvin B. Scott and Stanford M. Lyman, "Accounts," *American Sociological Review*, 33 (1968), 46–62.

44. Kassenbaum, *Delinquency and Social Policy*, p. 3.

> ... many of the connections between social structure and individual be-
> havior are not made through the mobilization of powerful personality drives
> to secure the performance of social roles, but rather through normative
> definitions of situations in which relatively weak and shifting motives are
> mobilized for the purpose at hand.[45]

Occasionally a view of human nature is implied, as when Douglas suggests that people label others as deviant because those who assign the labels cannot experience their own respectability and moral superiority unless there are others whom they can look down upon.[46] By and large, though, the concept is simply not used, and the implicit assumption is that human nature is highly pliable and hence requires the continuous reconstruction of the social *and* personal world.

Dynamics: In everyday life, individuals have a variety of possibilities for coping with their own and others' problematic behavior and for creating order. These strategies, in turn, have institutional counterparts.

On the personal level, the typical means for dealing with problematic (deviant) acts is for the offender to give an account of his or her behavior. This account can take two basic forms: (1) the individuals seek to deny the deviance by legitimating their behavior in terms of alternate values; or (2) they acknowledge the wrong and their culpability, as well as their underlying respect for the violated norm and willingness to make amends. A third intermediate possibility is to acknowledge guilt but plead extenuating circumstances. In the first case, offenders refuse to accept the deviant label by giving an account that seeks to legitimate their acts in terms that remove them from the category of deviant behavior. This can be done either by showing that an act conforms to *another* norm (perhaps a "higher" one or one belonging to a different culture or subculture), or by showing the act to be an accident and thus not their fault.[47]

On the institutional level, the deviant behavior may be defined out of existence altogether or explained away on a case-by-case basis. This is done by occupants of certain positions, whose jobs are to provide such accounts to agencies of social control on behalf of individuals (and often whole categories of persons) who habitually engage in conduct in need of legitimation. For example, social workers may do this for juvenile delinquents; doctors, for alcoholics; psychiatrists, for homosexuals; and

45. Arthur Stinchcombe, review of Erving Goffman, *Behavior in Public Places* in *American Journal of Sociology*, 69 (May 1964), 679.

46. Douglas, *Deviance and Respectability.*

47. See for example, Erving Goffman, *Behavior in Public Places* (New York: Free Press, 1963), and Peter McHugh, "A Common-Sense Conception of Deviance," in *Deviance and Respectability*, ed. Douglas.

so on. Thus, doctors who insist that alcoholism is a disease are putting forward an account that explains it as something different from deviant behavior because "sickness" supposedly excuses individuals from responsibility for their condition. However, because this places on alcoholics the obligation to cooperate in treatment, persons addicted to alcohol may in fact prefer a definition of the situation that sees them as choosing to drink.

The clients served by these professionals need not be the offenders but may be the society or the public. In this case, the professional's job is to prove that the offender's attempted legitimations are unacceptable. For example, a district attorney attempts to prove the defendant's account unacceptable to a jury.

Whichever definition of the situation prevails is significant in determining how a social problem will be treated. The label "deviant" tends to suggest punishment, whereas "sickness" advocates treatment. Consider the different treatment accorded an ordinary criminal and one judged insane. Thus, obtaining correctives deemed appropriate to a particular problem may be largely a question of putting over a particular definition of the situation, one which naturally goes with a certain set of correctives.

The procedures for putting over preferred accounts, as well as insisting upon the usual ones (that is, those favored by the establishment), range from clarifying classifications of people to bargaining, from trials and appeals to confrontations and demonstrations. Thus, the object may be to induce a school official to change a child's classification from the less hopeful prognosis of "retarded" to the more hopeful one of "learning disability." Or the goal may be to persuade an entire profession such as psychiatry to change its view of an entire category of persons (for example, to classify homosexuals not as "mentally ill" but as "different but normal").

Although each particular account may be settled, the process is basically unending, because new questions arise out of new challenges to the account. Thus, whereas a social problem may be reduced or redefined, social problems are rarely ever finally resolved. For this reason, this approach is basically pessimistic in that problematic conditions are seen as continuing to exist as long as there are ambiguities of meaning and changes in power relations—that is, as long as there is a language and a social situation.

The Neoconservative Approach

There has always been a conservative view, at least since the time of the ancient Greeks. Thus, in *The Republic*, Plato argued for an ideal society, ruled by an intellectual elite, and stratified according to "gold," "silver," and "brass" classes whose members would be denied political and economic equality, as well as social mobility. Individuals were to remain at their assigned posts for life, discharging their societal duty for the greater good of the societal whole. During the last generation in America, however, the rich conservative tradition underwent a fallow period, especially in the sociology of social problems. Only in recent years has the conservative school begun to regain its historical prominence. To distinguish this recent upsurge from earlier ones, the term "neoconservative" is used. The approach is still better represented among observers and analysts in the social sciences such as Irving Kristol, Nathan Glazer, and Daniel Bell, than among people who conduct empirical sociological investigations.

Societal Reality: Central to the neoconservative world view is the notion that the societal world is less malleable and more intractable than other approaches often assume. In part, it is a matter of unavoidable scarcity—there are always more social goals and ambitions than resources. Hence, some legitimation of restraint on demands must be maintained.[48] Similarly, there are psychological intractabilities: for example, you need a measure of inequality to reward the efforts of those who work harder, save more, and so forth.[49] Central to the neoconservatives' view of the building blocks of the societal world are the twin concepts of "elites" and "masses." The elites fulfill the entrepreneurial function essential for innovative, vigorous economic activity and the cultivation of culture, but above all, as the carriers of societal values they sustain the ongoing moral and political vitality of the community.[50] The relationship between elites and masses is not viewed as one of domination and subordination; the elites do not constitute a ruling class that exercises exploitative power over the masses. In a well-ordered society, the elites are to the masses as leaders are to followers: They wield, not power, but authority; each side is party to an unwritten covenant. It is the moral obligation of the masses to follow the lead of the elites, and the elites must be worthy of being followed. Social problems develop when one or both of the parties fail to live up to their side of the covenant. Thus, the masses may reject the authority of the elites and fall prey to egalitarian delusions, or the

48. Daniel Bell, "The Revolution of Rising Entitlements," *Fortune*, 91 (April 1975), 98–103.

49. Wilbert E. Moore and Kingsley Davis, "Some Principles of Stratification, Reply and Comment," *American Sociological Review*, 18 (1953), 394–397.

50. This line of thought was previously developed by Gaetana Mosca and Vilfredo Pareto.

elites may become decadent and may cease to represent the society's most deeply cherished values.

To play their roles properly, members of society must accept these roles willingly and draw meaning from them. This, in turn, necessitates a strong and cohesive normative culture that builds respect for authority into each individual's personality, inculcation of a sense of special responsibility in members of the elite, and a continual reinforcement of authority by punishing those who flout society's ideals, rules, and elites, while rewarding those who respect them.

The neoconservative notion of authority is not necessarily authoritarian or totalitarian; indeed the branch of neoconservative thought that appears to be in ascendancy at present in American social science is one that reckons its descent from Tocqueville. Like him, it is rather suspicious of strong, centralized, activist state power. Neoconservatives tend to distinguish between society and state and typically recognize not one but a variety of elites in different fields—political, intellectual, religious, economic, social, cultural, and so forth—whose memberships only partially overlap. Similarly, within each sphere there may be competing elites, each of which represents a somewhat different set of values within the dominant framework. In American politics, the leadership of the Democratic and Republican parties are seen as constituting such competing elites. Democracy, according to this view, is a political system in which, at regular intervals, two or more political elites representing different values compete for the public mandate, a pluralism *within* the confines of a broad national consensus.

To neoconservatives, most social problems are traceable to, or symptomatic of, a breakdown of authority on one or another of three levels: (1) individual conduct, (2) processes and agencies of social control, and (3) the fundamental moral order of society. Deviant behavior is viewed mainly as the product of a defective personality or character. Blame rests primarily with the individual deviant and not on society. Neoconservatives do recognize, however, a societal obligation to equip individuals with strong superegos and a bulwark of cultural values to protect them against the temptation of deviant acts. Similarly, agencies of social control are not to be allowed to become lax or to engage in misguided permissiveness, because if they fail to reinforce conformity with societal norms and rules with punitive sanctions where called for, individuals will not be motivated to behave properly. Finally, authority may be disturbed throughout society, to its very core, when during periods of rapid social change, decadence, or other society-wide dislocation the basic consensus on values begins to crumble.

Human Nature: The conservative's stress on maintaining authority to combat social problems is underlined by a pessimistic conception of human nature:

> History consists for the greater part of the miseries brought upon the world by pride, ambition, avarice, revenge, lust, sedition, hypocrisy and all the trains of disorderly appetites which shake the public.[51]

Many neoconservatives subscribe to a view of human nature as dim as that of their intellectual ancestor, Burke. Religiously oriented conservatives, such as James Burnham, put it in phrases reminiscent of the traditional doctrine of Original Sin.[52] Ernest van den Haag describes it in terms of the Freudian id:

> Although needful of society, we are not born helpful to it. Needing society we are born, nevertheless, asocial, if not antisocial. Therefore, the first aim of socialization is to bend the inborn drives of the infant into socially acceptable directions. Our inborn drives can disrupt society or be satisfied at the expense.[53]

Failure to tame infantile egoism is seen by some as ultimately responsible for the student radicalism of the 1960s, which had little to do with the causes ostensibly being championed, but was really a symbolic acting out of the students' anger at their parents for having saddled them with defective personalities as a result of permissive upbringing.[54]

A consensus-oriented social scientist may stress that persons who have been acculturated into a deviant subculture might quite as readily have been educated to be, say, soldiers; a structural-functionalist points to the scarcity of opportunities for legitimate careers for ambitious lower-class youths; and a Marxist states that the worst crimes are those committed by the elite against the people. Neoconservatives, on the other hand, assert that criminality and other forms of deviance such as alcoholism, drug addiction, and juvenile delinquency are caused by unleashed personal impulses, deficient moral upbringing, and "bad" genes. As such, undersocialized, badly integrated individuals are quite beyond the range of moral persuasion. Society can best deter them by appealing to their narrow self-interest via punitive sanctions. Theoretically, crim-

---

51. Edmund Burke, "Reflections on the Revolution in France," in *The Works of the Right Honorable Edmund Burke*, rev. ed., vol. 3 (Boston: Little, Brown, 1865), p. 418.

52. James Burnham, *Suicide of the West* (New Rochelle, N.Y.: Arlington House, 1964).

53. Ernest van den Haag, *Passion and Social Constraint* (New York: Stein and Day, 1963), p. 7.

54. A view reported by Kenneth Kenniston, "A Second Look at the Uncommitted," *Social Policy* 2:2 (July/August), 1971.

inals could be rehabilitated, but neoconservatives feel that the adult human character is too set in its ways for rehabilitation to work on a large scale.[55]

Dynamics: Authority vested in the super-ego, in agencies of social control and in a unifying normative culture thus serves, according to the conservative, as a kind of lid that contains the eruptive potential of human nature. Disintegration of authority, however, is seen as endemic to the modern condition, which is characterized by the loss of insulation of elites from the masses and consequent difficulties experienced by elites in exercising effective leadership.[56] The decline of traditional forms of authority, the erosion of status barriers among classes of people, and the widespread social and political mobilization make the elites directly vulnerable to the vagaries of the masses. Such a situation encourages the rise of irresponsible demagogues who will say and do anything to flatter the masses, but who in reality are unscrupulously manipulating them.[57]

The peculiarly social, as opposed to political, manifestations of a breakdown in authority, social order, and culture were perhaps most articulately analyzed by Emile Durkheim. First, there is a weakening of the ties (that is, the mechanisms of social control and integration) that bind the individuals to the collectivity and continually reinforce their allegiance to its values and norms. The weakening of collective bonds means that individuals become more autonomous. In the absence of social constraints, such as the do's and don't's society sets, people are thrown back on their innate nature, which results in an explosion of wants and aspirations. Durkheim labeled this condition "egoism" because it defines individuals in a weakened social order. A second manifestation of the breakdown of social order is a splintering of the *conscience collective,* or the system of moral regulation, due to social crises, such as economic depression or religious schism, which prevent people from acting the way they ought to by denying them the necessary means of acting appropriately. This condition, which Durkheim referred to as *anomie,* robs the overarching social order of a necessary harmonious relationship between life-styles and the means of achieving them. Both kinds of normative disruptions at the macrosociological level could be linked, Durkheim asserted, to seemingly individualistic, idiosyncratic forms of problematic behavior, such as suicide.[58]

More recently, the conditions Durkheim saw as characteristic of

55. On this viewpoint see James Q. Wilson, *Thinking About Crime* (New York: Harper & Row, 1975).

56. Robert Nisbet, *Twilight of Authority* (New York: Oxford University Press, 1975).

57. William Kornhauser, *Politics of Mass Society* (New York: Free Press, 1959).

58. Emile Durkheim, *Suicide,* trans. John A. Spaulding (New York: Free Press, 1951).

"egoism" have found a new theoretical home in the concept of relative deprivation. Relative deprivation refers to constant invidious comparisons that are said to be made by individuals and groups concerning one another's relative standing and to the feelings of injustice and deprivation experienced by those who come out behind, at least by their own measures. Although this same phenomenon might be described by conflict theorists in terms of group conflict, opposing objective interests, and exploitation and revolt, neoconservatives tend to see it as a more subjective process of status envy and competition. And whereas the alienation approach sees equality in the allocation of what the society has to give (income, status, power) as a radical solution to these social problems, neoconservatives suggest these be permanent features of human life because of an insatiable urge to have some things others do have but the ego does not, be it beauty, style, or whatever.

Almost paradoxically, and perhaps therefore indicative of the fundamental irrationality of human nature, the neoconservatives note, status competition among groups and individuals as well as feelings of relative deprivation actually intensify during periods of progress. One example often cited is the growing political militancy and antiwhite feeling among blacks during the 1960s, a period when, according to neoconservatives, blacks were making rapid material gains. Concerning the black "revolution of rising expectations," Nathan Glazer wrote:

> Something very strange is happening in the American racial crises. On the one hand, the concrete situation of Negro Americans is rapidly improving . . . on the other hand, as the Negro's situation improves, his political attitudes are become more extreme.[59]

Another "fictitious" social problem, in the sense that the neoconservatives see it as existing in the mind of the liberal intellectual or radical agitator and not in real social conditions, is the supposed alienation of the worker under capitalism. Thus, alienation is nothing more than a *deus ex machina* that the leftist intellectual invokes whenever he needs an explanatory cause. To blame alienation on the supposedly monotonous, fragmented character of assembly-line work is to ignore the fact that fewer than 2 percent of American workers now work on the assembly line. Thus, Ben J. Wattenberg writes:

> . . . perhaps the major danger today is only that we will be catch-phrased and crisis-mongered to death before all is done. It is time for a reassessment. . . . It is time to investigate the capital-lettered afflictions that seem to issue from every typewriter through the land, spreading apparent doom on an otherwise healthy society.[60]

59. Nathan Glazer, "The Negro's Stake in America's Future," *New York Times Magazine*, September 22, 1968, pp. 30–31.

60. Ben J. Wattenberg and Richard M. Scammon, *This U.S.A.* (Garden City, N.Y.: Doubleday, 1965), p. 305.

If the source of the problem is intellectual rhetoric, and if pruning it will cure our ills, then do neoconservatives simply deny the reality of all social problems? How do they respond to John Kenneth Galbraith's argument that while America is affluent, in the sense that many Americans are quite well off, the public sector—hospitals, schools, museums—is poverty stricken?[61] What about pollution, highway fatalities, crime, and so forth? Most neoconservatives recognize that these problems do exist and deserve consideration, but point out (1) that they are corollaries of the affluent society and (2) that they can be corrected by a larger gross national product, increased scientific progress, better administration, and so on.[62] In other words, correctives will be achieved not by change but by more of the same.

Beyond strengthening character building at home and in school, authority, and other mechanisms of social control, neoconservatives would approach the restructuring of society very cautiously. Neoconservatives feel that if there are to be attempts at social reform, it is best to accomplish these via the private sector because scientific expertise is abundant there and administrators are typically more efficient, cost conscious, and pragmatic than civil servants. Thus, to get more housing they favor outright grants to citizens to purchase their own houses in a free market, rather than for the government to build them. Neoconservatives remind us that many of the best intended interventions by government bureaucrats were not only unsuccessful but brought about a cure as bad or worse than the disease. For example, Medicaid and Medicare increased the costs of health care, and the Great Society helped cause a runaway inflation.[63] In addition, neoconservatives place greater value on social stability and constitutional freedoms than on egalitarianism, and they are not quite convinced that all three values can be maximized simultaneously.[64] They tend to see messianic attempts to reconstitute society as almost inevitably entailing the imposition of one group's ideas of what is good on the rest of society; they would prefer that individuals re-

---

61. John K. Galbraith, *The Affluent Society* (Boston: Houghton Mifflin, 1960).

62. Zbigniew Brzezinski, *Between Two Ages: America's Role in a Technocratic Era* (New York: Viking, 1971).

63. Harry Schwartz, *The Case for American Medicine* (New York: David McKay, 1972), and Robert A. Levine, "Rethinking of Social Strategies," *The Public Interest*, no. 10 (Winter 1968), 86–96.

64. Robert Nisbet, "The Pursuit of Equality," *The Public Interest* (Spring 1974), pp. 101–120.

mained free to pursue their own happiness in their own various ways, without governmental interference. Therefore, change will occur gradually and naturally, if it occurs at all.

AN EXAMPLE: POVERTY AS VIEWED BY
THE FOUR APPROACHES

About 24.3 million persons, or 12 percent of the total U.S. population, were living in poverty in 1973. Poverty is defined as an annual income below $5,038 for a family of four not living on a farm. By this criterion, although there are twice as many poor whites as poor blacks, a greater proportion of the black population than of the white population is poor: over 30 percent of all blacks but only 13 percent of all whites qualified as poor. Although urban poverty is perhaps more visible to the public at large, close to half of the poor live in rural areas. Old persons, female heads of households, and children also make up large percentages of the poor. Except during times of severe economic recession, able-bodied males make up only a small fraction of the poor. Thus, in 1970 only 12.3 percent of the poor who were able to work were unemployed; 9 out of every 10 of these were women, many mothers of young children.

Poverty is linked to other social problems, as both cause and effect. The poor's mental illnesses are more frequently diagnosed as psychoses, while mental illness among the nonpoor usually takes the form of less serious neuroses; in addition, the poor are more often treated in notorious state mental institutions rather than by private practitioners. They are less healthy physically than other segments of the population, and their children are more likely to die young.[65] The poor commit more serious crimes than do those of higher socioeconomic status *and* are more often the victims of such crimes. The four approaches discussed earlier offer different perspectives on the problem.

The concept of a "culture of poverty" sums up a view of poverty shared by many *consensus* theorists. They see in the poor's creation of a consensus pattern at odds with the dominant culture a major ongoing cause of poverty (though not necessarily its original source). Thus, the poor adapt to poverty by resorting to illegal activities that their subculture legitimates, such as bookmaking, prostitution, and drug peddling, and by becoming connoisseurs of the one luxury poverty makes abundant —empty hours during which one can lead an unregimented life free of

65. U.S.H.R. Committee on Ways and Means, *Basic Facts on the Health Industry* (June 28, 1971), pp. 124–125, 116–117ff.

the time clock and the office or assembly-line routines.[66] This explains both why the poor can endure poverty and how society can go on tolerating it. The outlook on life characteristic of the poor is said to furnish them with psychological comfort and at the same time forestalls rebellion. It also explains why the poor often reject opportunities for greater income and status that require them to give up their habitual ways of "making it," such as running numbers and drug pushing, and to accept new disciplines.

Among those who approach poverty with the tools of *structural-functional* analysis, two decidedly different approaches are apparent. Adherents of Talcott Parsons, a leading member of this school, generally define poverty as a form of deviance and view the behavior of the poor as the reverse of what is adaptive or functional. The deficiencies of the poor are said to include: (1) lack of such required modern personality traits as control over one's impulses and the drive to work, save, achieve, and plan ahead; (2) a restricted role repertory limiting their ability to adapt to changing work opportunities; (3) lack of role-skills, ranging from proper manners when job seeking to punctuality; and (4) deficient mental functioning as a result of poor socialization, including limited interest in new ideas and difficulty with abstractions and interpersonal relations.[67] If a large or growing proportion of society's members has these characteristics, the society's productive roles go unmanned, and it experiences economic difficulties of the kind one sees in underdeveloped nations as well as in underdeveloped parts of the United States, such as Appalachia.

Another line of structural-functional analysis is advanced by Frances Piven, Richard Cloward, and Herbert J. Gans. Though all three are closer to the alienation approach than to the structural-functional one, each has used structural-functional analysis to uncover the roots of poverty. Gans, for example, argues that poverty is functional to the existing societal structure.[68] First, it provides industrial society with a pool of low-wage labor to carry out such so-called dirty work as unskilled factory and farm labor, and domestic and janitorial work. Second, the poor support a sizable number of middle-class professionals, including thousands of social workers, who supposedly serve the poor, but whose

---

66. Eliott Liebow, *Tally's Corner: A Study of Negro Street Men* (Boston: Little, Brown, 1967); Oscar Lewis, *La Vida: A Puerto Rican Family in the Culture of Poverty, San Juan and New York* (New York: Random House, 1966).

67. Jack Roach, "Sociological Analysis and Poverty," *American Journal of Sociology*, 71 (July 1965), 68–75.

68. Herbert J. Gans, *More Equality* (New York: Pantheon, 1973); see also Frances Piven and Richard Cloward, *Regulating the Poor* (New York: Vintage Books, 1971).

relatively well paying, higher-status jobs would no longer be needed if poverty were eradicated.

Third, due to their lack of political and economic power, it is the poor who absorb the costs of growth and expansion in America. When urban renewal plans for middle-class housing are developed, it is often the poor who are forced to relocate to make room for it. Finally, the poor serve as an economic and social measuring stick against which the affluent can experience and take pride in their higher status.

That poverty is functional in these and other ways is reflected in the threat that such correctives as reallocation of wealth pose to the existing societal order. Thus, not only is poverty functional, but many of its alternatives are dysfunctional.[69] Note, however, that far from suggesting that poverty must be tolerated so that the existing social order can be perpetuated (an impression structural-functional analysis frequently creates, leading to the charge that it is inherently conservative), the conclusion is that if we are truly committed to doing away with poverty, the societal structure will have to be transformed.

To the Marxist wing of the *alienation* approach, the seeds of poverty are inherent in the capitalist economic system. It pits the objective interests of the bourgeoisie against those of the working class. Karl Marx described the inevitable dialectic logic of poverty in capitalist society as follows: Accumulation of wealth and capital and the expansion of industry generate an increased need for production. During expansionary periods, capitalist industry needs a surplus labor force from which it can temporarily hire hands to meet immediate needs. During periods of average or stagnant production, these laborers are superfluous and are laid off from their jobs, thus forming a "disposable industrial reserve army." When unemployed, these laborers have no income and are thrust into poverty. The cycle is renewed, however, when capitalist accumulation again increases, and the need for cheap labor arises again.[70]

Marx explained the origins of poverty as follows: The value of what is produced is seen as a function of the amount of labor invested in it, with the capitalist contributing nothing. All profit is thus surplus value extracted from the workers through exploitation; that is, by paying them less than their product is worth and by treating them as easily expendable cogs in the productive machinery. However, contemporary Marxists see the present situation somewhat differently than earlier ones in that, though most workers are exploited, *most* of the surplus value is

69. Herbert J. Gans, "The Positive Functions of Poverty," *American Journal of Sociology*, 78 (Sept. 1972), 275–289, especially 287.

70. Karl Marx, "Relative Surplus Population and Capital Accumulation," in *Poverty Economics and Society*, ed. Helen Ginsburg (Boston: Little, Brown, 1972).

extracted from particular subsections of the working class—blacks, women, and ethnic minorities in the United States, foreign workers in Europe, and Third World peoples in global terms.[71]

Yet, unlike liberal theorists whose concern is almost entirely for those who live in grinding poverty, the alienation approach's critique goes beyond the plight of what is identified as the subproletariat to include all inequality; stratification per se is a social problem. According to S. M. Miller and Pamela Roby, to focus on poverty is to imply that a basically wholesome, superaffluent society has a residual problem that some adjustments could resolve. The attitude that it is not nice for the wealthiest nation in the world to have several million poor citizens sidesteps the real issues. Among these are: "How great should the economic and social differences be among various groups in society? What are the bases of monetary and status rewards? In what ways can the mechanisms that disperse rewards be changed?"[72]

A related thesis, subscribed to by Lee Rainwater, Martin Rein, and Herbert Gans, suggests that the definition of poverty should not be fixed at a given income level (adjusted only for inflation effects on the value of the dollar), but tied to *median* income of the society, so that when the average American grows richer, what is considered poor is also upgraded.

Furthermore, poverty—and inequality—are viewed not as situations that are easily corrected by mailing large enough checks (the idea behind income maintenance), but as social, political, and personal conditions. The poor and underprivileged are short not just on cash and basic services,[73] but on assets (wealth, housing, savings) and on "self-respect and opportunities for education and social mobility and participation in many forms of decision-making."[74] Such pervasive injustice can be overcome only as society is fundamentally remade. David Gordon sums up the reasons as follows:

> Radicals suggest that capitalists would oppose a meaningful redistribution and equalization of income for two reasons. First, it would totally undermine the wage-incentive system in a society where work is fundamentally alienating. If workers can receive a decent income from the State without working, and if their work in society is unsatisfying, why should they work? . . . Second, radicals also argue that the State would not and could not meaningfully re-

71. Paul M. Sweezy, *The Theory of Capitalist Development* (New York: Monthly Review Press, 1942), pp. 59–62.

72. S. M. Miller and Pamela Roby, *The Future of Inequality* (New York: Basic Books, 1970), p. 6.

73. Lee Rainwater, *What Money Buys* (New York: Basic Books, 1974).

74. Miller and Roby, *The Future of Inequality*, p. 12.

distribute income in a capitalistic society because the State serves the interests of the capitalist class and because capitalists are interested primarily in maintaining or increasing their relative share of income.[75]

To *interactionists* and *ethnomethodologists*, poverty is a label placed on some members of society by others. As Georg Simmel, an intellectual father of this approach, stated it:

> ...the fact that someone is poor does not mean he belongs to the specific social category of the poor.... It is only from the moment that [the poor] are assisted ... that they become part of a group characterized by poverty. This group does not remain united by interactions among its members, but by the collective attitude which society as a whole adopts toward it....[76]

On one level, members of this school are concerned with describing how such labeling stigmatizes the individuals who are its object and affects their life. The definition of the situation projected upon them by those with whom the poor come into contact forces the impoverished person to engage in degrading but expected forms of behavior. The stigmatization is not an automatic result of low income, but is related instead to an imputation of moral character. Thus, some forms of poverty are considered romantic, as, for example, the poverty of hippies, students, and aspiring artists. Still another category is that of "working poor," a term used to describe persons who work and who are not recipients of charitable or governmental assistance, but whose incomes are low. Still another category is that of the "temporary poor," who refuse to take on the identity, typically, because they view their situation as anomalous— for example, the many unemployed aerospace engineers laid off in 1970– 1971. In marked contrast to these categories are those, who, as David Matza puts it, society characterizes as the "disreputable poor,"[77] those who remain unemployed or irregularly employed during periods of nearly full employment.

Ethnomethodologists are interested in uncovering the commonsense rules used by persons in everyday life and by their somewhat more formalized counterparts in agencies of social control, whereby persons are assigned to one or another category of poverty. Each typecasting carries with it a tacit branding of a person's moral worth or standing, which in

75. David Gordon, *Problems in Political Economy* (Lexington, Mass.: D. C. Heath, 1971), pp. 227–228.

76. Georg Simmel, "The Poor," trans. Claire Jacobson, *Journal of Social Problems*, 13 (1965), 139.

77. David Matza, "Poverty and Disrepute," in *Contemporary Social Problems*, ed. Merton and Nisbet, p. 615.

turn is associated with a prescribed appropriate treatment. A welfare chiseler, for example, is "untrustworthy," a type of character who is considered as appropriately treated with suspicion and surveillance.

Although *neoconservatives* differ among themselves in their viewpoints on poverty and inequality, there is widespread agreement that poverty in America is a problem but one that has been greatly exaggerated. Inequality, on the other hand, is basically not a social problem; the real problem is that it has been misperceived as such. Ben J. Wattenberg points out that amidst all the cries about poverty and injustice, Americans have more of everything that is to be had than ever before.[78] Others who claim that poverty in the United States is largely a case of relative deprivation point out that there is little starvation among the American poor and that compared with most citizens of Third World countries, or even with most of our own American ancestors, the average welfare family, with its TV set, telephone, and daily portion of meat, lives well. Nathan Glazer writes:

> Of course, we know there is poverty in New York City, but it is poverty relative to a standard of living defined as necessary to a decent life by individuals, groups, and the mass media.[79]

To obliterate the residues of poverty, a frequently proposed approach is expanding the gross national product, which should—albeit indirectly and over the long run—raise the standard of living of the poor as it raises that of the nation as a whole. Thus, the preferred conservative solution is to increase the size of the total pie rather than increase the proportions of some of the slices at the cost of the other bigger ones.

Raising the standard of living of all by increasing the total supply of wealth does not necessarily reduce inequality between individuals of social classes, which is all to the good as far as neoconservatives are concerned. They hold that some people deserve to receive more reward money than others (because of greater effort, the long training periods they must endure, and so on) and that these inequalities are for the collective good because they motivate persons of ability to produce and innovate more. Societies thrive when entrepreneurs are rewarded.

Finally, to neoconservatives, equality connotes leveling to the lowest common denominator. Robert A. Nisbet has pointed to the ill effects income redistribution could be expected to have on culture:

78. Wattenberg, *The Real America.*

79. Nathan Glazer, "The Culture of Poverty: The View from New York City," in *The Poor: A Culture of Poverty or a Poverty of Culture?* ed. J. A. Winter (Grand Rapids, Mich.: William B. Erderman's Publisher, 1971), pp. 29–48, cited from p. 36.

It is comforting to think that the only victims of a national policy of substantial redistribution would be those whose original tastes result in large yachts, Rolls Royces and Rembrandts. . . . The original, bizarre, or eccentric tastes of smaller fry will be the chief casualties, those which manifest themselves not in the yacht or Rolls Royce but in the experimental boat or automobile, in the writings and the paintings of the just-emerging artist, or in any of the countless spheres where the creative mind operates and must have the kind of support that can come only from those whose financial sacrifice is the measure of their support.[80]

CONCLUSION

Thus there are four perspectives on social problems. The first is basically optimistic that society can understand the way it functions—or malfunctions—and can correct disorders and gain or restore an equilibrium productive for most if not all its members, who are essentially malleable and, hence, adaptable.

The second perspective is rather downcast concerning contemporary problem-ridden society, which is more or less congenitally distorted and distorting and unable truly to resolve its problems until its basic structure is radically recast. Such recasting, though, is optimistically assumed to be followed by a more or less problem-free society.

A third view sees the roots of social problems in the universal difficulties of communication, ambiguities of meanings, difficulties of interpersonal transactions, and the abuses which occur as those are dealt with. Adherents of this approach are inherently pessimistic about our capacity either to understand the social world or to solve its problems in any deep or permanent sense.

The fourth perspective sees both individuals and society as quite intractable and unmalleable; hence, it is to some extent doomed to live with a fair measure of social problems. At the same time, they see fewer real problems than do other schools because they suggest that part of the problems experienced are drummed up by agitated minds, and when these rest, the problems will subside quickly. Also, whereas others see problems in inequality and the exercise of power, neoconservatives see them in the disintegration of authority and the excessive striving toward egalitarianism.

80. Robert A. Nisbet, "The New Equalitarians," *The Columbia Forum*, 4:1, New Series (Winter, 1975), 2–11.

CHAPTER 2
THE MAIN
FACTORS

Drawing on the major approaches discussed in Chapter 1, as well as on studies in humanist psychology[1] and cybernetics,[2] I have evolved a conception as to what principal factors shape societal perceptions of, and responses to, social problems. Because I see particular social problems as reflecting basic underlying societal factors, the central focus of this book, which unites all the subsequent chapters, is on the following question: Under what circumstances, in what ways, can people understand and control their collective condition? How this question is approached and what answers are put forth is of special relevance to understanding social problems. This is because the very concept of "social problems," that is, the notion that some societal conditions are problematic, while others are not, carries with it the implication that choice is possible, that conditions can be altered, that, to some extent at least, our societal direction can be guided. The term "societal guidance" is here used to characterize my approach. Social problems are often defined and distinguished from, say, natural catastrophes on the ground that they are socially created; this book stresses that what characterizes social problems is the idea that they are viewed as conditions people are expected to ameliorate or overcome.

In this activist sense, cancer is a social problem because contemporary society has accepted the search for a cure for cancer as its

1. Abraham H. Maslow, *Toward a Psychology of Being* (New York: Van Nostrand Reinhold, 1968).

2. Karl W. Deutsch et al., *Nerves of Government* (New York: Free Press, 1963).

responsibility. To this end, time, energy, brainpower, and economic resources are mobilized to research the cause of cancer, to build facilities and train personnel to use the findings of research in the care for those who have it, to redistribute resources in such a way that persons who need treatment will receive it, and so on. In contrast, we do not agonize over our inability to sprout wings for short flights in the city; it may be a shortcoming, but we do not feel that a societal effort to remedy this lack is either possible or needed. Thus, a comprehensive approach to social problems must concern itself not only with their sources, patterns, and consequences, but also with the strategies societies devise to combat them and the conditions under which these strategies are effective. Before describing our approach in terms comparable to those used in Chapter 1 to discuss a variety of earlier theoretical outlooks, we explore the historical background out of which the societal guidance definition of social problems rises and the characteristics of the era to which it seems to speak. Over the course of history, many afflictions were not perceived to be social problems until the belief arose that society could mobilize to do something about them. As long as people accepted the world as created and overseen by supernatural forces, they viewed society's condition—and afflictions such as tornadoes or hurricanes—as either states of nature or as God-given rewards and punishments, but not as problems for society to resolve. Paradoxically, then, the perception of a condition as a social problem reflects a measure of optimism. The extent of optimism with which problems are approached, however, has greatly differed from one historical epoch to another and within epochs, with regard to both the scope of the problems that require solution and the capacities for societal guidance.

Thus, the industrial revolution focused its world-can-be-molded mentality on nature. The French Revolution may be viewed as an early attempt to apply this mentality to the social environment as well. Only over the last hundred years or so have the efforts to review critically and redo society gained systematic backing, both in the form of expectant attitudes among the public at large and in organized movements for social change such as the labor and civil rights movements. The 1917 Russian Revolution was an ambitious, conscious, and confident effort to remake an entire social structure of a whole nation. The Soviet revolutionaries were seeking the abolition of private property, of religion, of differences in wealth and social standing, the withering away of the state, and the ushering in of the "new man," an optimistic societal engineering project if there ever was one. After World War II, similar highpoints of optimism were reached in the underdeveloped countries, during the struggle for national independence. It was widely believed that once the colonial powers had been cast out, most of the countries' other difficulties could be overcome.

In the United States, the New Deal and the Kennedy-Johnson era constituted high points of societal optimism. During the latter period, several hundred new domestic governmental programs were instituted in order to deal with a vast array of social problems affecting practically every aspect of personal life. Thus, the recognition that Americans eat, drink, smoke, take drugs, and worry excessively prompted a decision that these problematic habits were to be dropped, through governmental effort, and in short order. At the same time an extensive list was drawn up of collective problems to be overcome, from poverty, crime, and racial injustice to deficient education, health care, and housing. To complete the agenda, the American government undertook to export democracy, economic development, and peace to the non-Communist world.

Over the last decade, this buoyancy has been deflated. The United States (and other Western democracies) discovered that many of the social problems they took on did not yield, or yielded only marginally, to the interventions directed at them. Despite a prolonged effort by the government to discourage smoking, the proportion of Americans who smoke has not decreased significantly from 1964 to 1974.[3] Alcoholism, a favorite target of reformers, seems to be on the rise.[4] The number of new drug addicts reported by the police each year rose from 10,012 in 1964 to 23,881 in 1971; after 1971, this figure decreased for a while only to re-increase recently. Antipollution gains are modest.[5] The number of reported criminal offenses climbed from 3,353,000 in 1960 to 8,638,000 in 1973, an average annual percent increase of 10 percent.[6]

At the same time, new problems were recognized before old ones were overcome (for example, pollution, resource shortages, renewed inflation). Although optimism has been replaced with varying degrees of fatalism, there has been no agreement on why our capacity to deal with our problems and reform or remake society has proved rather limited. Should our failures be ascribed to our lack of political will, insufficient commitment of resources, absence of know-how (and inadequate social science), incorrigible human nature, or oppressive societal institutions?

Similarly, the fiftieth anniversary of the Soviet revolution celebrated an impressive growth in industrial machinery, in the standard of living, and in the size of the professional and white-collar groups, and yet prac-

3. *Statistical Abstract of the United States*, 1974, p. 87.

4. *Alcohol and Health*, Second Report of H.E.W. Secretary, June, 1974.

5. *Environmental Quality*, the Fifth Annual Report of the Council on Environmental Quality (Washington, D.C.: U.S. Government Printing Office, December, 1974).

6. *Statistical Abstract of the United States*, 1974, p. 147.

tically none of the original revolutionary goals had been accomplished.[7] Most of the underdeveloped nations, disillusioned by stacks of discarded five-year plans, have realized by now that development knows no rapid formula or master plan. And, whatever one thinks about the three frequently mentioned possible exceptions—Yugoslavia, China, and Cuba— even here progress has been made, at best, by fits and starts.

As this book is being written, a resurgent pessimism prevails. In 1974, Robert L. Heilbroner captured the spreading mood when he pronounced the outlook for man "painful, difficult, even desperate," and went on to say that "the answer to whether we can conceive of the future other than as a continuation of the darkness and disorder of the past seems to me to be no; and to the question of whether worse impends, yes."[8] I cannot tell what intellectual atmosphere will prevail by the time this book reaches the reader, but I am quite confident that a less dramatic, less easy to summarize, middle position is in line with the evidence before us. Societies are not easy to change. Their problems are difficult to remedy, and their basic structures not readily transformed. Yet our capacity to render our social condition more congruent with our deepest needs seems to be gradually growing. Out of the current pessimism, which may be a corrective reaction to the unbounded optimism of the past, may well arise a better balanced, more empirically valid, and normatively committed orientation to the dynamics of deliberate, or guided, societal change. Second, the trend away from wreaking our will on the environment and toward a search for better understanding of our societal and personal selves may intensify (see Postscript). Social scientists have a major contribution to make in this quest for a more realistic orientation to the world and a society more responsive to the needs of its members. The purposes of this book are to help forge the tools social science requires in this task and, above all, to serve the citizens whose participation is essential to any valid transformation of society toward a more easily guided society, one more able to solve its problems and overcome the conditions that generate these problems.

Before the variables that characterize societal guidance are introduced, the underlying assumptions used in developing the societal guidance approach are outlined. We shall explore the same three core issues faced with regard to the four approaches discussed in Chapter 1.

7. Barrington Moore, Jr., *Soviet Politics—The Dilemma of Power* (New York: Harper, 1965), Chap. 18; Isaac Deutscher, *The Unfinished Revolution: Russia, 1917–1967* (New York: Oxford University Press, 1967).

8. Robert L. Heilbroner, *An Inquiry Into the Human Prospect* (New York: Norton, 1974), p. 22.

THE ASSUMPTIONS OF
SOCIETAL GUIDANCE

Societal Reality

The central attribute of societal reality from the viewpoint of a guidance theory, one concerned with the factors that determine our ability to change that reality to our specifications, is that it is composed of three different layers: (1) the world of *symbols*, including values, culture, knowledge, meanings, as well as our rhetoric and political promises and threats (all elements studied by interactionists and ethnomethodologists as well as by consensus sociologists); (2) the realm of *objects*, including economic and technological resources and nature; and (3) the *action* space of behavior, roles, interpersonal links, and collectivities ranging from race to class (of particular interest to structural-functionalists, but also studied by interactionists and conflict theorists). For reasons that need not be spelled out here, we cannot change the laws of *objects* at all; we can only learn to use them instead of being ignorantly subject to their whims (try to modify the second law of Newton). In contrast, *symbols*, as John Locke stressed, are extremely pliable. We can readily create a mental image of a winged horse, using the concept of wings and the picture of a horse. Symbolic acts such as the writing and rewriting of presidential proclamations, charters, and laws, can be performed by the stroke of a pen.

Finally, the *action* space is intermediate in terms of relative degree of malleability; it is possible to reorganize a community, change race relations, or mobilize a dormant people, but to do so typically requires extensive and prolonged effort.[9] When we set out to change the world, to solve a social problem or abolish its root condition, a relevant question is, on what layer or layers are we acting: symbols, objects, or action? The efforts needed and the results that can be expected will vary accordingly. Thus, we could remove outmoded laws in one day (such as the one permitting involuntary institutionalization of mental patients), but we could only gradually change the social system of a school and could never alter the laws of gravity.

Although the world has always had three layers, its composition is changing in that societal reality is gradually becoming less object-bound and more responsive to symbols. The reasons are many and range from the growing weight of knowledge compared to that of material resources

---

9. For further discussion see Amitai Etzioni, *The Active Society* (New York: Free Press, 1968), p. 24 and chap. 2.

(yearly expenditures on knowledge grew very rapidly until recently stabilizing at a high 29 percent of the gross national product)[10] to the growing importance of education as compared to inherited wealth for social standing and mobility (although wealth still helps in getting a good education).[11] Important also has been the development of computers, communication satellites, and television as well as the rise in the proportion of the labor force who work more with symbols (the professions) as compared with those who work with objects (blue-collar workers). Finally, the increasing tentativeness of social relations has heightened the significance of symbolic links among persons.[12] Thus, we suggest that society is gradually becoming more pliable and more guidable; hence, in principle, it is becoming more responsive to our collective will and individual needs and less a victim of fate.

Human Nature

We suggest that it is fruitful to assume a universal set of basic human needs, having specific attributes that are not determined by social structure, cultural patterns, or socialization processes. If this postulate is accepted, it follows that because human needs are universal, whereas societies differ in their cultural patterns, stratification, polity, and role specifications, then societies also differ in the extent to which they are able to satisfy their members' needs.[13] We know that human beings can adapt to a large variety of social structures and cultural patterns. This, though, is not sufficient evidence that the ways in which their needs are satisfied are highly malleable, as long as the frustrations they suffer—or level of satisfactions they achieve—co-vary. In other words, people lived both in Athens and in Sparta, but this is not proof that each society was equally responsive to its members' needs. Adaptation may have exacted much higher costs in Sparta than in Athens.

Specifically, in company with Abraham Maslow and other humanist psychologists, we propose a tentative list of basic human needs, including

---

10. See Fritz Machlup, *The Production and Distribution of Knowledge in the United States* (Princeton, N.J.: Princeton Univ. Press, 1962), and Daniel Bell, *The Coming of Post-Industrial Society* (New York: Basic Books, 1973), for discussion of some conceptual and methodological issues in the study of knowledge. See Machlup, pp. 348–362, especially p. 362.

11. Peter M. Blau and Otis Dudley Duncan, *The American Occupational Structure* (New York: Wiley, 1967), p. 430.

12. Warren Bennis and Philip Slater, *The Temporary Society* (New York: Harper & Row, 1968), Chap. 4.

13. Abraham H. Maslow, *Motivation and Personality*, 2nd ed. (New York: Harper & Row, 1960), p. 35 ff.

a need for secure survival (food, shelter, protection), affection (or love), recognition (or dignity), and self-actualization.[14] Though these basic human needs are held to be universal, their foundation, except for the survival needs, is not seen as biological. The higher needs (for love, dignity, and self-actualization) may exist in the animal world in a very primitive way, but they are central to the life of human beings. How can such needs be universal but not biologically derived? The answer, in part, seems to be that having these needs is a prerequisite of being human. Thus, for instance, infants "adopted" by animals, and who grew up without affection and recognition, did not acquire the attributes of what is considered a human being, but instead remained crawling, barking, four-legged, doglike creatures.[15]

The thesis that people have basic human needs gains in plausibility as a result of several studies. They suggest that, contrary to popular belief, attempts to make people act in ways that are incompatible with their nature tend to fail or succeed only superficially. Thus, brainwashing, an encompassing and intensive effort, seems to have affected only a minority of those on whom it has been tried, and this minority included people who were already predisposed toward the views they were persuaded to accept.[16] Moreover, many of those who were swayed held their new views only as long as they remained in the particular environment where the efforts at persuasion had been made.[17]

Communist countries are of particular interest here. The USSR, for instance, now has more than 50 years of experience with a society that has tight control over the messages its educational institutions and its media carry; this message control is supplemented by well-heeled and highly regulated ideological machinery (for example, Marxist reading sessions) and by a closely linked reward structure (for example, party members, quota-breaking workers, and others who have proved themselves loyal gain various privileges). Nevertheless, the needs manifested in the behavior of the average Russian are surprisingly similar to those

14. Etzioni, *The Active Society,* p. 627.

15. See J. A. L. Singh and Robert M. Zingg, *Wolf-Children and Feral Man* (New York, Harper, 1942), for one view of a highly controversial subject. For a comment on the quality of evidence gathered on this subject, see Kingsley Davis, *Human Society* (New York: Macmillan, 1948), p. 204, fn. 3. Also see James C. Davies, *Human Nature and Politics* (New York: Wiley, 1963), p. 13, for an interesting piece of research on the question of basic human needs.

16. Edgar H. Schein et al., *Coercive Persuasion: A Socio-psychological Analysis of the "Brainwashing" of American Civilian Prisoners by the Chinese Communists* (New York: Norton, 1961); William J. McGuire, "Attitudes and Opinions," *Annual Review of Psychology,* 17 (1966), 475–514; Constance Holden, "Prisons: Faith in Rehabilitation is Suffering a Collapse," *Science,* 188 (May 23, 1975), 815–817.

17. Schein, *Coercive Persuasion,* p. 163.

of a Western person: They focus first on a quest for consumer goods and then on more affection, recognition, *and* autonomy.[18] Similarly, a study of Eastern Europe showed that acceptance of the "party line" is often shallow and expeditious.[19]

Hadley Cantril asked people in fourteen countries about their hopes, aspirations, and sources of happiness.[20] He found significant similarities in countries as divergent as Brazil, Egypt, India, Israel, the United States, and Yugoslavia. For instance, all respondents rated economic concerns higher than all others. With few exceptions, social, political, and international matters received very low ratings. Family and health received intermediate ranking.

Other studies found a positive correlation between happiness and one's position in social stratification as measured by factors such as income and education. This suggests that happiness is linked to satisfaction of the lower comfort needs, as well as to opportunities for satisfaction of higher needs—opportunities that tend to be higher in higher positions in the social structure.[21]

Still other studies found correlations between lack of satisfaction of basic needs and various forms of asocial or antisocial behavior and illness, the kind of behavior that, when inflicted on many persons, is considered a social problem. For instance, a study of auto workers found mental health to vary with the worker's job levels; the higher the skill, variety, responsibility, and pay of the job, the higher the average mental health. Among those holding positions offering less opportunity to satisfy basic needs, there was a high incidence of feelings of inadequacy, low self-esteem, anxiety, hostility, dissatisfaction with life, and low personal morale.[22]

18. See Jan S. Prybyla, "The Soviet Consumer in Khrushchev's Russia," pp. 252–260, and A. Aganbegian, "Living Standard of the Working People in the USSR and the U.S.A.," pp. 271–288, in *The Soviet Economy*, ed. Harry G. Shaffer (New York: Appleton-Century-Crofts, 1963).

19. For a view of the experience of people in Eastern Europe, see Czeslaw Milosz, *The Captive Mind* (New York: Knopf, 1953).

20. Hadley Cantril, *The Patterns of Human Concerns* (Princeton, N.J.: Princeton University Press, 1955).

21. Norman M. Bradburn and David Caplovitz, *Reports on Happiness* (Chicago: Aldine, 1965).

22. Arthur W. Kornhauser, *Mental Health of the Industrial Worker: A Detroit Study* (Huntington, N.Y.: Robert E. Krieger, 1965); and Alan McLean, *Mental Health and Work Organizations* (Chicago: Rand McNally, 1970). For a more general discussion of the relationship between economic conditions and happiness, see Richard Easterlin, "Does Economic Growth Improve the Human Lot? Some Empirical Evidence," in *Nations and Households in Economic Growth*, ed. Paul A. David and Melvin W. Reder (New York: Academic Press, 1974), pp. 89–126.

The existence of some needs, the disregard of which is very frustrating to the members of a society, has been widely recognized. But this conception usually is one of very flexible needs, which can be satisfied in a very large variety of ways. Thus, it has been suggested that people need a regular caloric intake and will find a starvation diet highly unpleasant, but that they could adapt quite readily to a very large variety of diets. In contrast, we suggest that most people, in all societies, find frequent caloric intake more satisfying than infrequent intake. More generally, we hold that any two societal structures, polities, or roles that differ significantly from one another will differ in terms of their responsiveness to basic human needs. We hold not only that a free society is more responsive to human needs than a totalitarian one, but that totalitarian societies differ in their "tightness" (for example, Russia under Stalin compared with Russia under Khrushchev) and that free societies differ in their measure of liberties (for example, the United States in the Joe McCarthy era compared to the United States in the John Kennedy era).

This concept has important implications for formulating solutions to social problems. A traditional approach is to assume that the individual's subgroups or subcultures are at fault, because of their genes, instincts, personalities, or irresponsible conduct and that efforts must therefore focus on these deviants who are unsatisfied and acting out their dissatisfaction (by rebellion, retreat, or illegitimate innovation), and further that the cure is to correct their attitudes via resocialization and social control. In contrast, our approach, while recognizing that these malfunctions may take place, also sees the equal possibility that society itself may be the source of the problem. If a society's institutional structure does not provide opportunities for satisfaction of basic human needs, or does not provide them to all members, the individuals and groups so deprived will become disaffected. They may then act in ways that will cause problems for the society. The nature of the need or needs neglected suggests the nature of the problem. Thus, economic deprivation, lack of deep interpersonal ties, or lack of opportunities for self-expression will each generate *different* kinds of problematic and change-demanding behavior, though there is no simple one-to-one correlation between the nature of the deprivation and the resulting reactions.

Thus, what is to be changed if the social problem is to be overcome is not necessarily the person or group, but society, its rules, norms, polity, economics, stratification, and other relevant features. Each problem area must be examined as to its sources: Does the problem lie in deficient socialization and social control, or in unresponsive societal structure, or in a combination of the two? If the problem is chiefly of the first kind, then improved schooling, rehabilitation, and policing should be helpful. Among the responses more appropriate to problems of the second kind are: (1) changing the law (for example, replacing laws that prescribe racial segregation with laws that ban it); (2) encouraging tolerance (for example, urging acceptance of homosexual liaisons between consenting adults); (3) reallocating wealth (for example, in order to reduce the rate of severe mental illness, traditionally higher among the poor);[23] and (4) transforming the society's "central project" away from production and consumption of material goods toward greater concern for the quality of life (see Postscript).

Theories about societies, however formal and neutral in their terminology, tend to have a normative impact on those who draw upon them for tools of social analysis. Theories without a conception of human needs (or those that see these needs as lacking specific attributes and thus being highly pliable) are open to a conservative interpretation, expecting individuals and groups to adapt to the society as it is. Theories that do assume autonomous human needs provide an independent basis with which to compare societies to each other in terms of their responsiveness to basic human needs. These theories further lead to a systematic consideration of the need to transform existing societies and cultures into more responsive ones, rather than to a focus on correctives that adapt people to roles that may not be able to fulfill their innermost needs.

Dynamics

We suggest that our societal world is growing increasingly more malleable, more changeable, whereas human nature poses a fixed set of needs that demand satisfaction. There remains one cardinal question: To what extent can we control our future through our efforts—through our own interventions in the world? Philosophically, this is a debate that has divided the voluntarists, who confidently assert that we can shape the future, from the determinists, who retort that at best we can only predict it. Voluntarism, the image of a person writ large, standing over a problem like a driver over a stalled car, assumes an actor who, at least in principle if not always in practice, is able to recognize the sources of a problem and deal effectively with it. Voluntarism goes with an engineering mentality that assumes that the dynamics of society can be mastered and turned to serve human purposes or, at the least, that tools and techniques can often be found that will enable us to fix things.

Determinism appears among those biologically inclined and takes the form of the attribution of dominant causality to genetic inheritance. Indeed, from differences in educational and status attainment to alcoholism and homosexuality, more and more social problems have recently

---

23. Whereas members of the middle class are more often neurotic, the lower classes are afflicted with more psychoses, the severest forms of mental illness. See A. B. Hollingshead and F. C. Redlich, *Social Class and Mental Illness* (New York: Wiley, 1958), p. 248. For a follow-up of this study, see Jerome K. Myers and Lee L. Bean, *A Decade Later* (New York: Wiley, 1968).

been reassigned genetic causes.[24] In its more purely sociological form, determinism appears primarily in the belief that history is unfolding according to a largely fixed script that can be marginally edited but not rewritten. Some determinists assert that technological and economic developments that we neither understand nor control are the social forces that in the twentieth century define both our problems and our capacities (or incapacities) to cope with them. Other determinists see contemporary societies basically as oversized tribes or communities that band together according to their own internal logic, which is not accessible to the will of individuals, groups, or the collectivity as a whole. Many determinist thinkers have been optimistic about the future (as, for example, many of the early social evolutionists who thought that progress proceeds independent of, and even despite, peoples' efforts). However, at a deeper level, determinism is passive because it discourages conscious attempts to bring about change.

We use the term "societal guidance" to refer to the total set of factors (or variables) that characterize our ability to guide, or to deal with, social problems and their conditions.[25] The term "guidance" is used rather than societal "control" because the latter assumes a downward, governmental, from-elites-to-the-populace direction, whereas we shall see that upward processes encompassing societal responsiveness to basic human needs, formation of an authentic consensus, and egalitarian distribution of power are cardinal elements of a model societal guidance system. For similar reasons, we avoid using the term societal "management," which, in addition to elitist connotations, implies a thoroughgoing rationalism, whereas we shall see that values and power are as important as knowledge and wise decision making. Finally, societal guidance differs significantly from societal change. Unlike the usual opposition between societal *status quo* and societal change, we contrast both with *deliberate* societal change. It's like the difference between stationary water, the flow of a river, and the ups and downs of the locks of a canal. It's like the difference between interest in given social relations (for example, kinship), social changes (for example, in fashion), and deliberate social efforts (for example, a civil rights movement).

24. For research on genetic causes of differences in educational achievement, see Arthur R. Jensen, *Genetics and Education* (New York: Harper & Row, 1973), and *Educational Differences* (New York: Barnes and Noble, 1973); also R. J. Herrnstein, *I.Q. in the Meritocracy* (Boston: Little, Brown, 1973).

25. I avoid terms such as "solving" social problems because these problems are frequently trimmed or cut, but not necessarily solved. I avoid the term "cure" and other medical images, because it is not as self-evident what the goals of the various interventions are for society as they are for the body. "Health" can be viewed as a desired goal. "Equality" is not equally attractive to all. But we need to understand interventions, whether or not we agree with their purposes.

If societies are to be more responsive, they must do the following:

1. They must acquire *knowledge* of the sources, patterns, and consequences of problem-causing conditions *and* of what guidance efforts
would be needed to overcome both the problems and their root causes.
(In the past, our partial understanding, often caused us to try correctives
which either failed to increase responsiveness of the social conditions to
human needs or actually reduced it.)

2. They must develop the strategies and institutions needed for effective
goal setting and *organization.* (Otherwise, a fine idea may backfire when
poorly or brutally implemented.)

3. They must provide the *power* bases to support the needed changes.
(Only few social changes will be accepted merely on their merit; most
require backing to overcome resistance to change from those whose vested
interests and entrenched beliefs lead them to oppose change.)

4. They must develop participation and authentic *consensus.* (Attempts
to rely on manipulated rather than authentic consensus accentuate the
difficulties of societal guidance.)

Because the chapters that follow are dedicated to these elements, it
is not necessary to dwell on them here, beyond clarifying their conceptual
origins. The factors are not an arbitrary list; they draw upon the approaches discussed in Chapter 1, and they hang together in the form of
a model of societal cybernetics. That is, I have borrowed from electronic
cybernetics suggestions as to what elements are needed for an effective
societal guidance mechanism: the capacity (1) to "read" the world, its
shape, and dynamics, (2) to digest this information, and (3) to feed it to
decision-making units that continually revise their implementation signals.[26] This mechanism is used in targeting torpedoes, for instance. A
ship is designated as the target. The torpedo's "eyes" (sensors) "read"
where the ship is and projects (in the torpedo's "mind," or computer)
where the ship is headed; the computer feeds back the information to a
data-processing unit, which concludes if and when the twain shall meet.
If necessary, the computer issues a directive to a power unit able to emit
direction-changing pulses to the torpedo's rudder and propeller. If necessary, the full cycle is repeated several times.

Significantly, this cybernetic model cannot be applied per se to
social systems or societies, because it leaves out half of the story, in terms
of sociological variables. *Unlike* torpedoes and other technical systems,
those elements subject to review and signaling in a society are not dead
matter but individuals and groups of persons. For both normative *and*

26. See R. B. Ash, *Information Theory* (New York: Wiley, 1965), and *Measure,
Integration & Functional Analysis* (New York: Academic Press, 1971); Jerry D. Card-
well, *Social Psychology: A Symbolic Interaction Perspective* (Philadelphia, Pa.:
Davis, 1971); Norbert Wiener, *Cybernetics, or Control and Communication in the
Animal and the Machine,* 3rd ed. (Cambridge, Mass.: M.I.T. Press, 1961).

practical reasons, their feelings, preferences, values, and interests must be introduced *systematically* into the analysis. Hence, the analysis must encompass the representative "upward" elements, which include such forces as political parties, labor unions, voluntary associations, leaders, and the media. Each of these has "downward" sides, as, for example, when the media helps shape what the people are, and does not merely report what it finds among the people. Similarly, the elected representatives do not merely represent; they also help shape the public's demands and receptivity to policy. Whereas both downward and upward flows are of interest, it is their upward role that turns cybernetic control theory into one of societal guidance.

The more relevant image here is not that of a torpedo but of a passenger ship. The core *metaphor* is of society as an ocean liner propelled by an undersized engine; thus it partly drifts with the ocean currents and is partly self-propelled. Meanwhile, a struggle goes on among the decks (first class, second class, and so forth) over where the various groups of passengers want the ship to go and over how the deck privileges will be allocated and by whom. The result is that the ship itself is continually being restructured as it sails on the high seas. Sailing the ship safely into port is clearly more than a matter of correctly determining latitude and longitude and working the rudder; it has to entail finding ways to reduce the struggle among the passengers and between the passengers and crew and finding a means for everyone to participate in reaching an agreement on the ship's future course. What makes for genuinely responsive upward participation, effective downward control, adequate societal information collection and processing, and the successful application of these mechanisms to bring about basic changes in society when needed is the set of questions the guidance approach tries to answer and the subject of subsequent chapters of this book.

Guidance theory focuses on factors that affect each and every social problem—such as the needed knowledge, the proper planning, the required motivation—rather than on the unique features of a specific list of social problems. Particular problems, however, can typically be characterized according to the factor that more than any other explains why the problem has not been resolved. Our failure to overcome poverty, for example, is more a question of a lack of resources and political will or insufficient power and mobilization, whereas our difficulties in treating schizophrenia or alcoholism are *relatively* more a question of inadequate knowledge. (However, I do not deny that knowledge about how to counteract the effects of infant malnutrition would certainly help lighten the consequences of poverty, just as more resources might help conquer alcoholism.)

In addition, social problems may be classified as being relatively more personal (suicide) or collective (the population explosion). The latter result primarily from unresponsiveness to the need to maintain harmony with the environment. Note, however, that the two tend to converge. Thus, a sharp rise in suicide can threaten a society's sense of self-confidence, whereas a population explosion is experienced by individuals as personal difficulties such as overcrowding, shortages, and so forth. Possibly a better dividing line is between the problems each individual or family must handle with whatever help the society can or does provide and those the community must handle with whatever aid individual members will lend. Alcoholism is a problem of the first kind; pollution of the second. The distinction speaks to the core question posed by the guidance approach: Where are the levers for change?

The following five chapters present the variables—knowledge, goal setting, organization, power, and consensus—that the guidance theory posits as essential to answering this question.

CHAPTER 3
KNOWLEDGE

In examining the role of knowledge in dealing with social problems, we ask three main questions, around which the three sections of this chapter are organized: (1) How potent is knowledge as a factor in dealing with social problems? There are two parts to this question: First, is knowledge reliable or does it largely reflect other factors, such as the interests of those who pay for it? Second, how "weighty" is knowledge, whatever its reliability, as compared to other factors, such as economic and political ones? Because these two considerations refer to the relationship of knowledge to other factors, they may be referred to as extrinsic considerations. (2) What different effects do the various ways of producing knowledge have on its effective use? Does better collection of data, more careful processing, and better theories yield more usable knowledge? Because these factors deal with issues that are internal to the social organization of knowledge, they may be referred to as intrinsic. (3) Under what conditions does knowledge flow effectively from the knowledge makers to the citizens and policy makers, so that they can use it in dealing with social problems? These considerations bridge the intrinsic and extrinsic aspects of knowledge.

EXTRINSIC CONSIDERATIONS:
THE RELATIVE SIGNIFICANCE OF KNOWLEDGE

The Trustworthiness of Societal Knowledge

The role of knowledge in efforts to overcome social problems could not be more obvious. The medical analogy comes to mind. When you experience the symptoms of what you think may be an illness, say, a fever and a rash, you call in an expert who diagnoses the condition by using technical indicators, such as blood and urine tests. The specialist then interprets the results in the light of some generalized concepts or theories, arriving at recommendations for intervention. To test the effectiveness of the intervention, the same basic application of knowledge is repeated: obtaining new readings on the indicators and then again interpreting the results. (Are the temperature and rash receding? Is the blood chemistry closer to normal?) If there is no improvement, additional tests are ordered, tapping other variables suggested by a theoretical conception of what else might be wrong, and the prescriptions for intervention are revised accordingly.

Modern society seemingly responds to its social problems in a similar way. Sharp rises in crime, drug addiction, child abuse, divorce, or pollution are viewed as alerting signals. Experts are called in, including university-based consultants, research corporations, and government specialists, who conduct various investigations and make recommendations. Certain of the recommendations are tried, their effects assessed, and so on. Thus, the full cycle of "reading" the problem of interpreting the signs on the basis of theoretical conceptions that serve to formulate suggested interventions, and of evaluating the results is found on the societal level. Thus, on the face of it, the medical analogy is quite appropriate. Indeed, it is widely subscribed to by the public and the media. It is frequently stated that we "should" be able to use our societal knowledge to lick our social problems in the same way that we conquered polio, tuberculosis, and malaria.

However, most social scientists hold a much less optimistic view of societal knowledge. Social scientists of all the approaches examined in Chapter 1 pondered the true significance of knowledge in determining both diagnosis and prognosis of our social problems, both in shaping personal decisions (for example, to stop smoking) and public ones (for example, to place higher priority on the quality of life). Conflict theory stresses the relative *in*significance of expert knowledge, which is not objective, but instead reflects the interests and outlook of those in power and therefore constitutes part of the problem rather than part of the solution. Marx suggested that only knowledge in the hands of the proletariat, or "the people," and chiefly after the proletariat has been liberated from its prerevolutionary subject status, is valid and useful. Many others have characterized those whom we currently turn to for prescriptions for our social problems as shamans, who, whether deliberately or unwittingly, help lull people into political quiescence by pretending to treat problems with their knowledge, which because of its distorted base, is not valid. Thus, Frances Piven argues that the advocacy planner, who supposedly works in the interest of the urban poor, "deflects conflict by preoccupying newcomers to city politics with procedures that pose little threat to entrenched interests. It is a strategy which thus promotes political stability in the city."[1]

Earlier we discussed a point ethnomethodologists make: There can be no solid facts; all are built on the shifting sands of human perception. Ethnomethodologists tend to suspect generalized facts and theories as being insensitive to the subtle nuances of complex realities. Neoconservatives point out that experts have often been found wrong, many millions of dollars too late.[2] Some would add that human beings are too irrational to be subject to scientific predictions. Structural-functionalists warn of the "unanticipated consequences" of our actions, eliciting unforeseen results that either undermine or reverse our intentions.

All this serves to warn us that one cannot naïvely assume that experts command or even that they necessarily seek the "truth"; it is naïve to assume that a fact is a fact is a fact, regardless of who uncovered it and how. Reviewing studies of the sources of innovation, John Walsh concluded: ". . . studies tend to reflect the interests and biases of those who perform them. Studies done in schools of business tend to stress managerial factors. Technologists are likely to stress applied research."[3] Walsh goes on to report that Project Hindsight, a study of the sources of technological innovation carried out for the Department of Defense, credited basic research with making only minor contributions, while two studies funded by the National Science Foundation (NSF), the federal agency entrusted with supporting basic research, found the role of basic research much more significant. It was not accidental that the studies came up with contradictory findings; they defined the uni-

1. Frances Piven, "Whom Does the Advocacy Planner Serve?" *Social Policy*, May–June, 1970, p. 35.

2. Daniel Moynihan, *Maximum Feasible Misunderstanding* (New York: Free Press, 1969).

3. John Walsh, "Technological Innovation: New Study Sponsored by NSF Takes Socio-Economic Management Factors Into Account," *Science* 180:4088 (May 25, 1973), 846–847.

verse of relevant data differently. The NSF studies went further back than the Department of Defense studies, thus covering not only the stage of technical planning, but the earlier, more conceptual phase, in which basic research was more likely to have played a significant role. In addition, the NSF studies encompassed less purely technological topics, such as the development of the input-output model in economics, whereas the Department of Defense studies focused more on hardware, such as the development of the Polaris submarine.

The point is not that all data are inherently untrustworthy, because they merely reflect a study's sponsorship. Scholars do free themselves in varying degrees from such biases. Neither the Department of Defense nor the NSF studies relied on "made-up" data; both were accurate and truthful in this sense. They reached different findings by defining their topics differently. The main lesson is that taking into account the sociological roots of data improves our understanding of the data and its limitations, even hidden biases.[4]

The Force of Knowledge

A corollary to the question concerning the extent to which societal knowledge reflects the world "as it really is" (and hence can be relied upon in dealing with social problems) and the extent to which it reflects the personal prejudices and social status of the knowledge seeker (and hence is unreliable) is the question of its relative significance in determining the dynamics of social change. Max Weber is portrayed as having engaged in a lengthy dialogue with the ghost of Karl Marx over this very question,[5] and the debate goes on among their followers. If knowledge is fashioned by class interests and serves chiefly to buttress the ideologies that give a moral and intellectual glow to these interests, as Marxists see it, then knowledge can have little causative power. In contrast, Weber rejected the notion that knowledge and ideas are fundamentally distorted by class conflict and held that class, status, and power, as well as knowledge, affect societal reality. In the same vein, Weber held that these social factors can be studied without having the knowledge of the observer fundamentally distorted by these forces. We do not presume to settle this classic debate. Hence, we shall not attempt to estimate how much of the variance in the characterization of social problems and in the formulation of corrections can be attributed to our knowledge or to economic

4. For additional discussion, see Robert K. Merton, "The Sociology of Knowledge," in *The Social Theory and Social Structure* (New York: Free Press, 1968), pp. 510, 542.

5. For a review, see Lewis A. Coser, *Masters of Sociological Thought* (New York: Harcourt Brace Jovanovich, 1971), p. 249.

and other social factors. Instead, it is simply assumed that knowledge is capable of playing a more than trivial role in the formulation of a society's atempts at societal guidance. We hence focus on what knowledge does do, on its specific consequences.

To illustrate our position with a concrete matter: It is often noted that the subjects which are being investigated reflect the preferences of those who control the research funds. For instance, a major impetus behind the passage of the National Cancer Act of 1971, which provided for increased applied and clinical research directed at conquering cancer, was a widespread belief in Congress and elsewhere that funds of the National Institutes of Health had in the past been poured so heavily into basic research that had few direct clinical payoffs. Specifically, funds had been used to study, not diseases afflicting large numbers of people, but rather those unusual ones that aroused research interest.

Thus, what we have learned, what we choose to study at any given point, and what we will get out of it is not largely the result of freewheeling scientific curiosity and serendipity. E.g., scientists studying lunar rocks very seldom happen upon a solution to industrial pollution or make any other such unpredictable breakthrough. Most findings are made in the area in which the scientist sets out to make them[6] and are *not* readily transferable to other areas.

Most directly, the targets at which scientific study is directed are greatly influenced by budgets.[7] The development of knowledge is very expensive. Scientists' salaries are high, computers are costly, and so are social science surveys. The Coleman Report on equality of educational opportunity (see note 24 below) alone cost nearly a million dollars. Because resources were available for decades to study space and weapons, and much smaller amounts for social problems,[8] most scientists gravitated to the space and weapons field, and this is where the greatest number of findings were made. Another example: Within the social sciences, funds were for many years more readily available for studies of mental rather than general hospitals; and indeed, until recently, there were scores of studies of psychiatric wards for each report on a medical one. In the private sector, most of the funds go toward improving consumer products —building a thinner TV set, concocting a new lipstick color or a perkier

---

6. S. C. Gilfillan, *Sociology of Invention* (Chicago: Follet, 1935); Richard Nelson, "The Economics of Invention: A Survey of the Literature," *The Journal of Business,* 32:2 (1959).

7. Jacob Schmookler, *Invention and Economic Growth* (Cambridge, Mass.: Harvard University Press, 1966).

8. Between 1953 and 1971, federal nondefense and nonspace outlays as a percent of the total research and development budget ranged from 4.7 percent to 13.9 percent; 1971 figure is an estimate. "National Patterns of R & D Resources," *Funds and Manpower in the U.S., 1953–1971,* National Science Foundation, NSF 70–46, p. 38.

mouthwash. An estimated total of $11.2 billion a year, or 40 percent of total national research and development expenditures,[9] are spent on such research.

It thus seems that the application of societal knowledge is not neutral; its direction and strength reflects. in part, other nonknowledge factors, such as power and economic interest. But we also hold that under the same social conditions, differences in the *internal* social organization of knowledge will make a difference, a subject we focus on next. In exploring the social organization of knowledge, we depict each factor and illustrate the effect of its absence, presence, and relative strength. Each factor must ultimately be viewed in the context of the others. Thus, although we begin by discussing how well we are able to get a reading on a social problem, and only then explore to what extent and with what result the available readings reach policy makers—needless to say, reliable readings not communicated, or unreliable readings well communicated, can only hinder the usefulness of knowledge in resolving social problems. The combination of effective reading *and* effective communication is what effective utilization of knowledge and, ultimately, effective societal guidance requires. The same holds for the other factors discussed in the next section. Thus, though it is necessary to introduce them one at a time, it must be kept in mind that they all work simultaneously. As the discussion now turns to internal organization of knowledge, a production analogue is followed: from raw material (the facts), to semiprocessing (interpretation), to final products (interventions, feedback, and evaluation).

THE SOCIAL ORGANIZATION
OF KNOWLEDGE

Reading the Problem

Citizens, policy makers, and experts faced with a social problem and seeking to evaluate alternate courses of action often do not have the basic information needed to gauge the scope, nature, and dynamics of the problem, or the effects of previous—or anticipated—interventions. It is like trying to perform surgery in a dimly lit room without seeing quite clearly what one is trying to reach or where the scalpel is cutting. The following examples illustrate the limits of our knowledge.

Among the rather elementary facts we often act as if we know, but in fact do not, are the following: Are few or many welfare recipients in-

9. *Research and Development for 1972, Funds in 1972, Scientists and Engineers, January, 1973,* National Science Foundation, NSF 74–312.

eligible for the benefits they are collecting? In the case of New York City, in which there is a high concentration of welfare recipients, a 3.4 percent ineligibility rate is suggested by the city's Human Resources Administration; estimates in Albany run to "more than 30%." A third party has suggested that neither statistic is worth 2 cents.[10]

Another example: We do not know whether or not long-term use of marijuana causes physiological or psychological damage, though much public policy is based on the assumption that it does.[11] We are not even really sure about heroin, though our public policy and millions of citizens have assumed otherwise for decades.[12]

Another example: A federal agency reports that "although the psychiatric profession is frequently called upon to predict the potential for dangerousness of persons brought before the courts, no scientifically reliable method for predicting dangerous behavior exists."[13] That means that thousands are incarcerated in notorious state mental hospitals against their will, without any reliable evidence that they are more dangerous than those released to the streets. Another example: We do not know whether the number and deployment of police (in cars or on foot) have any real effect on the rate of crime.[14]

The net effect of this lack of knowledge on social policy was summed up during a congressional hearing by a former special assistant to President Johnson who testified:

> The disturbing truth is that the basis of recommendations by an American Cabinet officer on whether to begin, eliminate, or expand vast social programs more nearly resembles the intuitive judgment of a benevolent tribal chief in remote Africa than elaborate sophisticated data with which the Secretary of Defense supports a major new weapons system.[15]

10. *New York Post*, August 4, 1972.

11. Thomas H. Maugh, "Marijuana: The Grass May No Longer be Greener," *Science*, 185 (August 23, 1974), 683–685.

12. Edward M. Brecher and the editors of *Consumer Reports, Licit and Illicit Drugs* (Boston: Little Brown 1972), pp. 21–32, especially p. 23.

13. Quoted from "Symposium on Dangerous and Mentally Disturbed Persons," *HEW News*, August 8, 1974.

14. James Q. Wilson, "Do the Police Prevent Crime," *New York Times Magazine*, October 6, 1974, pp. 18–19, 96–102. See also Wilson, *Thinking About Crime* (New York: Basic Books, 1975).

15. Joseph Califano in testimony at hearings on the Full Opportunity Act, conducted by the Subcommittee on Evaluation and Planning of Social Programs, U.S. Congress-Senate Committee on Labor and Public Welfare. Quoted in Clement Bezold, "Congressional Research Support and Information Services," U.S. Congress Joint Committee on Congressional Operations, 93rd Congress, second session, Appendix of Hearings (Washington, D.C.: Government Printing Office, 1974), p. 452.

Over recent years, the case has been made that social indicators should be developed in the form of standardized measurements to be taken at fixed times (for example, annually) to provide a regular reading on at least some basic facts.[16] Economic indicators (size of gross national product, amount of money in circulation, unemployment, prices) and population (birthrates, death rates, population growth) have existed for some time and have served to help both citizens and policy makers gauge the extent of progress and our problems. Thus, rather than debate whether or not people are unemployed, the discussion focuses on what level of unemployment is acceptable (the measure of the existing problem is relatively clear).[17] Such measures have also strengthened economics and demography, because a regular flow of quantitative data seems essential for the development of a science.

The development of *social* indicators in the area of public safety, education, health, housing, recreation, and so forth, is still in an early stage. The first report was issued in 1968, the second in 1973.[18] Thus far, the endeavor illustrates both the considerable technical difficulties involved in creating such measures and their value for societal guidance.

The difficulties are illustrated by the following contrast: According to police reports there were 198 violent crimes per 100,000 population in 1965, yet according to a survey of citizens, the rate was about 355, or more than 75 percent higher.[19] Which survey should be relied upon? Clearly many crimes are not reported by victims to the police and, so it seems, by the police to the statistical authorities.[20] At the same time, it

16. See the discussion on the call for social indicators in "Social Choice and Social Planning" by Daniel Bell, *The Coming of Post-Industrial Society* (New York: Basic Books, 1973); see also Eleanor Sheldon and Robert Parke, "Social Indicators," *Science*, 188 (May 16, 1975), 693–699 and Wilbert E. Moore and Eleanor Bernert Shelton, "Monitoring Social Change. A Conceptual and Programmatic Statement," American Statistical Association, Social Statistics Section, Proceedings of 1965 (Washington, D.C.: American Statistical Association, 1965), pp. 144–149.

17. We say "relatively" because such measurements are not precise. For example, two articles on long-term labor participation rates and forced part-time employment estimate that real unemployment is about 1.5 times the Department of Labor figure. See "End of the Boom," and "Tasks of the American Labor Movement," *Monthly Review*, 18:11 (April 1967), pp. 7 and 13 respectively.

18. See *Social Indicators, 1973*, selected statistics on social conditions and trends in the United States (Washington, D.C.: Office of Management and Budget, 1973), and *Toward a Social Report*, with introductory comments by Wilbur J. Cohen (Ann Arbor: University of Michigan Press, 1970).

19. *Social Indicators, 1973*, p. 46.

20. Marvin E. Wolfgang, "Uniform Crime Reports: A Critical Appraisal," *University of Pennsylvania Law Review*, 3:5 (March 1963), p. 709.

is possible that victims exaggerate when they report crimes to pollsters and survey researchers.

The difficulties hidden in the seemingly simple question, "What's what?" are often quite intricate. For example, arrest figures are commonly employed to measure both the level of criminal activity and that of police anticrime effort. But these statistics include (1) many people who were charged but found innocent; (2) many people who committed several crimes but were caught only once; (3) people who committed one crime but were arrested, released, and rearrested, and are counted as multiple arrests.[21] Thus, clearly, the level of criminality and/or policing may fall but the reading may rise (for example, if record keeping is improving and civil liberties are less often respected) or fall (if record keeping grows sloppier or people are arrested less wantonly).

Three kinds of measures are typically used to measure health-care delivery: (1) *input,* which includes the resources available for treatment (hospital beds, doctors, nurses); (2) *process,* that is, the procedures followed, (such as does the hospital regularly review the tissues removed by surgeons to verify if they are indeed pathological in most cases?); and (3) *output* measures (for example, how much actual improvement in health has been achieved?). All pose serious problems. Output measures are affected by many factors *other* than the medical treatment provided, especially by the wealth and social status of the person. Thus, a decline in infant mortality in an area may well mean that the population has become more middle class, not that local health programs have become more effective.[22]

Input and process health measures are indicative of the social efforts in this area of service, but not necessarily of achievements or outcomes. It has not been proved, for instance, that more hospital beds mean more or better medical care. Actually, studies show that the more beds there are, the more surgery takes place, even if the population is not sicker. Hence, very likely, more *un*necessary surgery takes place, meaning *lower-*quality care.[23] Thus, just as studies of schools have suggested that increasing a school's budget, number of teachers, books and variety of

21. Andrew Hacker, "Getting Used to Mugging," in *Readings in Sociology,* eds. Edgar A. Schuler, Thomas F. Hoult, Duane L. Gibson, and Wilbur B. Brookover (New York: Crowell, 1974) pp. 612–620.

22. Odin W. Anderson, *Health Care: Can There Be Equity?* (New York: Wiley, 1972) pp. 147–150.

23. M. I. Roemer, "Hospital Utilization and the Supply of Physicians," *Journal of the American Medical Association,* 178 (December 9, 1961), 989–993.

physical facilities[24] does not necessarily correlate with achieving better education, so, adding doctors, hospitals, and clinics does not necessarily produce better health.

Our point is not that it is impossible to learn the facts of social life, but that it is a much more demanding task than is often assumed. In addition, we wish to emphasize that the quality of knowledge available to deal with a social problem, which is one factor affecting the extent to which the problem will be resolved, is influenced, in turn, by the amount and quality of "raw material"—basic facts—available.

The sociologist also recognizes that the collection of data by itself has various social consequences that in turn affect the general social condition and various problem areas. Example: A nationwide assessment has been introduced to report regularly to policy makers, schools, parents, and taxpayers as to how well the schools were performing. The resistance on the part of school officials, even before the first reading was taken, was enormous, and the project got off the ground only after it was so rigged that the data did not identify specific schools. For over a decade the debate on this issue has continued subsiding only barely.[25] Opponents still argue that such testing encourages teachers to focus on preparing pupils for the tests, rather than on the desired curriculum; that the tests focus on some subjects (especially those easiest to measure) to the neglect of the more subtle, humanistic ones; that they unfairly malign those who are disadvantaged—not because of their having been poorly taught, but because of their disadvantaged backgrounds, and that the tests therefore favor white, middle-class children.

Proponents claim that even without testing, evaluations of pupils and schools are made anyhow, but that they are then based on hunch, gossip, and spot-checking rather than systematic data. They add that the tests are becoming ever more encompassing and bias free, that the resulting pressure to perform is desirable, and, finally, that the parents and general public who pay for the service are entitled to know what kind of education their children are getting.

A "golden mean" may be the best approach in this instance. Too much testing of the wrong kind may do more harm than good; yet some assessment is inevitable, and it would seem preferable that it be based on standardized data. Moreover, the very debate over the validity of the data focuses attention on the need to be guided by knowledge in making policy decisions. This has not always been obvious to many school prin-

24. James S. Coleman, Ernest Q. Campbell et al., *Equality of Educational Opportunity* (Washington, D.C.: Government Printing Office, 1966).

25. "National Assessment—Measuring American Education," *Compact*, 6 (February, 1972).

cipals anxious to protect their records or to parents and voters who are occasionally mobilized by emotional issues such as the sexual or political preference of the teachers rather than the quality of their teaching.

Also regular readings on social indicators would help balance the current emphasis on economic indicators. The economic measures tend to stress quantity of production rather than quality of life, neglecting the costs material growth exacts in terms of routinization of labor, environmental deterioration, and so forth. For instance, according to economic indicators, the mass production of autos swells the gross national product; however, by a combined social and economic measure, taking into account safety and the environment, railroads would be a more highly favored mode of transportation. Our public policy is still largely geared to economic indices. The nation still subsidizes autos (by paying for their "tracks" out of public funds), whereas railroads have to build and maintain their own tracks. In short, the scope and quality of the readings we take, and their side effects, affect our individual as well as collective knowledge of our condition, our problems, and our dealing with them.

Interpretation

If you have ever seen a computer tape or printout, a deck of IBM cards, or a sheaf of tables full of figures, you will realize that a pile of facts is not very informative in and of itself. Data are raw materials that must be processed to make sense. Processing may range from the simple, fairly mechanical operation of summing up the information to a highly intricate analysis of what a variety of statistical tests and mathematical models reveal.

The trouble is that in all interpretation, information must be deliberately sacrificed to allow for summary, the way we must forget about each individual tree in order to gain a picture of the forest. Second, all such summaries are subject to mathematical and analytic, as well as normative, slanting.[26] The more sophisticated the processing, the more this is the case.

One example will have to stand for the thousands that could be given. Reference is often made to N million poor Americans, as if poverty were a clearly defined concept. Actually, the number is significantly affected by how one chooses to draw the line between poor and nonpoor.

---

26. Those interested in examples of differing definitional and statistical interpretations can consult Paul B. Horton and Gerald R. Leslie, *The Sociology of Social Problems*, 4th ed. (New York: Appleton-Century-Crofts, 1970), Chap. 3, "The Interpretation of Data"; and W. Allen Wallis and Harry W. Roberts. *Statistics: A New Approach* (Glencoe, Ill.: Free Press, 1956).

In 1964, Mollie Orshansky developed an index of poverty for the Social Security Administration that was based on family size and composition, place of residence, and the proportion of family income needed to purchase a minimum adequate diet. This index set the poverty line for a family of six living in a nonrural residence at about $3,000.[27] The Conference on Economic Progress established a poverty line that applied to all families at $4,000.[28] The Bureau of Labor Statistics based its figures on a "modest but adequate standard of living" that varied according to place of residence.[29] In 1962, for example, for a family of four living in Atlanta, Georgia, the poverty line was set at $6,000.[30] Who is poor—those who earn less than $3,000, $4,000, or $6,000? Poverty, like pornography (and like other definitions of social problems) is at least in part in the eyes of the beholder and in the interpretations given to statistical data by those who set such definitions—the knowledge makers and those who retain them.

In addition, the research methods utilized, be they participant observation or less obtrusive behavioral observation, laboratory experimentation, or opinion surveys, affect the interpretations that make facts into social knowledge. Participant observation studies, such as *Tally's Corner*,[31] tend to be more emotive than are statistical analyses. Attitudinal surveys provide a picture of people's aggregate subjective feelings, usually in quantitative expressions. Experiments in laboratories (Stanley Milgram's studies showing that people will readily follow even cruel orders of an authority[32]) are typically more precise than field studies, but their real-life significance is not firmly established. Studies that use several measurements and several methodologies—for example, both attitude survey *and* behavioral observation—produce considerably more reliable knowledge, but are *much* less common than single-method studies. The rise of social sciences and the pressure to justify their scientific status hence stressed the reliance on methods that produce quantitatively neutral, hence, relatively "cold," knowledge. However, frequent reactions have set in, resulting in supplements and main works that are more emotive, communicative, comprehensible to the public, and mobilizing.

27. S. M. Miller and Pamela Roby, The Future of Inequality (New York: Basic Books, 1970), p. 35.

28. Horton and Leslie, The Sociology of Social Problems, 4th ed., p. 322.

29. Ibid.

30. Ibid.

31. Eliott Liebow, Tally's Corner: A Study of Negro Street Men (Boston: Little, Brown, 1967).

32. Stanley Milgram, "Behavioral Study of Obedience," Journal of Abnormal and Social Psychology, 67, 1973, 371–378.

Theories and Interventions

Scientists like to assume that the path to the solution of a problem leads from the collection of data and its interpretation, via a theory about its inner dynamics, to the location of causes or independent variables, and finally to the formulation of a solution. The theory (or model) summarizes our scientific data and understanding of the world to date and contains our working hypotheses as to causes and dynamics of the phenomenon.

How theories are expected to work is illustrated by the following example: The *American Soldier* studies carried out during World War II uncovered the puzzling finding that soldiers in the military police were more likely than those in the Air Corps to believe that a "Soldier with ability has a good chance for promotion in the army," even though the objective rate of promotion was actually much higher in the Air Corps. (Among non–college-educated noncoms, the difference was almost 2 to 1, while among college-educated privates and PFCs it was 3 to 1 in favor of greater perceptions of promotion opportunities in the MP unit.)[33]

To explain this finding, two sociologists formulated the theorem that a person's satisfaction with his condition depends in part on whom he compares himself with (reference group), not on the "objective grounds" alone. Thus, the Air Corps men, who saw quite a few members of their reference group being promoted but not themselves, were less happy with the rate of promotion than were the MP's, whose reference group encouraged fewer expectations.[34] The phenomenon was termed *"relative* deprivation."

Since then, in many quite different situations, other studies have found a similar discontent. For example, James C. Davies looked for a common source of a variety of revolutionary and rebellious outbreaks, such as the Russian and Egyptian (1952) revolutions and Dorr's Rebellion (a civil disturbance that occurred in 1842 in Rhode Island). He identified an economic "J-curve" depicting a long, gradual rise in prosperity followed by a sudden sharp downturn producing feelings of relative deprivation in the populace as having preceded all these outbreaks.[35]

33.   Samuel Stouffer et al., *The American Soldier* (Princeton, N.J.: Princeton University Press, 1949), vol. 1, 252.

34.   Robert K. Merton and Alice S. Rossi, "Reference Group Theory," in *Social Theory and Social Structure*, pp. 279 ff.

35.   James C. Davies, "Toward a Theory of Revolution," *American Sociological Review*, 27:1 (Feb. 1962), 5–19. See also Ted Robert Gurr, *Why Men Rebel* (Princeton, N.J.: Princeton University Press, 1970).

On the basis of such studies, when sociologists encounter similar situations, they apply the concept of relative deprivation, which conjures up these previous findings and explanation and allows them to make sense out of what others find startling. When asked to use this knowledge to help guide the formulation of correctives to social problems, sociologists would warn that the increased appropriation to the poor (or foreign aid to less developed nations) cannot be expected to lead to the widely expected gratitude, but to rising expectations and demands.

Thus, this piece of theory, and others like it, allow one to organize many seemingly disparate data, to better understand their underlying dynamics, and to avoid the frustration that tends to occur when things do not work as common sense predicts. Although theories clearly work in the sense just discussed, it is less clear how powerful they actually are. Many social scientists favor greater reliance on theory because they believe that this is the way the natural sciences have been developed:[36]

> How can we hope to develop effective traffic safety programs when the experts cannot even agree on the causes of accidents? . . . The State Department of Motor Vehicles reports that following too closely is the primary cause of accidents; the Thruway Authority blames driver inattention; the State Police cite excessive speed, while the United States Bureau of Public Roads asserts that accident involvement was highest at low speeds. . . . in addition, the National Safety Council reports that driver's failure to yield right-of-way is the primary cause of accidents.[37]

Yet social science theories have provided less than the hoped for basis for societal guidance, and, where followed, the results have often been unsatisfactory. The annals of public policy are littered with multimillion-dollar wrecks, which were first driven according to a social science theory.

One of the most controversial examples is the provision written into antipoverty legislation requiring that the poor be granted "maximum feasible participation" in the management of programs set up to solve their problems. The theoretical notions out of which this program idea grew were (1) that those who were to benefit from a program would be best able to formulate and supervise it (direct, or participatory, democracy); (2) that participation would be beneficial to the psyches of people heretofore typically in subordinate roles (an acting-out theory); and (3)

36. This is hardly the place to review the history and status of these sciences. That sciences may well have developed and do develop otherwise, see William J. Price and Lawrence W. Bass, "Scientific Research and the Innovative Process," *Science*, 164 (May 16, 1969), 803–806, and George Homans, *Social Behavior: Its Elementary Forms* (New York: Harcourt, Brace and World, 1961) pp. 8–11.

37. *The New York Times*, September 25, 1968.

that a new power base supported by federal funds could be created among the poor to counterbalance social elites (a pluralism of the power-base theory).[38] Many explanations have been advanced for why the program did not work (or is believed not to have worked; the data are far from clear-cut). The poor are said to have been too preoccupied with survival or fearful of the mighty to vote and elect their representatives to control the programs (only 2 to 3 percent did). Their representatives are charged with often having favored their own pockets or particular subgroups or with having been inept administrators. The local power elites are reported to have quickly formed coalitions to have the participatory clause removed and to undermine the whole program. Without going into detail about the various conflicting reports and interpretations of what happened and why, the very existence of such wide differences in interpretation suggests how bewildering a guide current social science theories often prove to be.

They tend to be weak because social sciences are less cumulative than the natural sciences, and their capacity to quantify variables is smaller (for example, try to quantify the output of liberal arts colleges—namely, enhance the humanistic dimension). In addition, social science theories are more likely to have normative underpinnings, ranging from Maoist radicalism to ultraconservatism. And, the social phenomena seem to be more complex than, say, that faced by astronomy, thus confronting social science theory with the following dilemma: "If predictive variables are too few, the theoretical models are too simple; and if there are too many, it is extremely difficult to understand their interaction."[39]

While the preceding weaknesses have often been reported, it is less often noted that, when it comes to formulating interventions to overcome social problems rather than merely constructing analytic models of the world, social science theories are particularly vulnerable. Theories advance by breaking up the phenomenon under study into analytic slices and then examining one slice—in effect, disregarding the others. Thus, econometrics assumes that "all other things" (for example, values, tastes, institutions) will be "held constant"; experimental psychology assumes that economic and social conditions are "controlled," and so on. Such specialization is essential for the abstractions typical theory building requires. Interventions, however, must be introduced into the real world, where *all* these factors—the economic, psychic, social, and the rest—play

38. Saul Alinsky, "The War on Poverty: Political Pornography," *The Journal of Social Issues*, 21:1 (January 1965), 41–48.

39. Aaron Wildavsky in a book review of Garry D. Brewer, *Politicians, Bureaucrats and the Consultant* (New York: Basic Books, 1973) *Science*, 182 (December 28, 1973), 1335.

a role, and where very few, if any, are ever constant or can be held still. Moreover, factors of various kinds interact and their mutual effects must be taken into account.

Wisely, few scientists claim that they can regularly and directly solve real-world problems. They claim: (1) that science is a value in its own right (it can provide aesthetic experiences and an intellectual pleasure akin to solving puzzles);[40] (2) that science enshrines and sustains an orientation to the world that requires being open to the new finding rather than prejudging, an orientation useful to citizens and policy makers as well as scientists; and (3) that *if* and when the various theories are pieced together and synthesized, they will provide the necessary total picture.

Such piecing together turns out to be extremely difficult, especially if it is to be accomplished in accordance with rigorous scientific procedures. What, in effect, happens instead is that interventions are typically formulated by *non*scientists, by professionals whose training is in problem solving, not truth finding, who *draw* on *several* sciences, and in addition mix in large doses of experience, professional lore, and distilled common sense. Thus, just as a sick person would be very unwise to call upon a professor of physiology *or* biology *or* chemistry, and well advised to call in a physician who knows *some* of each of these disciplines and lots of practical knowledge, so a builder calls in an engineer, not a professor of mechanics or electronics. Unfortunately, until recently, social scientists often tried to move directly from abstract theory to dealing with social problems. Although conscientious social scientists do warn their societal clients that for their suggestions to work, "all other things must be equal," this caveat is frequently ignored, and social sciences are blamed for the real-world failure of the attempted correctives to social problems.

The social sciences have not, however, been wholly lacking in attempts to provide synthesized, as distinct from analytic, knowledge. Thus, while social work theory has suffered because it, like the other professional disciplines, is considered less prestigious than the analytic disciplines and has long been excessively psychologistic, focusing on individual treatment, it has nevertheless, or so it seems, made more significant contributions toward the formulation of realistic interventions than have the analytic disciplines. For instance, knowledge has been accumulated about, and systematic consideration has been given to, such pragmatic questions as which works better, group or individual psychotherapy, community development or community mobilization, open or closed

40. J. Barzun, *Science, The Glorious Entertainment* (New York: Harper & Row, 1964).

wards for mental patients, low- or high-security prisons; fixed or indeterminate prison sentences, reliance on counterdrugs to block drug abuse or drug-free talking therapy, and so on.[41]

Other steps in the right direction have been taken by applied psychology, criminology, urban anthropology, and public administration.[42] Still, a systematic *policy* science focusing on movable variables and on systemic rather than analytic concepts, and committed to servicing rather than merely unveiling the elusive truth, has yet to come into being.[43]

Whereas most social science training still takes place in traditional single-discipline departments best suited for basic research,[44] a report by the National Academy of Sciences and the Social Science Research Council recommends that universities establish broadly based, multidisciplinary training and research programs in "applied behavioral sciences";[45] in short, what we call the policy approach. Several universities have already developed such programs (University of California at Berkeley, the John F. Kennedy School at Harvard).

Feedback and "Evaluation"

To complete the knowledge process, the effects of early interventions must be both ascertained and then taken into account in formulating subsequent interventions. Precisely because the scientific base is weak and the synthesizing disciplines young, it must be assumed that, as a rule, no policy on a given social problem will be adequately formulated the first time around. Most, if not all, will require considerable, perhaps fundamental, redoing once field experience has been gathered. In the research and development of relatively simple devices such as a new automobile or missile, the inability to know ahead of time, the need to rely at least in part on trial and error, on testing, is routinely assumed. One moves from pencil-and-paper sketches to the construction of small-

---

41. Patricia C. Sexton, *Spanish Harlem* (New York: Harper & Row, 1965), Chaps. 8 and 9; see also Paul Lazarsfeld, William Sewell, and Harold Wilinsky, eds., *Uses of Sociology* (New York: Basic Books, 1967), Chap. 7.

42. See Marvin E. Wolfgang and Franco Ferracuti, *The Subculture of Violence* (New York: Tavistock, 1967); see various issues of *Public Administration Review*, *The Journal of the American Institute of Planners* and *The Journal of the Behavioral and Applied Sciences*.

43. For additional discussion, see Amitai Etzioni, "Policy Research," *American Sociologist*, June 1971, pp. 8–12 and *The Active Society* (New York: Free Press, 1968), Chap. 4.

44. Among the interesting attempts to develop a "grounded" theory and methodology for such an approach, see Anselm L. Strauss and Barney G. Glaser, *The Discovery of Grounded Theory* (Chicago: Aldine, 1967).

45. *Bulletin, The American Academy of Arts & Sciences*, Vol. 24 (March 1971), 5.

scale models, or "prototypes," which are tested, and almost invariably the conception is revised in the process. Social science programs are still often sketched out and then immediately implemented, at multimillion-dollar levels. The reasons programs were and still are launched with little or no pre-testing include overoptimism concerning our capacity to anticipate and manage, social scientists' irresponsible oversell of their wares, and, above all, program heads' belief that only the supersell will pry the funds out of Congress, state legislatures, or city hall in the face of competing demands.

Also, once a multimillion-dollar program is fielded, *unlike* a small pilot program, it tends to generate sufficient vested interest and political pull to resist effective evaluation and, above all, change—not forever, but often for a considerable time during which there is a substantial expenditure. This phenomenon has been amply documented in the area of government contracting with the defense and aerospace industries, which promote their multibillion-dollar hardware—from aircraft carriers to skylabs. Its equivalent exists in the area of social programs. For instance, shortly after World War II, Congress set up the Hill-Burton program to fund the construction of new hospitals and the modernization of old ones to solve a serious shortage of hospital beds. After 25 years, the program has been so successful that, with few exceptions, the problem no longer exists. Indeed, the Department of Health, Education, and Welfare (HEW) recommended to Congress that the program be phased out.[46] Congress, however, insisted on continuing the program to the tune of $200 million a year. Congressmen are particularly fond of programs that involve construction, especially in their congressional districts.

Aside from political opposition to effective (as distinct from perfunctory) evaluation, there are considerable technical difficulties. All the problems of indicators, measurements, and theory referred to above reassert themselves. Moreover, there arise the difficult questions of (1) what goals a program's achievements should be measured against when it had no clearly stated ones to begin with and (2) how to distinguish between failures due to basic misconceptions and mistakes made in the ways a program was put into practice, ranging from incompetent administration to ignoring powerful opposition.

The poor quality of the resultant evaluations has been widely remarked. "Although there are notable exceptions, most of what passes for evaluative research in most fields of public service, such as health, social work, and education, is very poor indeed," Suchman concludes in his book on *Evaluative Research*. "By and large, evaluation studies of action or service programs are notably deficient in both research design and execution. Examples of evaluative research which satisfy even the most elementary tenets of the

46. Dr. Charles C. Edwards, "Too Many Politicians, Too Many Laws," *Modern Medicine*, 43:13 (July 1, 1975), 60.

scientific method are few and far between."... Levine, who headed the research and evaluation efforts of the Office of Economic Opportunity, remarks that "the state of evaluation of educational programs is such that we cannot even be sure that when favorable program results are obtained, they are the result of good program design ... [and not] merely a Hawthorne effect.... Wildavsky has caustically condemned the quality of most PPB policy analyses conducted by government staff. "The data inputs ... are huge and its policy output is tiny."[47]

Moreover, how does one evaluate a program that is constantly being modified, and do so at reasonable cost with sufficient speed to be of value?[48]

Despite these problems, the record suggests that a measure of evaluation tends to be more helpful than none. The mere fact that it is known that evaluations are being made helps. A case in point is the unnecessary surgery, quite commonly performed in the United States,[49] that endangers the lives and well-being of the patients on whom it is performed, swells the cost of health care, and uses up talent and resources needed elsewhere. A study found that when checks were conducted by outsiders (that is, not from the hospital under study), the percentage of surgical interventions later found inappropriate fell from 71 percent ($N = 162$) and 67 percent ($N = 156$) in each of the two weeks prior to the evaluation to 55 percent ($N = 76$) in the first week of the audit and to 19 percent ($N = 17$) in the ninth week.[50] It should not be so surprising after all that it makes a difference in behavior if one knows that somebody is carefully checking and cares, as against a free-for-all or a friendly committee composed only of one's peers.

In addition, even crude "first approximations" at evaluation help raise questions that otherwise might be ignored. For instance, an HEW study compared "control alternatives" for "motor vehicle injuries" and

47. Harold Orlans, Contracting for Knowledge (London: Jossey-Bass, 1973), p. 120. References to E. A. Suchman, Evaluative Research (New York: Russell Sage, 1967), and to R. A. Levine, "Evaluation of Office of Economic Opportunity Programs—A Progress Report," American Statistical Association Social Statistics Section, Proceedings of 1966 (Washington, D.C.: American Statistical Association, 1966), pp. 242–251, and to A. Wildavsky, "Rescuing Policy Analysis from PPBS," Administration Review ((March-April, 1969) pp. 189–202.

48. This question is raised by P. Marris and M. Rein, Dilemmas of Social Reform (New York: Atherton, 1967), pp. 198 ff. For additional discussion, see Carol H. Weiss, Evaluation Research (Englewood Cliffs, N.J.: Prentice-Hall, 1972), and Carol H. Weiss, ed., Evaluating Action Programs (Boston: Allyn & Bacon, 1972).

49. David Mechanic, Politics, Medicine, and Social Science (New York: Wiley, 1973), pp. 285–286. See also Erwin A. Blackstone, "Misallocation of Medical Resources: The Problem of Excessive Surgery," Public Policy, 22 (Summer 1974), 329–352.

50. P. A. Lembcke, "Medical Auditing by Scientific Methods," Journal of the American Medical Association, 162 (October 13, 1956), 646–655.

found startling differences in the expenditures each method required to avert a death. For the period from 1968 to 1972, each life saved by the introduction of seat belts cost only $87, while to achieve the same results through improving driver skills required $88,000.[51] Even if these figures proved to be off by quite a bit, nonetheless they are an eye-opener. We may not wish to rush right out and close driver education classes, but, surely, given an additional allotment of a million dollars for highway safety, the money would be more efficiently utilized by encouraging people to buckle their belts rather than by investing more in driver education.

Without some sort of evaluation, and revisions based on it, social interventions become akin to administering a medication without even checking to see whether it cured the ill, had no discernible effect, or aggravated the problem.

THE FLOW OF KNOWLEDGE: FROM MAKER TO USER

From Knowledge Makers to Policy Makers

Although it may seem self-evident that whatever knowledge is available must reach those who need it to solve their problems, or formulate new interventions, there are several powerful hurdles in the way. One problem is motivational. Many of the best investigating minds are committed to *basic* research[52] (in universities, or even in government agencies, such as the N.I.H. research complex in Bethesda, Maryland, whose annual basic research budget is nearly $2 billion). Here, rewards and promotion go to those who carry out studies that have no necessary applications and who *publish* results in scientific journals rather than communicate them to citizens or policy makers who might apply them. At present there is considerable stigma, as well as economic penalty, attached to both the "popularizer" of findings and to those who conduct applied research. This is reflected in the following survey finding: While only 1 percent of 2,051 scientists doing basic research expressed a desire to engage in applied research, 55 percent of 379 applied scientists wished to work in basic research.[53] Moreover, a grant to study an applied prob-

51. Elizabeth B. Drew, "HEW Grapples With PPBS," *The Public Interest*, 8 (Summer 1967), 16.

52. See, for example, B. Eiduson, *Scientists: Their Psychological World* (New York: Basic Books, 1962), and Anne Roe, *The Making of a Scientist* (New York: Dodd, Mead, 1963).

53. H. M. Vollmer, in Saad Z. Nagi and Ronald G. Corwin, *The Social Contexts of Research* (New York: Wiley, 1972), p. 71.

lem will often be "bootlegged" to turn it into basic research.[54] The Law Enforcement Assistance Administration reported at a meeting called by the U.S. General Accounting Office in 1973 that, despite using a variety of evaluation methods, it had been hard pressed to identify any results from research monies given on a "hands-off" basis to a number of selected universities.[55]

Another difficulty inheres in the lines of authority. People in charge deliberately distort data on performance to make themselves look better, depriving the citizens and the policy makers of significant information in the process. Thus, U.S. Army intelligence officials are reported to have "deliberately underestimated the number of Vietcong guerrillas, apparently to bolster their contention that the Army's controversial search-and-destroy tactics were successful. . . ."[56] Furthermore, the data were progressively diluted as they were passed upward from one echelon to the next higher one. Thus, a field report estimated the number of South Vietnamese families killed by American troops as 175 to 200, maybe 400. By the time it reached Army headquarters, the number had been reduced to 20 to 28.[57] A similar distortion of data as it travels upward from knowledge makers to policy makers has been reported in other parts of government, ranging from the White House staff[58] to the Food and Drug Administration, where, according to the testimony of eleven physicians and research workers before a Senate subcommittee, researchers who produced negative findings in studies of drugs to be offered to the public by the drug industry were harassed, transferred, and at times overruled by their superiors.[59] The Atomic Energy Commission was shown to have suppressed for at least 10 years studies by its own scientists that found nuclear reactors more dangerous than was officially acknowledged.[60]

54. Stephen Parks Strickland, *Politics, Science and Dread Disease* (Cambridge, Mass.: Harvard University Press, 1972). On "bootlegging," see H. M. Vollmer, *Adaptations of Scientists and Organizations* (Palo Alto, Calif.: Pacific Books, 1974), Chap. 10.

55. *Evaluation of Law Enforcement Assistance Administration Programs: A Conference Summary* (Washington, D.C.: National Academy of Public Administration and the U.S. General Accounting Office, February 22–23, 1973), p. 9. Quoted in Stuart Adams, "Evaluative Research in Corrections: Status and Prospects," *Federal Probation*, 38: no. 1 (1974), 18.

56. *The New York Times*, February 27, 1973.

57. *The New York Times*, March 27, 1970.

58. George E. Reedy, *Twilight of the Presidency* (New York: Norton, 1970).

59. *The New York Times*, August 16, 1974; also see Jacqueline Verrett and Jean Carpenter, *Eating May Be Hazardous to Your Health* (New York: Simon and Schuster, 1974), Chap. 3.

60. *The New York Times*, November 10, 1974.

It follows that the more one is able to motivate or retain researchers interested in social problems and in effective communication with policy makers, implementing organizations, and the public, the more effective societal knowledge will be in solving social problems—all other things being equal.

The Citizens: Can They Absorb and Apply Knowledge?

If better knowledge were available and more of it were accurately communicated, could the recipients adequately absorb and apply this knowledge? This question is explored with reference to policy makers in Chapter 4, "Goal Setting." Here we examine the citizens' capacity. Whether or not citizens are able to absorb the information needed to form a knowledgeable opinion and vote intelligently is a question that has often been raised. On the face of it, evidence abounds that citizens are rather ignorant. Studies show, for example, that many citizens (33 percent) do not know the name or party of their representatives, not to mention what they voted for or against in Congress.[61]

Warren Miller and Donald Stokes point out that the public generally knows very little about election candidates. And among people who intend to vote, almost half know nothing about either candidate. Furthermore, people know next to nothing about the positions candidates have on public policies.[62] They lack basic information. For example, only 21 percent answered correctly as to the content of the Bill of Rights,[63] only 19 percent could name the three branches of government.[64] Sixty-three percent of 38 communities opposed measures which were "obviously" good for them, such as, adding fluoridation to the drinking water to ward off tooth decay.[65] Approximately 63 percent of adult Americans could not name a single action undertaken by their school board during the last year.[66]

Yet, although it appears true that many Americans could not pass an elementary civics quiz, a closer look suggests that they *do* know and

61. See Warren E. Miller and Donald E. Stokes, "Constituency Influence in Congress," *The American Political Science Review*, 57 (1963), 45–56.

62. Ibid., pp. 54–56.

63. Robert E. Lane and David O. Sears, *Public Opinion* (Englewood Cliffs, N.J.: Prentice-Hall, 1964), p. 61.

64. Ibid.

65. Nelson W. Polsby, *Community Power and Political Theory* (New Haven, Conn.: Yale University Press, 1963), pp. 130–131.

66. *The New York Times*, March 24, 1975.

understand the basic information they need to make an intelligent election choice. If one stops to consider that each citizen has only one vote to cast for a particular office, it makes sense that he or she should use it to vote for peace and prosperity and against war, depression, and inflation, with most other matters fading in comparison.[67] And, while citizens are occasionally confused (or misled) as to which candidate and party supports which policy (for example, in the 1964 election the candidate who earnestly pledged deescalation of the Vietnam War immediately after his election turned around and escalated), by and large, they do get it right eventually. Johnson ended up by having to give up hope of reelection when the public support for the Vietnam War, and for him, waned; Nixon was forced to resign when a majority of the public and the Congress had come to favor his impeachment. Lincoln's observation that while you can fool some of the people some of the time, you cannot fool all of the people all of the time seems vindicated.

More important, the question of the citizens' competence to choose is quite frequently discussed in the abstract and is unconnected to facts of societal structure. Obviously, if people work the whole day at grueling jobs that leave them fit only for TV watching at night, and if they have quit school early in order to work because of economic pressures, and if they are affected by schooling and mass media culture that teaches them to value consumer goods over public affairs, they will be relatively "ignorant." Liebow's depiction of undernourished blacks working in construction who, worn out, come home to crowded, noisy hovels to collapse in front of the TV and dull their senses with beer,[68] the finding that the average American family spends 6 hours a day watching TV,[69] and James Coleman's conclusions from a study of ten high schools about the materialsitic values transmitted by many high schools and especially by adolescent peer groups[70] bear this out.

But, if they are longer and better educated and not forced to do such enervating work, people are both better able to inform themselves and more likely to participate politically. Studies have shown that the more educated and better off engage more in discussions about social problems and public policy and are generally more active in politics, are

67. On the argument that the voter is no fool, see V. O. Key, *The Responsible Electorate* (Cambridge, Mass.: Harvard University Press, 1966); for the other side of this debate, see Gerald Pomper, *Voters' Choice* (New York: Dodd, Mead, 1975), especially p. 206; and for some relevant evidence, see Lloyd A. Free and Hadley Cantril, *The Political Beliefs of Americans* (New Brunswick, N.J.: Rutgers University Press, 1967), especially p. 97.

68. Liebow, *Tally's Corner*, pp. 29–71.

69. Non-white households watch 16 percent more TV than white households, according to a 1974 Nielson survey.

70. James S. Coleman, *Adolescent Society* (New York: Free Press, 1961).

more likely to develop a sense of citizen duty, are more likely to have greater knowledge of, and more sophistication about, politics, and are more likely to join politically active and relevant as well as nonpolitical groups.[71] Thus, whereas only 41 percent of grade-school graduates could define the term "cold war" at one of its high points in 1950, 66 percent of the high-school graduates and 87 percent of the college educated could.[72] Proportionally, those able to tell the number of senators per state is rather similar.[73]

Finally, citizens are more motivated to inform themselves, the more they have reason to do so. A study found a high correlation between following politics regularly in the mass media and a citizen's sense of his "civic competence," that is, confidence in one's ability to affect political decision making. Among Americans reporting a high sense of civic competence, 59 percent reported a high exposure to political stimuli (following politics in the mass media and paying attention to election campaigns), whereas only 21 percent of those with a low sense of civic competence reported a high exposure to political stimuli.[74]

The Role of the Social Critique

Knowledge makers include not only those who collect, process, and interpret information, but also those who dwell upon its deeper meanings and relate them to the social values—the intellectuals. From society's viewpoint, its self-view and perspective on its problems and what is to be done is shaped not merely by new scientific findings, but by notions of what a decent society ought to be like. Both idealistic visions of a just and humane society and more specific programatic ideas play a core role in the societal efforts to cope with social problems. Thus, for instance, "motherhood," once a synonym for a sacrosanct concept, was cast as a possible harmful enterprise by those concerned with the population growth. In part, this is a matter of evidence that at present rates, by 1980, it is estimated there will be between 222 to 231 million Americans; by the year 2000, between 251 and 300 million.[75] However, whether such figures—and the society they entail—are a source of alarm, delight, or in-

71. Lester W. Milbrath, *Political Participation* (Chicago: Rand McNally, 1965), Chaps. 3 and 5.

72. Hazel Gaudet Erskine, "The Polls: The Informed Public," *Public Opinion Quarterly*, 26 (Winter 1962), 674.

73. Ibid.

74. Gabriel Almond and Sidney Verba, *The Civil Culture* (Boston: Little, Brown, 1965), p. 189.

75. *Statistical Abstract of the United States, 1973*, p. 6.

difference is significantly affected by what intellectuals make out of them. The role of the intellectuals in specific social problem areas can be seen in Michael Harrington's calling attention to poverty (it existed before, but he helped make it into an "unacceptable" condition);[76] in Daniel Moynihan's role in advancing a case for "benign neglect" of the blacks as a way to deal with race relations *after* some gains were made by the blacks and a white reaction has set in;[77] and in the role of Betty Friedan in calling attention to the plight of the woman.[78]

In many of these intellectual efforts, social scientists participated either as the front-line spokesmen and spokeswomen or as second-line participants, in providing arguments, insight, use of data, to advise, buttress, work out, and communicate a general perspective rather than merely a fact or finding.

Structurally, social scientists, especially those university-based and tenured, are well placed to act as social critics. Most policy makers and citizens work with basic assumptions about the societal reality, human nature, and the dynamics of social processes aimed at dealing with social problems they are barely aware of, or usually quite unwilling to consider, let alone change. The social scientists are, or at least ought to be, exempted from such preconceptions and pressures by virtue of their training and position.

The job security university tenure affords, the norms of academic freedom, and the open outlook upheld by the intellectual community at large tend to protect the social scientist as social critic from the repercussions that civil servants, politicians, or others in more vulnerable positions might likely have to endure as the result of advocating unorthodox views. Together with other intellectuals, social scientists are therefore potentially better able to exert leverage to reopen discussion on such "communities of assumptions." Thus, leading social critics were among the first to question the taken-for-granted notion that blacks were inherently inferior, when this was still a dominant assumption,[79] that criminals, homosexuals, and mental patients are intentionally "evil" or "different,"[80] or that punishment rather than therapy, reform, or tolerance is the way to deal with these "deviants" and their subcultures, suggesting

76. Michael Harrington, *The Other America* (Baltimore: Penguin Books, 1963).

77. Daniel P. Moynihan in a memorandum to Richard M. Nixon, February 1970. For Moynihan's view of the political context of this well-known phrase, see Daniel P. Moynihan, *The Politics of a Guaranteed Income* (New York: Random House, 1973), Chap. 2.

78. Betty Friedan, *The Feminine Mystique* (New York: Dell, 1965).

79. Gunnar Myrdal, *An American Dilemma* (New York: Harper, 1944).

80. David J. Rothman, *The Discovery of the Asylum: Social Order and Disorder in the New Republic* (Boston: Little, Brown, 1971).

instead that perhaps society should be changed, rather than all our efforts be directed at adjusting the person to it.[81] It was intellectuals as social critics who advanced the concept of a "quality-of-life society" (against the simple-minded notion of economic "progress") and of "world peace through world law," and who, in many other areas, raised the possibility of basic alternative assumptions.[82]

AN EXAMPLE: THE ROLE OF
KNOWLEDGE IN ALCOHOLISM

Alcoholism's credentials as a social problem are impeccable. About 40 percent of motor vehicle deaths appear to be attributable to alcohol. The economic costs involved in health care, traffic accidents, welfare payments to families of alcoholics, crime, and inefficiency at work associated in the United States with misuse of alcohol were estimated at $25 billion. Drunkenness, driving under the influence of alcohol, disorderly conduct, and vagrancy (an "alcohol-related offense") accounted for 3.3 million arrests in 1971. HEW figures show an association with alcohol in 64 percent of murders, 41 percent of assaults, 34 percent of forcible rapes, and 29 percent of other sex crimes. A high proportion of suicides are committed either under the influence of alcohol or by alcoholic persons. About 41 percent of the marriages of alcoholic persons are estimated as unstable, and the disruption in the home is alleged to create disturbed children who are then more prone to become alcoholics themselves. Children born to alcoholic mothers are said to be less healthy, less alert, and less well developed than other infants, and so they start out in life disadvantaged. Alcoholics and heavy drinkers tend to develop cirrhosis of the liver, heart disease, cancer, and other crippling or fatal diseases more frequently than does any other segment of the population.[83]

Reading the Problem

Despite all we know about the multiple problems associated with alcohol abuse, we lack many of the most basic facts needed to develop societal interventions to combat it. Take the apparently simple question of how many alcoholics are there to be treated? The 1972 Consumers Union

81.   Richard A. Cloward and Lloyd E. Ohlin, *Delinquency and Opportunity* (Glencoe, Ill.: Free Press, 1960); and Richard A. Cloward, "Illegitimate Means, Anomie and Deviant Behavior," *American Sociological Review*, 24 (1959), 164–176.

82.   See Etzioni, *The Active Society*, pp. 181–182.

83.   All statistics are for 1971 and are taken from *Alcohol and Health*, Second Report of the Secretary of HEW, June 1974.

Report's estimate was 5 million.[84] This is in line with the estimate of HEW in its 1972 publication.[85] However, *Alcohol and Health*, a 1971 report of the HEW secretary, estimated that there are 9 million alcoholics, and the Second Report of June 1974 put the figure at 10 million.[86] A text on rehabilitation covers the range by estimating the number of problem drinkers to be as few as 6 million or as many as 12 million.[87]

Accurate statistics are difficult to come by for a number of reasons. Individual cases of alcoholism are often far from easy to identify. Only 1 physician in 300 is reported to be able to recognize an alcoholic when he or she seeks treatment for some other illness.[88] A doctor can treat a patient for hepatitis, cirrhosis, ulcers, anemia, diabetes, tuberculosis, and muscle weakness, all diseases associated with heavy drinking,[89] without ever recognizing alcoholism as a causal or related problem.

The social shame associated with alcoholism hampers efforts to gather reliable data on alcohol-related deaths. Five hundred alcohol-related deaths are officially reported each year in New York City; however, according to Dr. Milton Helpern, the city's former chief medical examiner, this figure is "far below the actual number."[90] The actual number is not known, although one source estimated it at 3,500.[91] A major reason for our hazy knowledge is that out of compassion for the families of alcoholics, physicians are reluctant to list alcohol as the cause of death on the death certificates that are the prime source of such data.

Theories and Interpretation

According to one school of thought, alcoholics can be completely cured, even to the point that they will be able to drink in moderation. According to another school, "once an alcoholic, always an alcoholic," and the most that can be achieved are periods of sobriety; thus, the al-

---

84. Consumers Union Report, 1972, p. 245.

85. *Alcoholism and Its Treatment*, HEW publication 73-9025, 1972.

86. *Alcohol and Health*, second report of the HEW secretary, June 1974, p. 1.

87. Sally L. Perry, George J. Goldin, Bernard A. Stotsky, Reuben J. Margolin, *The Rehabilitation of the Alcohol Dependent* (Lexington, Mass.: D.C. Heath, 1970), p. 1.

88. A statement by the National Council of Alcoholism given to *The New York Times*, August 2, 1972.

89. *Alcoholism and Its Treatment*.

90. *New York Post*, October 23, 1974.

91. Ibid.

coholic should refrain from all drinking because any drinking might send him or her over the brink. The ambiguous nature of theorizing is illustrated by both schools relying on the same studies and statistics to support their opposing views. Thus, a 1974 review of 265 studies of psychologically oriented treatments of alcoholism covering 13,817 patients rated almost two-thirds of the patients improved. Of these, about half (4,591) had achieved total abstinence, while the other half had not.[92]

Most theories of alcoholism treat it as an illness rather than as a form of deviant behavior. In some respects, however, the disease model of alcoholism is a poor fit. A central defining characteristic of what we generally call illness is that the victim is not responsible for his or her condition. Yet, scarcely anyone seems prepared to accept such an assumption concerning alcoholism. Studies have shown that professionals and laypersons alike feel that alcoholics have inflicted their problem on themselves, at least in part, and that alcoholics must actively cooperate in their own treatment if it is to succeed.[93] Whereas the motivation to seek help is a prerequisite to treatment of most illnesses, the element of choice in asking or refusing help for alcoholism appears especially significant and problematic. Confusion about the extent to which alcoholics can be properly viewed as being held responsible for their condition has led to a curious situation: Alcoholism is the only recognized illness that is simultaneously a criminal offense.

Moreover, even within the framework of the medical model, there are a number of unresolved issues. A major one centers around whether the approach to treatment should be primarily physiological or psychological. Thus, there are those who see alcohol as an emotional crutch from which serious physical side effects may develop, whereas others hypothesize that individuals may have genetic or metabolic predispositions toward addiction to alcohol and that their addiction has little if anything to do with personality problems.[94]

From the different conceptions, different prognoses are derived. One major physiological treatment is to block the physical addiction and its

92.   Chad. D. Emrick, "Review of Psychologically Oriented Treatment of Alcoholism, I. The Use and Interrelationships of Outcome Criteria and Drinking Behavior Following Treatment," *Quarterly Journal for the Study of Alcohol*, 35 (1974), 523–549.

93.   A. S. Linsky, "Theories of Behavior and Social Control of Alcoholism," *Social Psychiatry*, 7 (1972), 47–52; Muriel W. Sterne and David J. Pittman, "The Concept of Motivation: A Source of Institutional and Professional Blockage in the Treatment of Alcoholics," *Quarterly Journal for the Study of Alcohol*, 26 (1965), 41–57.

94.   John A. Carpenter, "Issues in Research on Alcohol," in *Alcoholism*, ed. Ruth Fox (New York: Springer, 1967) pp. 16–23.

harmful consequences. Antabuse, a drug that reacts antagonistically to alcohol and induces nausea, is one method used; use of sedatives, vitamins, and electrical shocks are others. Among proponents of the psychological approach, behaviorists have put forth the theory that alcoholism is learned and reinforced behavior providing important rewards such as euphoria or decrease of depression or loneliness. Drinking is hypothesized as a reflex response to reduce an inner drive. The drinker is given aversion therapy based on shock treatment or drugs to make the experience of drinking painful. Freudians theorize that excessive drinking represents unconscious tendencies of self-destruction, oral fixation, or latent homosexuality, while Adlerians see in alcoholism a struggle for power. Depth psychoanalysis over a period of years is the recommended treatment.

Another approach credits a lack of meaningful relationships and of social and cultural support groups as a leading cause of alcoholism. Alcoholics Anonymous and various "talking therapies" such as group therapy, confrontation therapy, psychodrama, peer-group counseling, and so forth, have grown out of these and related insights. Still another school says that alcoholism stems from a combination of all three factors: biological, psychological, and sociological. Treatment should therefore combine therapies from all three areas.

Feedback and Evaluation

Attempts to evaluate alternate treatment programs so as to determine which are most effective are plagued by differences among the programs and program participants. Thus, programs define who is or is not an alcoholic differently, and, generally speaking, the looser the definition, the greater the rate of cure. Programs that are highly selective in the kinds of applicants they admit for treatment are also prone to have higher success ratios, though the types of persons who fit readily into their treatment plans may constitute only a small percentage of all alcoholics. Moreover, measures of effectiveness of treatment do not always take into account program dropouts or persons who fail to report for follow-up counseling after treatment (though such persons are likely to have different traits and attributes than those who stay in the program all the way through), and comparisons among programs often omit consideration of differences in attrition rates. Whether or not participants adhere to all aspects of the treatment regimen is often not sufficiently investigated. Failure to take into account such variables flaws many attempts to interpret the success or failure of treatment.[95]

As the situation stands now, all treatment approaches have some

95. *Alcohol and Health*, second report of the HEW secretary, June 1974, pp. 154–159.

data in their support, but none is conclusive. If any approach appears to have the edge, it is the kind of treatment offered by Alcoholics Anonymous.[96] Success in groups such as this, however, is primarily a matter of individual motivation and small-group dynamics, which develop naturally and are not readily subject to societal guidance.

From Knowledge Makers to Policy Makers and Citizens

Theoretically, one way to eliminate alcoholism is to eliminate alcohol. At one point, the advocates of such a coercive strategy gained a sufficiently sizable political base to introduce a ban on the production and sale of alcohol in the United States. Yet, not only did Prohibition fail to abolish alcoholism, it alienated moderate as well as hard drinkers and gave rise to a widespread defiance of the law. Yet even today, despite the repeal of Prohibition and the inroads made by experts in convincing the public and their governmental representatives that alcoholism is a disease, not a crime, the punitive approach still dominates societal efforts to combat alcohol abuse. Although the number of arrests for drunkenness declined 19 percent from 1960 to 1971,[97] the suggestion to turn over the treatment of alcoholics to social workers and medical centers, and thus relieve the burden placed on police, has yet to gain acceptance. In 1971, 909,000 persons were arrested for intoxication, and not as drivers.[98]

The public believes that most alcoholics are on skid row.[99] A picture of a dirty, disheveled bum asleep in a doorway or panhandling for spare change immediately comes to mind. Yet, indications are that these alcoholics represent only from 3 to 5 percent of the alcoholics in the United States. More than 70 percent of the millions of alcoholics remain in the community and continue to perform their accustomed roles —paying taxes, sending their kids to college, and working as salesmen, bank presidents, housewives, teachers, farmers, clergymen, and physicians —with varying degrees of disturbance. Alcoholics exist in all classes with, it seems, roughly equal frequency. Denial of alcoholism, especially by middle- or upper-class persons and their families constitutes a major hindrance to the problem's identification.

96. Paul E. Kaunitz, "On the Other Hand," *Medical World News*, 15:39 (November 8, 1974), 124.

97. FBI, *Uniform Crime Reports, 1971* (Washington, D.C.: U.S. Government Printing Office, 1971).

98. Ibid., p. 153.

99. *Alcohol and Health*, report of the HEW secretary, December 1971, p. 1.

The Critique

Together with humanists, social scientists have played a major role in providing the public and the public authorities with the concepts and ideas that redefine alcoholism not as a crime, but as a personal and social problem. However, they differ in their views on where to put the blame (for example, on weak parents or an alienating structure). Whereas their concepts clearly have not gained full approval, nevertheless, they are increasingly endorsed and very gradually translated into changes in public policy and citizens' perspectives.

IN CONCLUSION

We saw the role knowledge—its content, organization, and social place and power—plays in approaching and dealing with social problems and in formulating the needed changes in the society and its programs to deal with the problem. We saw mainly negative examples—for example, what happens when knowledge is poor or not communicated—and few positive ones, because the needed knowledge still is often either lacking entirely or has some inherent limitations or is not communicated or not used. The main point, though, is not to point to the present state of this factor, but to illustrate its role in dealing with social problems.

CHAPTER 4
GOAL SETTING

AN ILLUSTRATION

Assume you are about to enter college. A number of questions concerning your plans for the future are bound to cross your mind: what subject should you major in; should you choose a major yet; what do you wish to become; what career do you plan to follow—or do you prefer to wait and see what kinds of jobs are available once you graduate. The range of answers to such questions discloses three main approaches toward using what we know to set goals and to lay out a plan that will organize the next steps to be taken to lead to the realization of our goals.

The first approach is to plan well ahead. Suppose I plan to become, say, a physician. To be admitted to medical school, I'd better study hard and get high grades. I'd better choose the proper mix of natural science courses and liberal arts in order to better show my talents and "breadth." I should find out what my college will do to help me get into the desired medical school, and so forth. We shall call this approach "rationalistic," because it assumes a high capacity to know and use knowledge, to set goals, and to formulate and implement a plan in line with knowledge and desires.

At the opposite extreme is the approach that says that the best way to learn and grow into a mature person is from experience and trial and error. One may try a natural science major for one semester or year, but may well switch to another one. As it is impossible to predict what one wants to do in the longer run, it is surely premature, indeed wasteful, to plan now for steps to be taken 2, 3, or 4 years hence. Who knows? It may be that there will be no market for doctors by the time I graduate, and a year hence I may drop out of college altogether and work for a while, and so on. We call this taking one step at a time or, more formally, "incrementalism." It assumes that we know little about the future, that our goals may change as we progress, and that commitment to a plan sacrifices a flexibility that the unpredictable future renders essential.

Finally, there is an intermediary approach. It forgoes detailed planning, in favor of guidelines. For example, because I might well be boxing myself in by fixing definitely on a career choice now and may yet want to change my mind for all kinds of unforeseeable reasons, my strategy will be to keep a range of likely career options open. Though I've lately become immersed in existentialist philosophy and am contemplating someday writing the "great American treatise," in the back of my mind I still think I might eventually want to become a doctor. Therefore, in between my philosophy courses and experimentation in other directions that might interest me at any one time, I make sure I take enough science courses to satisfy premed requirements. Alternatively, I might sit down and broadly evaluate my interests and talents, not as yet in terms of a major, but rather, at this point, in terms of qualitative or humanistic pursuits versus quantitative or scientific ones, of working with people versus working alone. This approach, reconciling the two previous ones and using guidelines instead of rationalistic plans or incrementalist trial and error, could be called "mixed scanning." Each of these approaches has a societal parallel.

THE THREE APPROACHES ON
THE SOCIETAL LEVEL

Societies have no minds, hearts, or hands, but they do make collective decisions about how to handle their social problems, either directly, via societal intervention, or indirectly, by affecting what individuals can and cannot do about their problems. The process has a variety of names. "Goal setting" refers to the process whereby those in charge of various government agencies, schools, voluntary agencies (such as nonprofit welfare and therapeutic agencies), hospitals, and a hundred thousand other organizations decide to what ends they wish to dedicate their efforts.

The process requires that vague commitments of a normative and political nature be translated into specific commitments to one or more specific courses of action. Thus, out of a growing concern with minority and women's rights grew "affirmative action," a policy seeking to encourage or force employers actively to recruit a proportional number of women and minorities in all job categories and at all levels. Similar development from general goals to specific program objectives can be found in the history of all attempts to resolve social problems if we roll them back to their formative stages. Other terms used to refer to the same process are policy making, decision making, planning, and programming.[1]

Although the process is sometimes more intensive and visible, and sometimes less so, it is nevertheless a continuous one. Goals are constantly set and reset; programs are formulated and revised, and so forth. At the same time, no cabinet, city council, or neighborhood meeting ever starts afresh, completely open as to what endeavors to correct social problems it is willing to consider. The range (and specifics) of the alternatives considered is affected, albeit in differing degrees, by the values the citizens and decision makers hold and the power relations among them. These factors are discussed in subsequent chapters. This chapter deals with how, within the limitations set by such background factors, a specific course of action is worked out. Or, viewed from another angle, because decision making and goal setting introduce an element of choice, it is the most deliberate and voluntaristic aspect of societal guidance. As such, it raises a question concerning the extent to which social actors can decide what direction they will take versus the extent to which they are compelled to follow a course set by forces beyond their control.

The three models of goal setting and decision making explored here —the rationalistic, the incrementalist, and the mixed-scanning models— are each compatible with particular assumptions about the extent of free choice possible. Rationalistic models tend to posit a high degree of control over the situation on the part of the decision maker. The incrementalist approach, often referred to as the art of "muddling through," assumes much less command over the situation. The guidance model combines elements of both in a way that is neither as hopeful as the first nor as pessimistic as the second.

The Rationalistic Approach

According to the rationalistic mode, an actor becomes aware of a problem, posits an alternative state of affairs as a goal, and "rationally" sets out to achieve it by carefully weighing alternative means and choosing among them according to an estimate of their respective merits.

The process requires beginning with a plan or blueprint for action that lays out logical steps to the goal—reducing the problem. Planners

---

1. For a discussion and illustration of all these, see Alfred J. Kahn, *Theory and Practice of Social Planning* (New York: Russell Sage, 1969), and *Studies in Social Policy and Planning* (New York: Russell Sage, 1969).

draw on the concept of a system, that is, on the notion that societal units and their problems are interrelated. Thus, for instance, public support for housing will affect employment (perhaps being adopted in part to stimulate the construction industry when it is in a down phase), race relations (possibly increasing conflict over placing and allocation), and so on. Planners stress that interventions are likely to backfire if these system linkages are ignored. Thus, government financing of many of the health services rendered to the poor and aged through Medicaid and Medicare, proved much more costly than expected. By injecting huge sums of government money into a health care delivery system characterized by a serious maldistribution of resources without simultaneously instituting administrative controls on cost and utilization of services, these two programs are widely considered to have accelerated the long-standing medical price inflation. Having previously pushed the cost of quality medical care out of the reach of large numbers of the poor and the elderly, this inflationary spiral was now beginning to threaten the ability of the middle class to afford care.[2] A somewhat humorous case in point arose in New York City in the closing days of John Lindsay Administration with the introduction of high-intensity sodium lamps as a deterrent to crime and the simultaneous planting of fifty thousand trees to make the city greener. The lights stimulated the growth of the trees to a point where existence of the trees was threatened. Citizens were soon divided between those who wished the lights removed to save the trees and those who wished the trees axed to save the lights.[3]

Because of such system linkages, rationalistic planners tend to oppose restricting one's deliberations to one social sector. They typically also favor central authorities that will see to it that plans are implemented. Such comprehensive planning was at the root of the Model Cities program, which was designed to coordinate and guide all the services provided in the designated cities, at least those provided to the inner-city poor. The Department of Housing and Urban Development, in collaboration with city government, was to furnish the central authority. A more modest variety of the same basic approach is found in operations research, where it is assumed that a problem area can be "modeled" and systematically attacked, at least intellectually, although the solution may have to be implemented by a variety of persons or groups.

Rationalist planners rail against the administrative pluralism so characteristic of the way the United States deals with social problems. Here is a typical news story:

2. See, for example, *Determinants of Expenditures for Physician's Services in the United States 1948–1968* by Victor R. Fuchs and Marcia J. Kramer, Department of Health, Education and Welfare, Health Services and Mental Health Administration, National Center for Health Services Research and Development, December 1972, p. 19.

3. *New Yorker*, May 5, 1975, pp. 90, 91.

Although almost $5 billion a year is spent by Federal, state and local governments to help handicapped youth, a two-year study by the Rand Corporation has found that the programs lack direction and coordination. Moreover, the study shows that the programs fail generally even to identify those eligible for aid and inequitably serve those they find.

Because the parents of handicapped children are confronted with a bureaucratic maze of overlapping jurisdictions and because no central agency coordinates the many programs, thousands of youths needing help are not getting it, according to the study.

The first part concludes that the programs serving handicapped youths are "varied, fragmented, uncoordinated and not responsive to an individual's total needs."

"The sheer number of institutions dispensing funds and services contributes to a situation in which no one plans, monitors or controls the handicap service system in any comprehensive fashion," the report states.

Although he sees the need for more spending in these areas, Dr. Kakaha [director of the study] believes that complementing coordination is required rather than an overhaul or dismantling of the existing system.[4]

Similar charges of fragmentation, overlap, and disarray have been directed at most programs concerned with correcting social problems, from welfare to housing, to education, to public safety. Take health, for example. Health services are provided directly by the federal government via the Veterans Administration and indirectly through federal funding and supervision of scores of programs focusing on, among other things, hospital construction, health-care standards, and health manpower training. Their proliferation has been such that, during the Johnson Administration alone, Congress is said to have enacted 51 major pieces of legislation administered through 400 different authorities.[5] The states also have their own departments of health and play a significant role in the administration of Medicaid. In addition, the cities' health departments deal with such matters as venereal disease and standards of hygiene in restaurants, as well as municipal hospitals and clinics. In addition, there are numerous voluntary (nonprofit) hospitals and clinics, proprietary (profit-making) institutions, and membership-based health facilities run by universities, labor unions, religious orders, and dozens of other groups. Over and above these health-care delivery units, there are several coordinating agencies, including comprehensive health-planning agencies and various health councils, which tend to be weak and ineffectual and thus barely reduce fragmentation.

Criticism of rational planning focuses on the disparity between the requirements of the model and the capacities of decision makers.[6] Societal

4. The New York Times, February 12, 1974.

5. Rosemary Stevens, American Medicine and the Public Interest (New Haven, Conn.: Yale University Press, 1971), p. 505.

6. Charles E. Lindblom, The Intelligence of Democracy (New York: Free Press, 1965).

decision makers, as critics point out, frequently do not have a specific, agreed-upon set of values that could provide the criteria for evaluating alternatives. Values are fluid; they not only affect, but are affected by, the decisions made. In actual practice, the assumption—implied in comprehensive planning—that values and facts, means and ends, can be clearly distinguished seems inapplicable. This is illustrated by the debate over the question of whether or not smoking marijuana is harmful and, hence, whether or not its use should be prohibited, decriminalized, or legalized. One of the questions at issue is whether or not marijuana smoking impairs driving skills; if so, legalization would hence precipitate more auto accidents. One question that then arises is: Suppose some impairment occurs after heavy use; should *all* marijuana consumption then be banned, even if alcohol use is not, despite its high correlation with auto accidents? Clearly, matters of fact (degree of impairment) are mingled with foggy terms (How much is "heavy?") and emotional value issues ("If you take my toy away, why not yours?"). Similar examples are to be found in practically all social problem areas.

In addition, information about consequences is, as a rule, not merely incomplete but rather limited. Typically, decision makers—critics of planning say—have neither the assets nor the time to collect the information required for rational choice. While new technologies, especially computers, increase our capacities for collection and processing of information, even they cannot carry out all the computations required by the rational model. Note, for example, that computers have been taught to play rather mediocre chess, at best. Yet, a chess game is enormously more simple than any societal situation. In chess, there are only two sides; the rules are explicitly stated and not subject to change; there are only sixty-four squares; the power of each piece is clearly defined; their positions and movements are clearly visible. In contrast, societal players are numerous and society's laws changing and changeable; turfs are poorly defined; power relations are in constant flux; information is often vague.

There have been few follow-up studies to check the validity of prediction and forecasting, a core element in all comprehensive plans. The results of those studies that have been made are eye-opening. Some of the most thought-provoking research concerns predictions in the stock market. It shows that random selection of stocks to invest in (that is, assuming that we are unable to know *anything* about the future behavior of the various stocks involved) leads to the same or superior investment as does following the advice of the majority of professionals.[7] The reason these studies are relevant to the social problems field is that the stock market

---

7.   James H. Lorrie and Mary T. Hamilton, *The Stock Market: Theories and Evidence* (Homewood Ill.: Irwin, 1973), Chap. 4.

is comparatively easy to study; compared with most other systems whose behavior we try to anticipate, it has considerably more "known" features. For example, there is continuous flow of readings about the state of the system and its individual components on every working day, indeed, several hundred readings for each day. Moreover, the data are in quantitative form and are readily amenable to statistical processing and analysis. By comparison, data on social problems are much less available, reliable, or quantifiable.

Finally, the critics of comprehensive planning argue that, rather than being confronted with a limited universe of relevant consequences, decision makers face an open system of variables, a world in which many potential consequences cannot be anticipated. Hence, decision makers, by attempting to adhere to the tenets of the rationalistic model, will become frustrated, will exhaust their resources without coming to a decision, and will remain without an effective decision-making model to guide them. A study of the ways in which the most successful U.S. military weapons were developed reveals most to be last minute improvisations—for example, putting the engine of one plane into the body of another or, in some instances, mixing components of six different systems.[8] In short, most were *un*planned combinations.

Long-range planning in minute detail used to be in vogue among socialist planners (the USSR still issues a total 5-year plan), among bureaucrats in many underdeveloped nations, and among U.S. federal government administrators. (In the mid-1960s all federal agencies were required to adopt a Defense Department designed Planning-Programming-Budgeting system, or PPBS.) Recently, however, this approach has been increasingly subject to question. Plans in socialist republics are increasingly serving as guidelines rather than dictates. Many developing nations have stopped drafting master plans, and in Washington the PPBS has been phased out in many areas.

Aside from considering rationalistic planning impractical, its critics consider it undesirable. It tends to entail centralization and the imposition of one set of values to the neglect of all others. Although the master plan may in theory have been arrived at democratically, and its centralized implementation should therefore be acceptable, centralization in effect, tends not to allow different groups and values to have an effective voice. Above all, because plans are inevitably modified in the process of implementation, pluralistic input tends to be excluded at these significant latter phases; once the plan has been approved, frequently only those who implement it can generally change it.

8. Chalmers W. Sherwin and Raymond S. Isenson, "Project Hindsight," *Science*, 156 (June 23, 1967), 1571–1577.

The Incrementalist Approach

A much less demanding approach, referred to as "disjointed incrementalism" has been advanced by Charles E. Lindblom and others.[9] Incrementalism seeks to adapt goal-setting and decision-making strategies to our limited cognitive capacities and to reduce the scope and cost of information collection and processing. Lindblom summarized the five primary requirements of the model as follows:[10]

1.   Rather than attempt a comprehensive survey and evaluation of all alternatives, the decision maker focuses solely on those policies that differ incrementally—that is, only in a few respects—from existing ones.

2.   Only a relatively small number of policy alternatives are considered.

3.   For each policy alternative, only a restricted number of "important" consequences are evaluated.

4.   The problem confronting the decision maker is continually redefined as conditions change. Incrementalism thus allows for countless ends-means and means-ends adjustments that in effect, make the problem more manageable.

5.   As such, incremental decision making is described as remedial, geared more to the alleviation of concrete present-day social imperfections than to the promotion of future societal goals.

Incrementalism is presented not only as the best strategy, but also as the one typically followed in pluralistic societies, as contrasted with the comprehensive planning favored by totalitarian societies. Influenced by the competition model of the market, incrementalists reject the notion that institutions can consciously formulate policies that express the collective "good." Policies that truly express the collective good can only result from a give-and-take among numerous "partisans" (various interest groups and other active groupings). The measure of a good decision is the extent of agreement on it among all those it affects and who can in turn affect its implementation. Poor decisions are those that exclude actors potentially capable of resisting or deflecting the projected course of action. Thus, at least from this viewpoint, prohibition was a grave misdecision.

That there is no central authority or plan does not necessarily mean anarchy, the incrementalists argue, because "partisan mutual adjustment" provides for coordination among the multiplicity of decision makers; in effect, this compensates for the inadequacies of the individual incremental decision maker and for the inability to make decisions effectively from

9.   Lindblom, The Intelligence of Democracy, pp. 137–139, 175.

10.   Ibid., pp. 130 ff.

one center. How mutual adjustment works, when it does, to the extent that it does, is illustrated by a study that examined the way several hospitals serving the same neighborhood coordinated their activities.[11] Boards and formal meetings were found to play a relatively minor role. Instead, a certain amount of coordination was achieved by hospital administrators keeping a keen eye on one another and adjusting their policies accordingly. Thus, when it became known to the director of hospital A that hospital B was closing its maternity division, hospital A expanded its maternity ward. And, relying only on an informal give-and-take, it was arranged that one hospital would provide the ambulance service for all those in the area. Thus, without there being a neighborhood "health czar" or even a coordinating committee, self-interest, information, and informal contacts provided a certain measure of neighborhood health "planning" arrived at voluntarily by the hospitals in the area.

Although, to its proponents at least, such incremental decision making is not only a realistic account of how the American polity works, but also the most effective approach to societal decision making, critics argue that decisions reached in this way necessarily reflect the interests of the most powerful, because partisans invariably differ in their respective degrees of power. The demands of the underprivileged and politically unorganized are therefore underrepresented, if not ignored.

Furthermore, incrementalism is not conducive to *basic* societal innovations, because it focuses on the short run and proposes only limited variations from past policies.[12] Whereas an accumulation of small steps could lead to a significant change, there is nothing in this approach to guide the accumulation; the steps may be circular (leading back to where they started) or unrelated (pointing in many directions at once, but leading nowhere). Kenneth Boulding comments that, according to this approach, "we do stagger through history like a drunk putting one disjointed incremental foot after another."[13] Home health services are a case in point. Experts are widely agreed that, where possible, it is preferable to provide care for the aged and disabled in their communities and homes rather than in institutions.[14] Home health care tends to be more humane, less open to abuse, and seems to be less expensive. In order for

11. Murray Milner, *Interorganizational Inequality and Cooperation: Health Care in an Urban Area* (Center for Policy Research, 1973).

12. Yehezkel Dror, "Muddling Through—'Science' or Inertia," *Public Administration Review*, Vol. 24 (1964), pp. 154, 155.

13. Kenneth Boulding in a review of David Braybrooke and Charles E. Lindblom, "A Strategy of Decision," *The American Sociological Review*, 29 (1964), pp. 930–931.

14. "Nursing Home Care in The United States," Subcommittee on Long-Term Care, U.S. Senate, November 1974, pp. 57–64.

home health services to be a workable alternative to institutionalization, a full package of services must be available. In addition to home visits from health professionals and paraprofessionals, visiting nurses and various social services may be needed. These might include visits from a social worker (who would counsel the patient on how to obtain other needed resources or help bring the patient out of a depression), companionship (providing access to a senior citizen's center), or various "aids in living" for persons lacking in mobility (ranging from an allowance to have groceries delivered, to housekeeping services, to meals-on-wheels). Although every individual may not need every service, home health care cannot substitute for institutionalization if only a narrow range of services is provided. Similarly, if many different vendors are supplying the various services, coordinated comprehensive treatment is difficult to come by.

Yet, out of the 2,800 home-health-care programs in the United States, by far the majority provide only for home visits by skilled personnel (visiting doctors and nurses and physical therapists). Semiskilled home health aides are not generally provided; neither are homemaking and housekeeping services. Only 21 percent of the programs offer any social services, let alone the full range.[15] And, these often do not provide health care.

Incrementalists do recognize one kind of situation to which their model does not apply—namely, major or fundamental decisions such as a declaration of war. These are viewed, however, as the proverbial exceptions that prove the rule. Yet, whereas incremental decisions do greatly outnumber fundamental ones, the latter's significance for societal decision making is obviously not adequately measured by their small number. Consequently, it is a mistake to view nonincremental decisions as insignificant. Moreover, the fundamental decisions often set the context for the numerous incremental ones. Thus, as we are accustomed to think of it, the Supreme Court's 1954 school desegregation ruling in *Brown* v. *Board of Education of Topeka, Kansas*, that separate but equal education was not possible and hence that schools must integrate their black and white pupils, was—in the segregated context of the time—a fundamental decision setting a social and political context, as well as a legal precedent, for later civil rights action. In the case of the American participation in the war in Vietnam, in which each additional commitment of troops, material, and money to the battle was incremental, often declared to be "the last," one can look back and identify relatively fundamental decisions, such as the passage of the Tonkin Gulf Resolution and, before that, the commitment of infantry, often recognized as the "pull-wire" that once introduced, gradually drew in the other pieces of the commitment into the scene.

15. Ibid., p. 59.

It is not enough, therefore, to show, as Richard Fenno noted, that Congress generally makes only small changes in the federal budget from one year to the next (a 10 percent or less difference appears typical).[16] These incremental changes often represent the unfolding of trends initiated at critical turning points. Fenno's own figures show an almost equal number of changes above the 20-percent level, per year, as below it; seven changes involved increases of 100 percent or more and 24 changes concerned increases of 50 percent and over.[17]

Although Congress and other societal decision-making bodies do make many incremental decisions without acknowledging the fundamental ones implied, what appears to be a series of incremental decisions is often, in effect, the implementation or elaboration of a fundamental one. For example, the U.S. space budget was $888 million in 1960, $2,387 billion in 1962, $5,900 billion in 1964. It peaked at $7,689 billion in 1967.[18] Though the budget increases may be viewed as merely impressive increments, the basic decision to take part in the space race was made in 1961, after President John F. Kennedy addressed a joint session of Congress and set space exploration as a goal *for the next decade:*

Now it is time to take longer strides—time for a great new American enterprise—time for this nation to take a clearly leading role in space achievement which, in many ways, may hold the key to our future on earth. . . .

. . . I believe that this nation should commit itself to achieving the goal, before this decade is out, of landing a man on the moon and returning him safely to the earth. No single space project in this period will be more impressive to mankind or more important for the long-range exploration of space. And none will be so difficult or expensive to accomplish.[19]

It is true that Congress could have reversed itself. But once a major commitment was made, an agency set up, and vested interests coalesced, such a reversal would have been very difficult. In effect, the 1961 decision was one for a $25 billion project that would last a decade.

Narcotics control is another significant area in which the passage of a law, the 1914 Harrison Act, constituted a fundamental decision. The enactment of this law radically reversed previous policy and set the context for an era, from which we have yet to emerge, in which a moralistic and punitive approach to drug use has dominated. Prior to the im-

16. Richard F. Fenno, Jr., *The Power of the Purse* (Boston: Little, Brown, 1966), pp. 266 ff.

17. Ibid.

18. *Statistical Abstract of the United States, 1972* (U. S. Dept. of Commerce, 1972), p. 531.

19. *The New York Times*, May 26, 1961.

position of controls under the Harrison Act, at least 200,000 U.S. citizens, and perhaps as many as 1 million, were addicted to opiates. Many of them were respected members of society.[20] The Harrison Act cut off all sources of legal supply to addicts. Commissioner Harry Anslinger and other officials of the Narcotics Division of the Treasury Department promulgated a very narrow and punitive interpretation of the Harrison Act and proceeded to launch a 30-year crusade full of moral fervor and factual misinformation against opiate addiction and later against marijuana use. Although the Supreme Court ruled in 1925 that the Harrison Act did not prohibit doctors from treating addicts by prescribing drugs, the activities of the Narcotics Division had by this time forced doctors to give up such treatment, thereby forestalling the development in the United States of a medical rather than criminal mode of dealing with the problem, as had been done in Britain.[21]

Theorists of incrementalism argue that incremental decisions tend to be remedial; small steps are taken in the "right" direction, or, when it is evident that the direction is "wrong," the course is readily altered. But if decision makers are to evaluate their incremental steps, which they must do if they are to decide whether or not their endeavors are effective, their judgment will require evaluative criteria and a longer-run perspective, which the incrementalists hold are not available.

It seems to me that while actors make both kinds of decisions, the number of fundamental decisions and their importance is significantly greater than incrementalists admit. Moreover, when the fundamental ones are missing, incremental decision making amounts to drifting, to action without direction. A more guidance-oriented approach to decision making requires two sets of mechanisms: (1) higher-order, fundamental policy-making processes that set goals and basic directions and (2) incremental decisions that both prepare for fundamental decisions and work out the details after the basic ones have been reached. Such a perspective is provided by mixed scanning.

Mixed Scanning

I suggest that mixed scanning, rather than incrementalism, provides both a realistic description of the strategy used by actors in a large variety

20.   John A. Clausen, "Drug Abuse," in *Contemporary Social Problems*, 3rd ed. Robert K. Merton and Robert A. Nisbet, eds. (New York: Harcourt Brace Jovanovich, 1971), pp. 187, 218–219; see also Gerald L. Robinson and Stephen T. Miller, "Drug Abuse and the College Campus," *The Annals of the American Academy of Political and Social Science*, 417 (January 1965), 101–109.

21.   On the British, see Edwin M. Schur, "British Narcotics Policies," in *Combatting Social Problems*, ed. Harry Gold and Frank R. Scarpitti (New York: Holt, Rinehart & Winston, 1967), pp. 447–461.

of fields and the most effective strategy for actors to follow. First, to illustrate this approach in a simple situation: Imagine we are about to set up a worldwide weather observation satellite system. The rationalistic approach would call for an exhaustive survey of weather conditions by cameras capable of detailed observations. In addition, review of the entire sky would be scheduled as often as possible. This would yield an avalanche of details, costly to analyze and likely to overwhelm our analysis and action capacities (for example, seeding cloud formations that could develop into hurricanes or bring rain to arid areas). Incrementalism would focus on those areas in which problematic patterns have developed in the recent past and, perhaps, on a few other regions deemed especially susceptible to problems.

A mixed-scanning strategy would include elements of both approaches by employing two cameras: a broad-angle camera that would cover all parts of the sky, though not in great detail, and a second one that would focus in on those areas revealed by the first camera to require a more detailed examination. Whereas mixed scanning might miss areas where only detailed pictures could reveal trouble, it is less likely than incrementalism to miss trouble spots in unfamiliar areas and is more practical than covering every bit of sky in each scan.

Applying this idea to the evaluation and implementation of social policy, the social efforts to cope with social problems, and the conditions which generate them, the first consideration is to formulate *general guidelines*. Thus, for instance, faced with resource shortages, inflation, unemployment, and energy problems, the United States in 1973–1975 faced the question of whether its domestic effort should give first or high priority to a new industrialization drive. Project Independence was an attempt to formulate such a drive by investing upwards of $600 billion into new technologies (designed, for example, to extract oil from shale, energy from sun, and so forth); in short, the emphasis was on capital rather than on consumption goods. Such a drive to create a new technology would, in essence, have placed the United States in the situation it was in in the 1870s–1890s; developing resources would again become a, if not *the*, central national purpose. In contrast to the increasing emphasis in the late 1960s and early 1970s on "quality-of-life" issues, efficiency, profitability and competitive considerations would regain their former high priority. Such a deemphasis of antipollution efforts has indeed occurred (polluting industries asked and, in some cases, received deferment of enforcement standards in view of the *economic* needs); the same applied to auto safety standards.

Various consumer and environmental protection agencies and interests, and to a lesser extent those concerned with affirmative action (for example, expanding employment opportunities for women and racial and ethnic minorities), have continued to fight for an increased emphasis on quality-of-life goals. These groups contend that these values are so important, that, if need be, they should be given priority over economic productivity.

In effect, no guidelines were set, no general direction was agreed upon. Instead, policies were formulated that moved the country in both main directions, but not effectively forward in either. For instance, a major effort was made to inject funds into the construction of highways, although autos are particularly unsuited for the energy-saving, environmental conservation era, while public transit continued to be neglected.

Should a guideline have been formulated in favor of quality-of-life as against re-industrialization, this would have suggested several policies without dictating specific details. Thus, public trust would have been preferred over private, environmental protection and safety programs would have been continued in full vigor, etc. Each policy, then, would have to be worked out in detail which, in turn, might often require a prior measure of trial-and-error, of experimentation, of modification as programs were implemented. In this way, the ad hoc adherence to the status quo typical of incrementalism is avoided through reliance on innovative, holistic guidelines, while the traps of trying to anticipate and plan ahead in an unrealistically detailed manner are also avoided.[22] The Congress' shift from reviewing each program on its own merit to an overall budget review, in addition to program-by-program review, in principle, offers a new opportunity for such guided decision making.

Effective decision making also requires that sporadically, or at set intervals, investment in broader scanning be increased to check for far remote and better lines of approach. Annual budget reviews and State of the Union messages provide, in principle, such occasions. An increased investment of this type is also effective when actors realize that the environment radically changes or when they see that the early chain of increments brings no improvement or even a "worsening" in the situation. If at this point the actors decide simply to drop the course of action, the effectiveness of their decision making is reduced, because through broader scanning they may discover that a continuation of the "loss" is about to lead to a solution. In many therapeutic relations and rehabilitation programs, for example, there are periods during which trust is developed but little visible progress is apparent. Time seems to be wasted. To drop the relationship at this point may often be to terminate it just as it is starting to bear fruit.

On the societal level, scores of social interventions are believed to have been stopped short of their take-off points, when the first few years of low-level funding did not bring about the desired changes. An evalua-

22. For a discussion on this see Etzioni, *The Active Society*, Chap. 12, especially pp. 282–290.

tion of the federally funded educational programs of the 1960s (Title I, Head Start, Job Corps, federal aid to higher education) concluded with two related observations: (1) that most of the educational legislation set time limits on the authorizations that were far too short to produce the expected changes; (2) that fundamental changes in education required the allocation, at least initially, of far more resources than were thought to be necessary when the programs were designed. Thus, when funds were divided equally among all disadvantaged children, only $150 per year above regular school expenditures per child was available for compensatory programs, whereas the more effective programs required an extra $600 to $900 per child.[23]

The strategy of mixed scanning assumes that both the observer and the actor have a capacity to evaluate decision-making strategies and to determine which is the more effective. Incrementalists, however, argue that because values cannot be scaled and summarized, "good" decisions cannot be defined, thus rendering evaluation difficult if not impossible. Yet, a closer look at actual public policy suggests that, in fact, decision makers, as well as the observers, can summarize their values and rank them, at least in an ordinal scale. For example, many societal projects have one primary goal, while other goals, which are also served, are secondary. For instance, finding an economic way to desalt ocean water is a primary goal; strengthening applied science is a secondary target of the same endeavor.

Actors evaluating the extent to which the *primary* goal has been realized may make this assessment their basis for judging a policy or program, more or less ignoring secondary effects, or when they compare projects they can award several times greater weight in contributors to the primary goal as compared to secondary ones.

When there are two or even three primary goals (for example, teaching, therapy, and research in a university hospital), actors can still compare their efforts in terms of the extent to which they realize each primary goal. They can establish that project X is desirable for the research effort but not for teaching, whereas project Y is very supportive of teaching but not of research, and so forth, without having to raise the additional difficulties of combining the effectiveness measures into one numerical index. In effect, they proceed as if the various purposes had identical weights.

Finally, an informal scaling of values and goals is not as difficult as the incrementalists assert. For instance, to set priorities in focusing its regulatory attention, the Consumer Product Safety Commission developed a procedure for ranking hazardous products. Product-related injuries are monitored through an information-gathering system called the National Electronic Injury Surveillance System (NEISS), which draws upon data from 119 hospital emergency rooms selected to make up a statistically valid sample of the American population. The information is coded according to 850 product categories and 250 injury categories. Injuries are rated on a scale from 1 to 8. A certain number of cases are selected for follow-up, in which instance investigators visit the injured person's home, reconstruct the accident sequence, and try to photograph the product or obtain samples of it. To arrive at a product's ranking, both frequency and severity of injuries are taken into account, with injuries to children and older people given extra weight. Listed according to their rank, the "ten most wanted" products were judged to be bicycles, stairs, doors (nonglass), caustic cleaning agents, tables, beds, football activity, swings and slides, liquid fuels, and architectural glass. Although different assumptions about what is salient would yield different listings, this does not mean that any particular listing is without guiding merit; rather, that each is suited to a different purpose.[24]

Another major relevant consideration regarding the question of whether an actor must limit his or her decision making to incrementalism or is able to add to it and enrich it by an overlay of fundamental overviews and guides is the quantity and quality of knowledge and decision making resources. Included here are the availability of data, of staff to collect and interpret data, and of computers and other technologies. By and large, domestic agencies have been weaker in their decision making capabilities than has the Department of Defense and NASA, which is one reason why these domestic agencies have tended to lose out in budget allocations. They could make less of a case, plan less well, and so on. Similarly, Congress is much weaker than the federal executive. Many congressional committees can allocate only one *part-time* staff person to evaluate a program critically. In contrast, the executive can assign hundreds of staff personnel or contract major outside studies to justify a program; in addition, the executive can conduct campaigns among the citizens to gain support for the programs it favors.

Finally, the more encompassing and inclusive a society's public efforts, the more it requires fundamental reviews and guidelines and the more it is harmed by more incrementalism. Although all modern societies have a greater capacity for control than did premodern societies, they differ sharply in their capacity to build consensus. Democracies must accept a relatively high degree of incrementalism because of their greater need to gain support for new decisions from many and conflicting groups, a need that reduces their capacity to formulate and follow a long-run

---

24. Steven Kelman, "Regulation by the Numbers," *The Public Interest*, no. 36 (Summer 1974), 83–102.

plan. Other than during a crisis, it is easier to reach consensus on policies that are only incrementally different from existing policies than to gain support for major policy departures. The role of crises thus becomes highly significant to change. Crises serve to build consensus for major changes of direction that are overdue (for example, desegregation). The Woodrow Wilson International Center for Scholars, in proposing the creation of institutions for strategy policy assessment, noted that only in times of great crises have there been arrangements in the U.S. government for "systematic, long-range, integrated planning." The writers cited "inertia, jurisdictional jealousies, the demands of the four-year election cycle, and perhaps an innate suspicion of the planning process itself" have led to a situation in which "quick fixes, crisis management, and damage limitation have been operative concepts."[25]

Totalitarian societies are more centralized and tend to rely on forms of power that are less dependent on consensus. They plan more but are inclined to overshoot the mark. Democracies first seek to build up a consensus before acting, and so they often end up doing less than necessary later than necessary. In contrast, totalitarian societies, because they are less capable of consensus building or even of assessing the various resistances, usually try for too much too early; they are then forced to make post hoc adjustments. The revised policies are often scaled down and involve more concessions to societal resistances than did the original ones. Whereas totalitarian misplanning may frequently squander resources, some initial overplanning and later scaling down is as much a decision-making strategy as is disjointed incrementalism.

For a democratic society to become more effective in coping with its problems, it has to rely less on incremental decision making, with its associated passivity and drift, and must move toward becoming an *active society*. An active society would differ from typical present-day democratic societies in its much greater capacity for examining and implementing basic "transformational" changes. It would differ from totalitarian societies in that it would link the greater knowledge-producing capabilities not to rationalistic attempts at total planning, but to mixed scanning. In addition, it would remain open to the fact that details often cannot be anticipated and that only guidelines can be used. Finally, as the next three chapters will explain in greater detail, such an active society would need to devise suitable implementation mechanisms (see Chapter 5). It would need to build a power base capable of effecting some redistribution of resources (see Chapter 6). And finally, to ensure

25. Woodrow Wilson International Center for Scholars, Washington, D.C. August 9. 1973. A Proposal for Developing a Capability at the National Level for Srategic Policy Assessment. Inserted in *Congressional Record* on February 25, 1974, p S2116.

responsiveness, it would need to establish consensus-building mechanisms able to carry a high volume of communication (see Chapter 7).[26]

AN EXAMPLE: URBAN RENEWAL
AND CITY PLANNING

The city is often seen as a kind of hothouse for social problems, in that it is characterized by high concentrations of the poor and disadvantaged, by crowding and anonymity, by crime and drug abuse—all made worse by the difficulties imposed by sheer size. Undisciplined, rapid growth is often diagnosed as a major source of the city's woes. The various strategies of city planning that have been part of efforts to impose order on this chaos illustrate the three styles of goal setting just discussed.

Rationalistic Approach: City Master Plans

A typical master plan of a city provides a minutely detailed account of desired future growth.[27] It includes demographic and economic analyses as well as projections of the city's industrial development and population trends based on a notion of the optimum size to be planned for. Included are sections depicting each major deficiency and a suggested corrective: decrepit housing and recommended building plans; lack of open space and land-clearing projects; traffic congestion and new thoroughfares; jumbled growth and suggested zoning regulations, and so forth. Maps, codes, draft legislation, cost projections, even rhetorical appeals to citizens are similarly incorporated into the plan.[28]

In addition, the typical plan also contains detailed designs for various subcities or "neighborhood units." Industrial and commercial districts are separated from residential areas and given separate designs. Schools, shopping facilities, parks, and so forth, are assigned accordingly. All major public and private activities are encompassed. Several hundred such plans were drawn up in the United States alone over the last four decades. "In terms of its impact, however, the master plan has been a failure. Although individual recommendations have often been implemented, no master plan has ever become a blueprint for the development of the city."[29]

26. For additional discussion, see Etzioni, *The Active Society*, pp. 481–484.

27. Herbert J. Gans, *People and Plans* (New York: Basic Books, 1968), p. 57.

28. See references cited, Ibid., pp. 75 ff.

29. Ibid., p. 61.

The plans broke down, first of all, because the initial processes of goal setting that led to their creation were neither responsive to real needs of the residents nor the outcome of an authentic consensus-building process. In the absence of agreed-upon goals or expectations, the plans were often "all things to all men," leading eventually to frustration when none of the goals were attained. "To members of different publics, the renewal program, for example, was a program of slum clearance, reclaiming of blighted areas, upgrading of substandard housing, remodeling of 'downtown,' construction of public buildings, solution of traffic problems, house preservation."[30] Typically, the planners forged ahead, taking as a basis for the plan primarily white, middle-class, Protestant values, their own or those who retained them, oblivious to the possible inappropriateness of these values to the majority of city residents. Often, the underlying values were technocratic. Neighborhoods were designed with reference to transportation routes or geographic factors, but not from a cultural viewpoint, aiming, say, at preserving the integrity of an ethnic enclave. Yet, ethnic groups are a strong basis of social cohesion, organization, and action; when such groups cut across planning districts, they have tended to conflict with the plan and oppose its goals.[31] For example, the master plan may call for the children of particular geographic units to attend a particular school, but parent groups, often organized along ethnic lines, demand otherwise.[32] Having disregarded the often disparate wishes and needs of various groups, especially the blue-collar class, ethnics, and senior citizens, there has been little reason for these neglected constituencies to cooperate with the planners or to support their plan.

Master planners tend erroneously to assume the existence of a powerful central authority capable of enforcing their designs and regulations; therefore, they disregard the role of political processes when it comes to implementations. For example, planners are inclined to put a much higher premium on open spaces and low-density living than most voters and most real estate interests. As a result, most city plans are met with little wide or enthusiastic support among the citizens, though this support is needed if the plans are to be protected from special interest groups. Actually, often those pieces of the plan that are implemented— for example, zoning regulations—are those that realtors or homeowners favor, while other pieces are neglected. Thus, lacking the omnipotent

30. Kahn, *Studies in Social Policy and Planning*, pp. 169–170.

31. Nathan Glazer and Daniel P. Moynihan, *Beyond the Melting Pot*, 2nd ed. (Cambridge, Mass.: M.I.T. Press, 1970), pp. lxxxiii–lxxxv.

32. Norman I. Fainstein and Susan S. Fainstein, *Urban Political Movements* (Englewood Cliffs, N.J.: Prentice-Hall, 1974).

authority the plan's implementation requires, incremental follow-through is the most that has often been achieved.[33]

Incrementalism

Cities without master plans, or cities with master plans that have been in large measure disregarded, nevertheless use spot planning, especially in certain problematic areas. Planning for an expressway, a subway line, a change in zoning regulations, or slum clearance are cases in point. Such small-scale, single-sector plans are often far more realistic, taking into account more of the relevant data and offering several alternative schemes rather than one approach. In doing so, they take goal setting out of the hands of the planner and allow clients to choose from among the alternative plans the one that best suits their purpose.

At the same time, however, these plans have often been myopic in that they have not taken into account the interactive effects of their own impact on other features of city life. Expressways moved the traffic more rapidly but increased pollution, put more pressure on downtown parking space, and made it possible for the more affluent members of the city (who were once a major source of tax revenue) to move to the suburbs where they were still within easy commuting distance to the city. Slum clearance did create new housing, but much of it was too expensive for the former residents of the area; thus it created serious social dislocation, increased alienation, and led to larger welfare rolls.[34]

The story of the "114th Street Project" is illustrative. In 1965, a group of businessmen set out to renovate one block of Harlem, on 114th Street between Seventh Avenue and Eighth Avenue. Using foundation and federal monies, $7.2 million was invested in sandblasting the exteriors of the old buildings and in refurbishing the interiors of the 458 apartments that the block contained. To avoid disturbing the social fabric, work was carried out in a few buildings at a time; during this period, the families were accommodated in vacant apartments on the block. A visitor 5 years later reported that the "physical change is dramatic . . . the atmosphere of decay has been supplanted by a cheerfulness that is marked by clean windows, tidy curtains and other indicators of an improved standard of housekeeping."[35] Incidences of throwing garbage out of back windows had persisted, but such a practice was no longer

33. For a study that illustrates well the follies of master planning and the life of incrementalism, see Martin Meyerson and Edward C. Banfield, *Politics, Planning and the Public Interest: The Case of Public Housing in Chicago* (New York: Free Press, 1955).

34. See Scott Greer, *Urban Renewal and American Cities* (New York: Bobbs-Merrill, 1965).

35. Charles Bartlett, *Chicago Sun-Times*, July 14, 1969.

as common as it once had been. Incinerators were more often used. A Block Council was in operation.

Social rehabilitation of what used to be known as a block of hookers and pimps was a main goal. However, 5 years after the start of the project, drug abuse had been added to the block's problems. At least forty-five families included a drug addict, according to one source. Fear of addicts had replaced the previous concern with the malfunction of services, especially lack of heat in the winter.[36] Plans to develop a playground and a garden in lots behind the block failed to materialize as funds promised by the city did not come through. Although yellow hopscotch squares were painted on the asphalt, a planned day-care center had not yet been built.

The incremental nature of the project is evident in several ways. Different facets of the proposed plan were to be financed from different sources—voluntary, federal, and city—a common American feature that is detrimental to a more comprehensive effort. Only pieces of the block program were implemented, with others being postponed, though it now seems unlikely some will ever be accomplished. Most significantly, it was assumed that a block could be treated as an isolated unit separate from the larger slum fabric. The encroachment of addiction illustrates the difficulties inherent in such an approach. At the same time, it appears that physical living conditions were improved and that some social and presumably psychic gains were also made.

Mixed Scanning

The whole city-planning field, though still oscillating between total planning and incrementalism, seems to be veering toward mixed scanning. In the first place, planners now emphasize "flexibility" instead of "forms,"[37] which in practice means they no longer expect to be able to evolve a priori a master plan that will stand for decades, if not centuries. Instead they evolve guidelines and directives—for example, in favor of a variety of housing patterns instead of a preference for either high rises or small townhouses, and so forth.

Second, plans now more often attempt to combine long-run guidelines and priorities with a detailed working out of specific facets of the plan. Thus, a long-run goal such as reversing the flow of the middle classes and their tax revenues from the central city to the suburbs suggests a series of specific steps, including emphasizing improvements in those governmental services or aspects of urban life that strongly concern middle-class residents, such as the quality of the public schools and safety

36. *The New York Times*, August 14, 1969.

37. Peter Wolf, *The Future of the City* (New York: Waston-Guptill, 1974), p. 163 ff.

in the streets. If the goal is to attract less polluting, light industry or to realize the city's potential as a tourist center, other actions are implied, such as deflection of trucking routes in the first case and expansion of the airport in the second.

Third, there is an increasing awareness of the need to take into account the public's *variety* of needs and preferences, thus opening the plan to politics, in the broad sense of the term; fewer attempts are made to insulate the plan from such "interference." Community participation is invited, or at least tolerated, with reference both to basic goals and directions and to particular details.

Last, there is a considerable mix of attempting to remove blight and of actively pursuing positive goals—of adding onto existing systems (adding a lane to the highway) as well as trying out innovations (monorails, citizen participation, and so forth). Along these lines, one outgrowth of the ecology movement has been the trend toward environmental impact review. This calls for subjecting new additions to the urban landscape, whether public (for example, expressways or monorails) or private (for example, oversized skyscrapers or new factories), to scrutiny both by technical experts and the public. Such scrutiny is designed to bring to light what, in addition to its stated purposes, a project's likely effects on the city's other facets are likely to be. Projects whose predicted negative consequences are judged to outweigh their positive ones may be banned entirely or they may be redesigned to eliminate or mute the undesirable side effects. Environmental impact review thus embodies the total planner's concept of the city as urban system within which each individual component has "interaction effects" that must be taken into account, while providing, as well, a structured setting for the "partisan mutual adjustment" among conflicting interests that incrementalists consider so vital. Environmental impact assessment can be considered narrowly (for example, primarily in terms of clean air and water) or it can be considered in broader sociological and economic terms (for example, what effect will the building of a complex of governmental offices or a shopping mall have on the character of a neighborhood?).[38]

IN CONCLUSION

The effort to "get a fix on a social problem," on its causes and consequences, may thus proceed either by attempts at broad, deep, detailed attack (the master plan), or by a series of steps taken one at a time

---

38. For additional discussion, see John Friedmann and Barclay Hudson, "Knowledge and Action: A Guide to Planning Theory," *American Institute of Planners Journal*, 38 (1974), 2–15.

(incrementalism), or by moving back and forth between general guide-lines and specifics (mixed scanning). The results depend in part on the structure of the acting unit (the society, the city), on whether it is centrally guided or pluralistically managed, and on the proportion of the total volume of activities that are guided at all. Next, the planning resources available to an actor are relevant. Obviously, the poorer the planning resources, the less can be planned, although societies and sub-societies that have planned most are often those that are less endowed with such resources. Given a specific structure and set of capabilities, the overplanner will waste resources and generate alienation, while the under-planner will not overcome a social problem; obviously a middle course is preferable.

CHAPTER 5
ORGANIZATION

IMPLEMENTATION AS A PROBLEM

The wisest decision, the most carefully laid out plan, the best intentions never transform themselves into a changed piece of societal reality, moving from a problematic condition to one that is problem free. Hence, once a plan, decision, or intervention is formulated, the unavoidable question is, how will it be put into effect? In the past, implementation was often thought to be a relatively simple matter: A nationally televised speech by the president would focus attention on the problem; enactment of a law would modify people's behavior; and setting up a worthy model would inspire emulation. In recent years, however, it has become increasingly evident that implementation is a complex enterprise. This is so because implementation entails moving from the highly malleable symbolic world of knowledge makers, planners, and decision makers to the much more change-resistant societal reality of resource scarcities, vested interests, power relations, and the commitments of individuals and collectivities to values that may be incompatible with a particular program or aspects of it. Resistance may be as active and violent as the resistance of those who demonstrate against the busing of children to implement court-ordered school desegregation. It may be mildly criminal and "underground," as is disregard of the gambling laws. Or it may be passive and withdrawn, as when prison inmates refuse to participate in educational or psychiatric rehabilitation programs. Actually, resistance to change, faced by almost any effort to deal with social problems, can and does take every form of behavior known to social science. To study modes of implementation is, therefore, to study the conditions under which the relevant individuals, collectivities, or organizations cooperate in the realization of the desired changes, or at least refrain from hindering them, and to study ways resistance may be taken into account or otherwise dealt with.

ALTERNATIVE MODES OF COMPLIANCE

From an analytic viewpoint, as we have shown in greater detail elsewhere,[1] implementation can be advanced through one of three kinds of compliance strategies (or through various combinations of these "pure" types): coercive, normative, or utilitarian. *Coercion* entails forcing compliance. This tends to generate resentment on the side of those affected and therefore is an approach that exacts high personal and social costs. Thus, mental patients do poorly in "closed" wards (where they are locked in). Incarcerating criminals is more effective in embittering them than in rehabilitating or deterring them.[2]

Normative techniques rely on invoking commitment to existing norms or on instilling norms. They include education, persuasion, rehabilitation, and psychotherapy. Normative appeals are obviously much less costly than coercion, but have another failing. They tend to assume an a priori, positive commitment to solving the problem on the part of those asked to implement a particular course of action. With the exception of young children, if the persons involved hold values opposed to those the implementation promotes (for example, religious opposition to birth control), they will tend to resist the attempted intervention. It follows that normative means are most effective when people are amenable to the offered solution from the start; that is, they often cannot be relied upon whenever there is deep-seated opposition. This is unfortunate, because normative means, when they *can* be employed, generate little or no alienation. Also, normative techniques tend to heighten commitment to the course of action, which is helpful to a social program in ways that are wholesome for the persons involved.

Many interventions rely on *utilitarian* means, especially financial incentives and administrative decrees or regulations intended to shape the calculated decisions of those affected. Unlike coercion, utilitarian incentives do not force persons to do what is desired, but instead arouse

---

1. Etzioni, *The Active Society*, pp. 354–359; Amitai Etzioni, *A Comparative Analysis of Complex Organizations*, rev. ed. (New York: Free Press, 1975), pp. 3–100.

2. Etzioni, *A Comparative Analysis of Complex Organizations*, pp. 49–50.

their self-interest by paying them or alter the situation in which they function in such a way that unless they do what is desired of them, they cannot obtain something else they want. On an institutional level, the federal government obtains concessions from state and local governments and corporations by making grants contingent on compliance with federal regulations such as enforcement of nondiscriminatory practices. On an individual level, by rigging welfare payments in such a way that it pays more to work than to remain on the state's rolls, the government hopes to motivate welfare recipients to seek jobs.

Utilitarian means are less alienating than coercive ones but do not generate as much commitment as do normative ones. Whereas the reward or outcome is welcomed, the steps that must be taken are, as a rule, not desirable in themselves. Unlike normative incentives, utilitarian ones generally leave intact a person's basic preferences. For example, high pay does not make hard physical labor desirable in itself the way, say, a philosophy extolling working with one's hands does for those who believe in it or learn to embrace it.

The large variety of agencies, organizations, and social movements advocating or implementing social changes to overcome social problems differ in the means of compliance they rely upon. Most emphasize one kind of compliance over the two others; the choice of method depends in part on the extent to which what they are trying to accomplish will be undermined or encouraged by one of the various compliance techniques. Thus, prisons rely on coercion to maintain order, thus generating high resentment among most inmates. This resentment in turn blocks the prisons' rehabilitative goals and, in the long run, impedes efforts to achieve "law and order" as well. In contrast, many of our best schools, as well as progressively run mental health clinics, rely predominantly on normative means to achieve their educational or therapeutic goals, because without the positive involvement of the participants, the school or clinic cannot function effectively. In situations where routine and continuous effort as well as some measure of involvement are required (for example, factory or clerical work), reliance on utilitarian means might be most effective. (This is the reason volunteer fire departments do well as long as fires are infrequent. When fires occur frequently, even daily, firefighters are typically put on a payroll.)

The tendencies toward such compliance specialization are quite strong; nonetheless, exceptions exist. Thus, to the extent that the prime role of the prison is seen as protecting society from dangerous persons, prisons are likely to emphasize coercion. Yet prisons are frequently also expected to rehabilitate their inmates, either through job training or schooling that aims at enabling them to become useful citizens when they are released or by changing their attitudes and reforming the antisocial tendencies thought to be responsible for getting them into trouble. Because coercive means are unsuited to accomplishing these goals, attempts have been made to rehabilitate inmates by paying them to attend classes (utilitarian means) or by recruiting them into psychotherapeutic or religious programs designed to inculcate positive attitudes (normative means). Other mixes of compliance techniques are typical of many programs dealing with such things as drug and alcohol addiction, mental health, and delinquency. Hence, when one seeks to understand the procedures used to tackle a social problem, it is useful to start by asking which are the specific goals pursued and the compliance means utilized. Are they compatible or incompatible?[3] And to what effect?

THE SECTORS

The social science literature is rich in debates over which compliance means to use in a particular situation (for example, should welfare clients be *forced* to work at jobs found or created for them or should they be *encouraged* to retrain for jobs they can get on their own?). Even more often, especially in the area of public policy, the debate focuses on which sector to rely on. Should interventions be introduced through the private sector (where profit plays a key role), through the government sector (where regulation and financial sanctions as well as coercion are widely used), or through the voluntary, nonprofit sector (where normative means play a relatively larger role)? The differences among these three sectors—from the viewpoint of their role in dealing with social problems—go far beyond the relative weight given to the various compliance means by each sector. Sectors can*not* be seen simply as an implementation of one kind of compliance strategy. Differences among them encompass matters of philosophy, economic interests, and traditions. They are often expressed in an age-old debate as to who is "better" able to deal with social problems—the private sector, the government, or the voluntary sector? The debate encompasses matters of fact (Which sector is more efficient?), of value (Are profit making and rendering a human service compatible? Can the government be trusted?), of political outlook (radical or liberal or conservative), and of party loyalties (Democrats have in the past tended to rely more on the government than Republicans).

Comparison of the sectors is further complicated by the different sets of goals used to assess the performance of each sector in dealing with social problems, as well as by the lack of strong evidence on many specific points. Thus, some argue that the government accomplishes more for

---

3. For additional discussion, see Etzioni, *A Comparative Analysis of Complex Organizations*, pp. 103–120.

social justice, while others assert that the private sector is more economical. Both *may* be right.

The Private Sector

To state that one should rely on the private sector to solve a social problem is to rely motivationally on individual initiative and the profit motive and institutionally on the business community, the corporations, "the market." This is the approach with which the majority of Americans feel most comfortable. In a 1967 survey, 79 percent of Americans in a national random sample agreed with the statement, "We should rely more on individual initiative and not so much on governmental welfare programs," while only 12 percent disagreed (9 percent expressed no opinion).[4] Similarly, 49 percent agreed (versus 38 percent who disagreed and 13 percent who "didn't know") that "social problems here in this country could be solved more effectively if the government would only keep its hands off and let people in local communities handle their own problems in their own ways."[5]

At the same time, more and more Americans favor giving the private sector a greater role. In a 1972 random sample of Americans, 83 percent said they wanted business to provide leadership in eliminating poverty, whereas in a 1966 survey only 66 percent had held this view; 84 percent of the respondents wanted business to give leadership in fighting racial discrimination (the 1966 figure was 69 percent).[6]

Those who feel that solutions to social problems should be sought via the private sector see the market not only as the most efficient mode of implementation but also as the one most compatible with freedom and individualism. The arguments advanced for implementation via the private sector are similar to those advanced for incremental goal setting (pp. 86–90) and the neoconservative approach (pp. 20–26).

Accordingly, proponents of the private sector argue that each individual is the best judge of what he or she needs and wants. Whereas some important "public" goods must be produced via the state (Milton Friedman lists protection of the nation and the individual from coercion as the main ones[7]), other goods are seen as best achieved individually or

---

4. Lloyd A. Free and Hadley Cantril, *The Political Beliefs of Americans* (New Brunswick, N.J.: Rutgers University Press, 1967), pp. 24–30.

5. Ibid., p. 24.

6. Harris Survey (December 1972), *Current Opinion*, vol. 1 issue 3 (March 1973), p. 25.

7. Milton Friedman, *Capitalism and Freedom* (Chicago: University of Chicago Press, 1962), p. 23.

through the aggregation of individual preferences and efforts, as in a market free from government interference. Several reasons are given for this viewpoint: first, market decisions allow each person to get what he or she wants; second, government decisions require collective action, and hence only a few alternatives can be considered. Thus, whereas we each can buy the kind of car *we* want, we can have only one national or state-wide welfare policy (or a few options); this means that many of us might have to settle for a policy other than our preferred one. Furthermore, the realization of collective goods and policies requires confrontation and conflict between opposed interests, which wears thin the fabric of society. Broadening the range of matters taken out of the hands of the private sector "strains further the delicate threads that hold society together."[8]

The government is viewed as both too powerful and too fumbling. As new missions are taken over by the government, it accumulates more and more power, eventually gaining hegemony. This leveling of "intermediate powers" destroys those natural groupings that are the sociological bedrock of individual liberty, leaving citizens exposed to unrestrained state power, and hence to tyranny. Although private charity may be inadequate in terms of the size of the poverty problem, it is held up as still preferable when compared to the repressiveness of welfare departments' "midnight raids" on mothers they support, to make sure no "able-bodied" potential breadwinners are living with them. In this area, private charity is viewed as a way to eliminate the degradation of endlessly filling out forms to establish one's eligibility for aid and other indignities and the fostering of dependency on the state that welfare is said to cause.

At the same time, the government is considered to waste resources and time, because its personnel—the bureaucrats—are not motivated to serve the citizens. After all, they are salaried and tend to be either tenured or politically appointed. Their fear of rocking the boat leads them to become "ritualistic overconformers" who hide behind mountains of memos and insist on going by the book.[9] Moreover, conservatives argue that, once in place, antipoverty bureaucracies and others oriented toward social problems tend to experience "goal displacement," with their main concerns becoming *their* survival and self-aggrandizement. Thus, they develop a vested interest in the continuance of the problems they ostensibly seek to correct or, at the least, a stake in exaggerating the problem's prevalence and seriousness. Such agencies push upward the public expenditure spiral, hence the need for more taxation that in turn under-

8. Ibid., pp. 23–24.

9. Robert K. Merton, "Bureaucratic Structure and Personality," in *Social Theory and Social Structure* (New York: Free Press, 1968), p. 254 ff.

mines the work ethic and the motivation to innovate. Thus, having set out to solve social problems, they become a major source of social problems. In contrast, the private sector is thought to be capable of accomplishing the same missions at a fraction of the cost because competition motivates businessmen to raise their individual incomes through increased efficiency and cost controls. The genius of the market profit motive, opportunities for individual initiative, lies in their ability to harness individual self-interest in resolving social problems.

An illustration of how the market forces can be harnessed to overcome a social problem is provided by housing allowances. In January 1973, the White House suspended subsidies to construction firms to build houses for the poor and adopted instead, on a small-scale basis, a program that involved awarding cash allowances directly to poor families so that they could obtain their housing in the market place. Both participants and officials were reportedly pleased with the results.[10] The new program cost much less. The average rental paid by participants from their own funds was $18.96, while the remainder was made up by allowances averaging $95 a month, or about 40 percent of what it takes to subsidize a new public housing unit each year. Two major reasons lay behind the savings. First, the families had a financial incentive to find a bargain apartment because they had to pay the difference between the allowance and the rent; still, they were not motivated to accept substandard housing because the allowance had to be spent for housing. Second, direct cash payments circumvented the corruption that appeared when the government subsidized private contractors and landlords.[11] Furthermore, the poor appreciated the program because it allowed them to obtain housing much more quickly (they did not have to wait for new construction) and to choose their own apartments and neighborhoods, and because it gave them leverage (the threat of moving) over landlords who refused to make repairs or provide services. Also, proponents claimed that the program removed much of the stigma of being assisted (because neither landlords nor neighbors need know); this was not a "low-income housing project." Finally, by naturally spreading recipients over a wide area, the program prevented the kind of massive political resistance to low-income subsidized housing that had been emerging in areas where residents exerted political pressure, demonstrated in the streets, and threatened violence to ban the construction of low-income housing in their neighborhoods.

In contrast, the difficulties accompanying private sector attempts to solve social problems are illustrated by evaluation studies of "performance contracting," where providers are paid according to their achieve-

10. Malcolm E. Peabody, Jr., "A New Way to House the Poor: Housing Allowances," *New Republic*, March 9, 1974, pp. 20–23.

11. Ibid., p. 22.

ments in rendering a needed service, for instance, in the "delivery of educational services" in public, especially ghetto, schools.

In 1970, contracts were signed for experimental programs in fifty-four school districts in twenty-four states, in places as different as the Bronx, New York, and Taft, Texas. Private companies were retained to use a combination of teaching machines, special teaching materials, and incentives for both students and teachers, to jack up "performance" as measured by test scores. Thus, in Grand Rapids, Michigan, children were given plastic wafers, exchangeable for cash, for their achievements; in Hammond, Indiana, the reward for a correct answer was a cookie. It was also agreed with companies that, not only would payment flow for higher scores, but there would be no pay if there were no improvements.[12]

The first problem was outright cheating. Anxious to make a buck, some of the companies provided the children with answers to the test questions. Where no cheating was found, no systematic improvement was measured as compared to control groups. More precisely, in 212 classroom populations, negative results were found in 25 percent of the performance contract classes, positive results in 15 percent, while in 60 percent no significant differences were found between the performance-contract and control classes.[13] Where higher scores were attained, closer inspection often revealed neglect of most subjects other than those tested, extending even, in one case, to physical education.

As a result, the program came under fire from educators for being very narrow in its approach to education, concentrating exclusively on inculcating the kind of "cookbook knowledge" that is easily quantifiable. The companies were faulted for ignoring the less quantifiable humanities curriculum, as well as for not providing students with training in reasoning and critical thinking to be applied to new situations they would encounter in later life. Doubts were raised whether such gains could be meaningfully quantified and hence tied to rewards. Finally, many educators doubted the ethical implications of rewarding the children for their achievements with free time in a room full of toys, transistor radios, and TV sets, as if their achievements had no intrinsic value.[14]

The Government

While philosophically the majority of Americans favor reliance on the private sector and oppose expansion of the government as a means

12. H. W. Ray, *Final Report on the OEO Experiment in Educational Performance Contracting* (Columbus, Ohio: Batelle Memorial Institute, March 1972).

13. Ibid.

14. Ibid., pp. 364–365. For an argument that the evaluation of these experiments was not conclusive, see Robert D. Marmin, "OEO's Performance-Contracting Project," *Public Housing*, 22 (1974), 2167–2188.

to combat social problems, the federal government has taken the lead ever since the Great Depression. For decades, the recognition of a serious new social problem has been followed by the introduction of one or more federal programs to attack it. President Lyndon B. Johnson alone started 435 new federal programs. His successor, President Richard M. Nixon, though a proponent of the private sector, also added additional federal programs—for example, the Law Enforcement Assistance Administration was created in 1968 to fight crime, and the Environmental Protection Agency in 1970 to deal with pollution. Government bureaucracies —federal, state, and local— currently employ approximately 14.5 million civilian workers, or one out of every six American workers.[15] The government spends more than $300 billion a year, roughly one-third of the gross national product. In 1975 there were more tax dependents (civil servants, military, disabled, unemployed, retired, on welfare) than nongovernment workers, 80,655,000 vs. 71,650,000.

The political beliefs of individual Americans are inconsistent in that a philosophical opposition to the government is accompanied by support for its continuous *expansion*. The 1967 survey already referred to, which found the majority of Americans endorsing a "cut in government" on philosophical grounds, also found that when asked about a variety of specific governmental programs directed at social problems (such as Medicare, federal aid to education, low-rent housing subsidies, urban renewal, and federal unemployment and antipoverty programs), 65 percent of Americans favored these programs, 21 percent neither favored nor opposed them, and only 14 percent opposed them.[16]

The argument for the governmental approach centers around the claim that the government can act as guardian of the public interest over and above the narrow self-serving interests of particular segments of society (for example, business, labor, the wealthy, and various ethnic groups) and as the champion and protector of those social groupings who do not have the power needed to ensure their getting their share of the societal pie in free market competition (for example, blacks, women, the aged, and the handicapped). Just as a private-sector approach tends to go hand in hand with a philosophy of incremental decision making, so those who favor reliance on government tend to urge a more rationalistic emphasis (see pp. 81–85). Thus, advocates of the governmental approach point out that only government has the resources to design truly systematic and comprehensive long-range plans and, even more important, has the power to carry them out.

15. "Washington's Bureaucrats: 'Real Rulers of America,' " *U.S. News and World Report*, November 4, 1974, p. 38; see also Daniel Bell, "The Revolution of Rising Entitlements," *Fortune*, 91 (April 1975), 100–101.

16. Lloyd A. Free and Hadley Cantril, *The Political Beliefs of Americans* (New Brunswick, N.J.: Rutgers University Press, 1967), p. 32.

To the argument that government is the champion of the weak, advocates of the private sector reply that citizens should stand on their own feet. What they lose in aid, they will gain in freedom. Proponents of government counter by asking how can people be expected to "pull themselves up by their bootstraps" if rapid technological change has made their skills obsolete or if discrimination has handicapped them educationally or otherwise made them unable to compete.

Moreover, to exercise freedom of choice in independent market decisions, an individual needs information. But without government intervention, the needed information is often not accessible. For instance, only under government pressure and over business opposition did food processors begin listing ingredients on packages and cans; it was the government that forced cigarette makers to print warnings on the health hazards of smoking on cigarette packs and advertisers to delete false and misleading product claims. Without government regulation, the producers of soft drinks might use materials that are cancer producing; producers of cribs might make them with slats wide enough for babies' heads to get caught in; aeronautics firms might make planes whose doors drop off.[17]

Those who argue in favor of greater reliance on government to combat social problems also point out that many needed services are difficult to provide on a for-profit basis, and attempts to render them profitable may result in higher cost, if not exploitation and scandal (as has occurred in many proprietary nursing homes).[18] In some areas, such as pollution, business is a direct cause of the problem and is quite unlikely to correct it voluntarily. In other social problem areas—such as mental health, alcoholism, or cancer research—private efforts are insufficient, and the government must step in if the gap is to be bridged.

Finally, one of the deepest roots of social problems, some would say the most tenacious one, is the societal structure of power and privilege of which the private sector is a centerpiece. If a more egalitarian distribution of wealth is desired, the private sector cannot be relied upon to contribute much more than charity, that is, small amounts. Only the government can achieve significant reallocation through its power to tax.[19]

---

17. For documentation, see Harold Schmeck, Jr. "Cyclamate Peril Denied by Maker," *The New York Times*, November 14, 1974; "Alarm Over Air Accidents: A Look at the Record," *U.S. News and World Report* (February 3, 1975); "Baby Cribs by Simmons Found Unsafe by U.S.," *Wall Street Journal*, August 19, 1974.

18. Mary Adelaide Mendelson, *Tender Loving Greed* (New York: Knopf, 1974); Claire Townsend, *Old Age: The Last Segregation* (New York: Grossman, 1971). See also, for example, John Hess, "Medicaid Billed for Rolls Royce with a Chauffeur," *The New York Times*, January 30, 1975, p. 1.

19. For additional discussion, see Edmund S. Phelps, ed., *Private Wants and Public Needs* (New York: Norton, 1965); Richard Musgrave, *The Theory of Public Finance* (New York: McGraw-Hill, 1959); and Etzioni, *The Active Society*, pp. 519 ff.

Proponents of the governmental approach are divided among themselves over what level of government to rely on: federal, state, or local. Federal programs are faulted for being excessively centralized. Washington-based administrators are thought to be too remote from those they serve, unfamiliar with local needs, and insensitive to local demands. And, the constitutionally mandated division of power between the states and the federal government is widely viewed as a vertical check and balance, safe-guarding individual freedom, equivalent in importance to the horizontal separation of powers among the executive, legislative, and judicial branches. Many Americans have consequently been alarmed at the growth of federal as opposed to state government, especially during the New Deal and Great Society eras of intensified effort to overcome social problems. Accordingly, they favor returning power to states and municipalities.

In line with this philosophy, the local governments, the states and cities, have recently been mobilized to an increasing extent to replace the federal government as the main carriers of domestic programs, under what is known as revenue sharing. Federal programs, from the Office of Economic Opportunity to the Department of Housing and Urban Development, were cut, and checks were mailed to about 35,000 local governments, to help them take care of the local social problems.[20] By and large, unlike federal grants, which can be used only for particular purposes (for example, to build a hospital or to help retarded children), revenue-sharing money has few or no strings attached.

Proponents of revenue sharing have argued that domestic missions, unlike national defense and space exploration, are chiefly carried out by local (state and city) agencies and that the demand and cost of such domestic services have risen rapidly ($28 billion in 1950 to $171 billion in 1971).[21] At the same time, the national government has virtually preempted the most productive source of revenue—the personal income tax, 91 percent of which is collected by the Internal Revenue Service. With domestic issues gaining greater attention relative to foreign affairs and outer space, the imbalance between the federal concentration of funds and local control of programs that deal with social problems was thought to warrant correction. Federalization of domestic programs might have been one way to accomplish this, but the ideological opposition to a still bigger central government made this politically unattractive. Instead, proponents of revenue sharing have favored transferring funds from the federal level to the states.

20. For an extensive look at the notion of revenue sharing, see the entire issue of *The Annals of the American Academy of Politics and Science*, 419 (May 1975), especially 103; also see Richard P. Nathan, Allen D. Manvel, Susannah E. Calkins et al., *Monitoring Revenue Sharing* (Washington, D.C.: The Brookings Institution, 1975).

21. *Statistical Abstract of the United States, 1973*, p. 410.

Yet, state and local governments seem to be, on average, seriously more deficient than the federal bureaucracy. For example, when a House subcommittee on legal and monetary affairs studied the results of giving the states $1.5 billion to upgrade law enforcement, it concluded that the states' programs are riddled with inefficiency, waste, maladministration, and, in some cases, corruption.[22] It further concluded that the program "had no visible impact on the incidence of crime." Among the patterns established were diversion of funds for political purposes, exorbitant consulting fees, contracts awarded without proper bidding, and misappropriation for other purposes than those of the program.

Manipulation of state and local programs by lobbies is also a problem. One of the main reasons that automobile manufacturers are anxious that safety standards be locally rather than federally enforced is that they can more readily get their way with local legislatures and enforcement agencies. The same holds for polluters. Since 1965 the federal government has called to account about 4,000 industries and cities for contributing to heavy pollution and found that almost all of them had state permits for their level of discharge. What happens to national guidelines concerning equality of employment and civil rights when left to the states to implement is illustrated in a report about the attempt to set up birth-control services for welfare clients, as required by the 1967 amendments to the Social Security Act and 1968 HEW guidelines. The guidelines state that all "appropriate" welfare recipients should receive family-planning services that "specifically include medical contraceptive services, social services, and educational services." Yet, a 1971 study showed that only twelve states complied, and three of these spent only $100,000 each on their programs.[23] In light of such findings, not more but less adherence to national guidelines must be expected as public funds become more locally controlled.

Moreover, there is good reason to believe that the red tape is longer and more snarled in many states and cities than it is in Washington. For example, in New York City, according to former Health Commissioner Joseph U. Terezio, it took 9 months and eighteen clerical steps to hire one X-ray technician (before the city hospitals were cut loose of the city's bureaucracy and set up as a semipublic corporation). The average time for completion of purchase requisitions was 88 days. And, despite all the comments about the cumbersome Washington bureaucracy, it turns out that state governments, with less than one-third the budget, have four-fifths as many employees.

22.   U.S. House of Representatives Report No. 92–1072, *Block Grant Programs of the Law Enforcement Assistance Administration*, 1972.

23.   *The New York Times*, December 13, 1971, p. 36.

A study of state legislatures conducted on a nonpartisan basis found many legislatures to be inept, understaffed, poorly paid, and in disarray.[24] Alabama ranked worst, primarily because it was so dominated by the Governor. Wyoming ranked forty-ninth; its legislature meets only forty days, including weekends, every other year, and it is not empowered to extend its sessions if business is incomplete. New Hampshire's lawmakers were paid $200 a year, which suggests either that they were affluent or were not expected to do much work. Almost all state legislatures were found to be more dominated by their governors than was Congress ever alleged to be dominated by the president.

But perhaps even more important, a major shift of funds cannot occur between levels of government (or from the government to the private sector) without affecting the distribution of funds among economic classes, races, regions of the country, or without determining which social problems will be attended to more vigorously than others. The Great Society federal domestic programs focused on the poor, the minorities, and the inner cities. Greater implementation of social programs by the states and municipalities entails a considerable shift of funds away from social reform, social justice, and redistribution purposes (welfare, housing, education) and toward general services (garbage collection, police and fire protection).[25]

The Third Sector

The choice faced by those who must administer programs in the area of social problems, and by the citizens who concern themselves with such programs, is commonly posed as one of choosing to rely either on the private sector or on the public sector. This view tends to conceal the important fact that there are really three sectors: the private, the governmental, and the nongovernmental public sector, which encompasses several hundred thousand voluntary associations and corporations. Three-fourths of Americans belong to at least one such association.[26] We refer to it as "the third sector."[27] The third sector tends to provide, on average,

24. Citizens Conference on State Legislatures, *State Legislatures: An Evaluation of Their Effectiveness* (New York: Praeger, 1971), especially pp. 51–53.

25. For an argument that our position is unwarranted, see Daniel J. Elazar, "The New Federalism: Can the States Be Trusted?" *Public Interest*, no. 35 (Spring 1974), p. 89.

26. Eli Ginsberg et al., *The Pluralistic Economy* (New York: McGraw-Hill, 1965); see also NORC Poll of March, 1974, on Group Membership.

27. We first coined the phrase "third sector" and described it in the article, Amitai Etzioni, "The Untapped Potential of the 'Third Sector,'" *Business and Society Review*, no. 1 (Spring 1972), 39–44; and Etzioni, "The Third Sector and Domestic Missions," *Public Administration Review*, 33 (1973), 314–323.

higher quality service than the government sector, is more costly than the private sector, and serves only segments of the population affected by social problems or in need of service.

Post-secondary schools can serve as our example. Most states now have systems of community and 4-year colleges as well as universities. Among the latter are some very fine institutions, such as the University of California and the University of Wisconsin, in whose affairs the state usually does not intervene, but the majority are intended primarily to provide low-cost higher education to large numbers of students. Generally the state institutions are less concerned with excellence or with innovation than are such not-for-profit colleges as Oberlin, Antioch, Swarthmore, Reed, and the Ivy League and Seven Sisters schools. Thus, as one study of a representative sample of all four-year institutions granting liberal arts degrees in the U.S. in the mid-sixties found, such third-sector colleges are more selective in student admissions than state-run institutions; have more faculty with degrees from better institutions; and have a more productive faculty in terms of research.[28] Thus, while on *average* the third-sector colleges may have higher academic standards, they do much less than the state schools to promote equality of access and are typically much more expensive.

The for-profit institutions encompass business and technical schools as well as modeling and correspondence courses. They enroll some 3 million students yearly. Their focus is not so much on education as on job training, and they attract a much wider segment of the population than either the third-sector or state colleges. Sometimes they may be closely associated with a particular business or industry and can help their graduates find jobs. But the for-profit educational sector is also regularly racked by scandals involving contracts whose fine print enables the companies to extort from their students.[29] In most cases, the lion's share of the tuition money does not go toward providing educational services but toward attracting new clients—in many cases, low-income victims. A study of the for-profit education industry found that profit-seeking schools spent only about 20 percent of their budgets on instruction, but up to 60 percent on marketing.[30]

Nursing homes provide another similar illustration of the emphases characteristic of each sector. Among social workers and other specialists

28. Peter M. Blau, *The Organization of Academic Work* (New York: John Wiley, 1973.

29. "Profit-Making Schools," *Washington Post*, June 23, 1974. This article was the first in a series by Eric Wentworth.

30. Ibid. (The study is by Edubusiness, Inc., 1970).

surveyed, most agreed that old people are generally better off in voluntary (not-for-profit) nursing homes than in proprietary (for-profit) ones, though they are best off in their own homes.[31] Voluntary nursing homes are reported to be costlier than proprietary ones.[32] Yet, because voluntary homes include all charges in one bill, whereas proprietary homes arrange for separate charges for room and board, medical services, and drugs, direct cost comparisons are difficult. In addition, voluntary homes typically provide more space per patient. And, although voluntary homes admit patients who, on average, are more seriously sick or disabled when they first arrive, patients in proprietary homes are reported to deteriorate more rapidly.[33] Inspectors generally find patients in proprietary homes to be less active and less well.[34]

Children's programs on commercial television have been sharply criticized by educators and social scientists for their hard-sell advertising aimed at turning children into product salesmen and for their excessive violence which may be psychically harmful to children. Third-sector (that is, public or educational) children's television programs have been highly praised for their educational value, especially in the case of minority children and those from low-income families. A study of 8,000 pupils who watched the educational network's *Electric Company* found that 85 percent of the teachers of these children noted reading gains among their pupils that were directly attributable to the program. About 36 percent reported increased ability to decode words, 25 percent mentioned improved spelling, and 38 percent cited improvements in basic sight vocabulary.[35]

Thus far we have discussed only nonprofit corporations; voluntary associations made up of volunteer members rather than paid employees are also an important part of the third, nongovernmental public sector. Prime examples in the social problem field are various self-help organizations—for example, for alcoholics, gamblers, and smokers—and drug-free rehabilitation programs, which are associations of persons seeking to overcome their own destructive addictions or dependencies. Other volun-

31. *The New York Times*, October 10, 1974.

32. *The New York Times*, December 10, 1974.

33. Leonard Goffesman, "Nursing Home Performance as Related to Residence Traits, Ownership Size, and Source of Payment," *American Journal of Public Health*, 64 (March, 1974), 269–276.

34. *The New York Times*, October 10, 1974.

35. Robert E. Herriott and Roland J. Liebert, "The Electric Company," *In-School Utilization Study*, Vol. 1 (New York: The Children's Television Workshop, August 1972).

tary associations have been formed to better the self and public images, as well as to further the economic, political, and social rights of groups that have traditionally been discriminated against. Examples are PUSH, which works on behalf of the poor and minorities, NOW, on behalf of women, and the Gay Activist Alliance, on behalf of homosexuals. Other voluntary associations have been organized to represent the interests of the public at large against the political power of private interests in such areas as consumer and environmental protection.

The Pluralistic Society

While the debate rages over the relative merits of each sector as the single best method of solving our problems, societal reality combines sectors in various ways.[36] The three sectors simultaneously compete with —and complement—one another. Thus, government-supported elementary and secondary schools provide free public education, but parents eager to buy more, or better, or different (for example, religious) education, and able to pay more, send their children to third-sector schools. Where special skills (e.g., languages, secretarial, computer programmers) are desired, profit-making schools are often chosen.

This is not to imply that the balance is working out perfectly, or even well; only that if any one of the sectors were to vanish, the total mix—whose proportion may well deserve to be altered—would be inferior, at least from the viewpoint of some significant social purposes.

Equally important, the sectors are forever forming new amalgamations. Government regulation of the private sector is increasingly encompassing and intense. Thus, in recent years, the government has required the private sector to shoulder more of the social costs of environmental protection as well as occupational and consumer safety; that is, private firms are less able to ignore the social problems. Similarly, many third-sector institutions now depend in some measure on government funds and hence must respond, to a degree, to certain government dictates. Thus, colleges and universities often rely on the government for research funds, scholarships, loans and student work programs, as well as for capital expansion such as dormitory and library construction. Threatened cut-offs of these funds serve as points of leverage, for instance, to induce colleges to hire more women and minorities.

Unhappiness with the extent and quality of governmental regulation, or guidance, of the private and third sectors has led to a large variety of suggestions to find other ways to increase the guidability and responsiveness of these sectors, including the election of some public directors to for-profit boards (General Motors) as well as to those of the

36. See Ginsburg et al., *The Pluralistic Economy*.

third sector (Harvard); suggestions that the churches vote stocks they own according to social considerations, not just business sense (the proxy voting organized by Saul Alinsky and others); selective boycotts of products (the United Farm Workers' lettuce and grape boycotts); consumer representation on boards of universities; and greater right of access to information by consumers and citizens (the right to examine one's credit rating and the right to see one's college files).

A detailed review of these efforts would entail many volumes, each much larger than the present one. We can only briefly summarize the major point, which is: No single approach has so far proved an across-the-board success from the viewpoint of all the major goals, including quality of service, social justice, and economy. Greater emphasis on one of these, and greater reliance on one of the sectors, tends to entail some "costs" in terms of relative neglect of other considerations. For example, quota hiring of disadvantaged minority members and women undermines the seniority system.

Recently it has been fashionable to favor the third sector over the governmental approach. Yet the activities of the voluntary associations tend to be intermittent and fragmentary. The membership of voluntary organizations is often not widely representative of the community at large. Voluntary programs tend to be small, and hence not widely available. Participation is highly selective. The services provided by nonprofit corporations tend to be costly. In contrast, lower quality service but more equality of access is a major value the government tends to foster (as in the offer of free public elementary and secondary education to all citizens).

AN EXAMPLE: HEALTH SERVICES

The American health-care delivery system is highly pluralistic: all three sectors are deeply involved in providing and financing health care, though the particular mix varies greatly from service to service. Thus, of the more than 6,046 general hospitals in the United States in 1972, 12 percent were private, for-profit institutions, 6 percent were federal, 27 percent were local, 2 percent were state, and 54 percent were private, not-for-profit.[37] Among long-term care facilities, nursing homes are run on both a for-profit and not-for-profit basis, with the greatest increase in recent years in the for-profit sector; mental hospitals are run by the states, the voluntary, and the for-profit sectors; and the federal government, through the Veterans Administration and the Public Health

---

37. Reference is to the short-term hospitals; see *Hospital Statistics, 1972*, American Hospital Association, p. 22.

Service, operates other long-term care facilities for wartime disabilities and for communicable diseases.

The participation of the various sectors in the financing of health care has changed greatly in recent years. In 1950, 68 percent of the cost of personal health care service was paid by the individual, 20 percent by federal, state, or local governments, 8 percent by private health insurance, and 4 percent by philanthropy and other sources. Following the passage of Medicare and Medicaid in the mid-1960s, the governmental share in 1970 rose to 35 percent, the proportion paid by private health insurance increased to 24 percent, and the burden on the individual was reduced to 39 percent.[38]

As is to be expected, each sector has its defenders and detractors. As with comparison of the sectors in other areas, the data are often inconclusive. Above all, assessments are generally different in terms of different purposes.

Quality, Cost, and Social Justice

If quality of service and integrity are used as the criteria of evaluating "output," the third sector ranks high, possibly, *on average* higher than the two other sectors. Government hospitals—such as those run by the Veterans Administration, as well as county hospitals—are not considered to be on a par with voluntary ones. Private (proprietary) hospitals, are often of lower quality than voluntary ones. Ten experts on hospital care were asked, "If you or your family required major hospital services— diagnosis or treatment—which twenty-five hospitals in the United States would you select as representative of the best?" The following hospitals were selected as the ten best: Massachusetts General, Boston; Johns Hopkins, Baltimore; University of Chicago, Chicago; Columbia Presbyterian, New York; New York Hospital, New York; Barnes, St. Louis, and Henry Ford, Detroit; Mount Sinai, New York; St. Mary's, Rochester, Minn.; and University Hospital, Ann Arbor, Michigan, and University of Minnesota Hospital, Minneapolis. All of these hospitals are nonprofit teaching institutions, and all are in the third sector.[39]

There is also some *statistical* evidence that voluntary hospitals are superior to proprietary ones in quality of care. In 1962 and 1964, a random sample of medical records of families of teamster union members who had received care in New York City hospitals was submitted to a medical audit. The review committee judged 85 percent of those treated

38. *Basic Facts on the Health Industry*, prepared by the staff of the House Committee on Ways and Means, June 28, 1971, p. 24.

39. *Ladies Home Journal*, February 1967.

in voluntary teaching hospitals to have received optimal care; however, only 54 percent of those admitted to voluntary nonteaching hospitals and 47 percent of those admitted to proprietary hospitals received optimal care. The committee also judged admission to the hospital as justified in 94 percent of teaching hospital cases, in 87 percent of the voluntary hospital cases, and in 74 percent of the proprietary hospital cases.[40]

Cost of care also differs greatly among the various types of hospitals. Long-term psychiatric patients stay an average of 103 days at a cost of $2,967 in proprietary hospitals versus 514 days and an average cost of $5,072, in state hospitals. Federal short-term hospitals cost $1,077 per case compared to $592 for voluntary hospitals.[41] The indications are that, along with variations in quality and efficiency of care, different types of hospitals also cater to different types of patients and illnesses. For example, proprietary hospitals tend to treat patients who are less seriously ill, and to provide fewer services, than do government or third-sector hospitals.[42]

The rising cost of health care has led to greater government role and regulation in recent years. Expenditures on medical care in the United States rose from $26.4 billion in 1960 (representing 5.3 percent of the gross national product—GNP) to $67.2 billion (7 percent of the GNP) in 1970.[43] Total health costs are expected to rise to 10 percent of the GNP by 1980.[44] The growth of the federal government's role in financing care for those populations who need the most and costliest care and who are least able to pay for it—the elderly and the indigent—in addition to federal subsidization of hospital construction, are often held responsible for the cost spiral of the late 1960s. Some see the increasing share of medical costs borne by third parties in general, be they the

40. M. A. Moorehead et al., "A Study of the Quality of Hospital Care Secured by a Sample of Teamster Family Members in New York City," (New York: Columbia University School of Public Health and Administrative Medicine, 1964). See also Milton Roemer, A. Taker Moustafa, and Carl E. Hopkins, "A Proposed Hospital Quality Index: Hospital Death Rates Adjusted for Case Severity," *Health Services Research*, 3 (Summer 1968), 96–118.

41. Duncan Neuhauser and Fernand Turcotte, "Costs and Quality of Care in Different Types of Hospitals," *Annals of the American Academy of Political and Social Science*, 399, (January 1972), 52–53. These data are for 1970.

42. DHEW Social Security Administration, Office of Research and Statistics, *Background Information on Medical Expenditures, Prices and Costs* (September, 1974 [Preliminary]), pp. 28, 37–38.

43. House Committee on Ways and Means, *Basic Facts on the Health Industry* (June 28, 1971), pp. 8–9; see also Theodore Chester, "United States Hospital Costs in International Perspective," *Annals of the American Academy of Political and Social Science*, 399 (January 1972), pp. 73–81.

44. Chester, "United States Hospital Costs in International Perspective," p. 74.

government or, more often, nonprofit or commercial health insurers, as a major factor in causing a very rapid increase in the cost of health care; this is because neither physicians nor patients are motivated to hold down costs when others are paying them.[45] (Neither the government nor the insurance companies have found effective ways to institute cost-control mechanisms.)[46] Thus, the cure—more public support—is viewed as the source of a major problem: Primary health care is out of the reach of millions of Americans, including the middle classes. Others favor the opposite route as a potential solution: all Americans should be covered by a national health insurance, which will entail *more* government intervention.

Interpenetration of the Sectors

Increasing interpenetration of sectors is evident in several ways. Tighter governmental regulation of the two other sectors is reflected, for example, in the abolition of the exemption of voluntary hospitals from the National Labor Relations Act (these hospitals now must permit unionization of their employees) and in the passage of freedom of information acts in some states, such as California and New York, calling for public disclosure of hospital finances. Similarly, the recently legislated Professional Standards Review Organizations (PSROs) mix government and voluntary mechanisms by requiring committees of physicians to verify the need for services of all Medicare and Medicaid (that is, state-paid) patients prior to admission to hospitals for nonemergency services.

A quite different form of interpenetration is seen in the area of consumer participation. Various attempts have been made in recent years to democratize the management of health-care delivery institutions. The idea is to make them more responsive to the needs of patients and of the community at large by placing consumer representatives on advisory or trustee boards of voluntary hospitals, prepaid medical plans, OEO clinics, and Comprehensive Health Planning agencies.[47] The results have been rather mixed. Except in the case of medical cooperatives, which give all

45. *Medicare and Medicaid Problems, Issues and Alternatives*, report to the staff of the Senate Committee on Finance, February 9, 1970; *Nursing Home Care in the United States; Failure in Public Policy*, report prepared by the subcommittee on long-term care of the Special Committee on Aging, United States Senate, November 1974.

46. Edward M. Kennedy, *In Critical Condition* (New York: Simon & Schuster, 1972); R. B. Stevens and R. Stevens, *Welfare Medicine in America* (New York: Free Press, 1974).

47. Citizens Board of Inquiry into Health Services for Americans, *Heel Yourself*, 2d ed. (Washington, D.C.: American Public Health Association, 1972).

patients voting rights and are governed by a board of elected representatives who contract with physicians for services,[48] consumers are rarely effective in getting their views to prevail. And even where consumers are in charge, consumer participation has generally been found to wane with an organization's increasing size and age. Where physicians and administration retain the upper hand, with consumers having more than negligible decision-making power, tension and continual jurisdictional disputes are common. The professionals accuse the consumers not only of disregarding the need for expertise but of wanting all the power without being able to sustain the energy necessary for exercising responsible authority. The consumers, in turn, charge that the physicians and administrators only wish to consult them about relatively unimportant matters (for example, the use of vending machines in waiting rooms) and use consumer representation chiefly as community morale boosters or for public relations purposes. In many instances, the consumer representatives have even less power, as in cases where the providers set up a consumer advisory council and decide what powers to give it, whom to appoint, and when to convene it. Consumer representatives on such advisory councils often complain that they are denied access to the most elementary information they must have to fill their role.

IN CONCLUSION

When all is said and done, there is no one superior way to administer to a social problem. Persuasion, rewards, and occasionally force are and may be used, depending on the social purpose and conditions. Similarly, no society relies only on the private sector or on the government or on the voluntary third sector; each sector is used, often for different purposes or different segments of the same problem population.

Finally, the sectors are no longer as separate as their titles, proponents, and opponents tend to imply. Government, private business, and voluntary agencies and associations all intertwine in many different ways to fashion the administrative tools used in coping with social problems. Overall effective results may be best achieved where implementation is pluralistic, but efforts as a whole are guided by the government, through legislation and enforcement. These last two factors are in turn evaluated by the citizens and reshaped in line with their preferences, a subject explored in the remaining chapters.

48. Ibid., Chap. 4.

CHAPTER 6
POWER

INTRODUCTION

We have seen that inadequate knowledge, excessively rationalistic or incremental goal setting, and ineffectual organizational tools may seriously hinder the coping with social problems. In addition, the success or failure of societal guidance, which affects collectivities and persons, depends on another factor—the need to heed the preferences and to gain the cooperation of those whose problems are to be solved. If public support is lacking, especially when "solutions" are imposed from above, success in overcoming social problems is unlikely and will tend to require a large investment of resources if not outright coercion. Therefore, even when expert knowledge of what needs to be done is keen, when goal-setting and decision-making strategies are both realistic and forward looking, and when administrative processes are technically well designed, there is still the question of who is to guide these processes toward which values.

The answer, as some civic textbooks have it, is not that each citizen has an equal say. The fact that one person has one vote does not mean that every person has an equal say as to where the society is headed or what it will do about its social problems. Three main factors determine how much leverage each individual and each group in society exercises. One is the nature of the relationship between citizens (or groups of citizens) and the government, the principal instrument of societal guidance. Is the relationship one in which, chiefly, the government designs interventions and then "sells" them to, or imposes them on, the citizenry? Or do citizens actively and effectively participate in formulating the course the government follows? This is the subject of the first section (Governmental Power) of Chapter 6.

Second, whatever amount of power the citizenry as a whole has *vis-à-vis* the government, particular groups and individuals have different shares of this power. No two groups of citizens have an equal say on anything; certainly not on the government's approach to social problems or the execution of interventions to affect them. And such groups often take action not directly mediated (although it is always indirectly affected) by the government. Thus, management and unions, women and men, whites and blacks work out their relationships in part directly with each other, through cooperation, negotiation, or conflict. Clearly, their respective power profoundly affects the outcome. Parents and children may discuss —or fight—over the family's budget, but the outcome is more determined by the parents. Corporate and consumer representatives may discuss product safety (for example, how to avoid dangerous toys), but the two groups hardly have an equal say over the outcome. Actually, power differentials play a double role: originally, such differentials are one *source* of social problems, ranging from economic exploitation to psychic stigma, from acts of violence to status manipulations; later, they are a factor shaping *responses* to the problem, explaining in part why some suggested interventions are welcomed, others merely tolerated, and still others blocked. This is the subject of the second section (Social Power) of Chapter 6.

Finally, members of society relate to the government and to one another in terms of their agreement or disagreement on social values and the relative significance of such values. That is, while they face each other as power wielders (or as persons with little power), they also face each other as members with different views. Individuals who agree with each other as to what is to be done may try to reach agreement with other groups as to the direction society should take by means of educational and political campaigns designed to influence values. These processes of "consensus building" are discussed in Chapter 7.

THE GOVERNMENTAL POWER

Alternative Viewpoints

Although the capacity to exercise direct public policy relating to social problems is diffused to some extent throughout society and is lodged in a large variety of institutions and their so-called private governments (boards of corporations, hospitals, colleges, schools, voluntary organizations, and so on), the single largest concentration of such power resides in the state. The state encompasses all levels of public government from federal to local and controls the institutionalized means of coercion (the police, FBI, jails, and courts). Through its taxing power, the state has direct control over roughly one-third of the economy and indirect control over the rest. Its policies largely determine whether the economy is going to be in high or low gear, inflated or deflated, growing or regressing. Its leaders have greater access to national media and more power to persuade and inspire than most, if not all, other sources.

Who decides for what purposes this enormous power is to be used? How do problems come to be assigned relative priority for government action? Whose needs, interests, and values are taken into account—and to what extent—when interventions are proposed and decided on?

One view is that each citizen, by casting his or her ballot, has a say on the direction in which the government is to move. When the votes are tallied, the majority opinion becomes clear, and this is the direction government policy takes until the next election. No social scientist of any stature subscribes to this civic textbook view of democracy, for reasons that will become evident shortly.

A second view is that of the pluralists. Their approach to power analysis is similar to the consensus theorists' and/or functionalists' approach to social analysis. Pluralists hold that there are in the political arena a large variety of groupings, in which citizens who have similar needs or vested interests or who support the same cause unite to press their demands on the government. There are private pressure groups (such as the American Association of Manufacturers, the American Medical Association [AMA], and the Farm Bureau), civic and public interest groups (Americans for Democratic Action [ADA] and Common Cause), and less well organized groups (various social movements), each pulling and tugging the government toward the objectives they espouse.[1] According to the pluralist theory, the government focuses on those problems and in ways that represent the direction favored by the confluence of these vectors.[2]

A third approach, the political analysis of the alienation approach, sees the government as reflecting, not a balance of many contending political forces, but a preponderance of a single one. As the "executive committee of the ruling class," the state uses its military, economic, and ideological powers to advance the interests of the establishment (the proprietary class). The result is that most people's problems are not at-

1. These objectives do not necessarily concern their immediate self-interest. Thus, churches fight for the poor, many of whom are not church members, and ADA, composed largely of whites, fought hard for civil rights for blacks.

2. David A. Truman, *The Governmental Process* (New York: Knopf, 1951); and Robert A. Dahl, *A Preface to Democratic Theory* (Chicago: University of Chicago Press, 1956).

tended to; the captain of the ship listens chiefly to those on the uppermost deck.

Though opposed on most points, both the pluralist and alienation views consider state power to be chiefly reflective of the distribution (or concentration) of power in society. In contrast, neoconservatives portray the state as an autonomous power base, which has grown in size and has appropriated, at an alarming rate, power previously exercised by a great variety of individuals, groups, and institutions. Citizens' appeals for government action are deflected, distorted, or deadened by the numerous layers of bureaucracy they must traverse. Neoconservatives fear that government may level all concentrations of power intermediate between it and the individual citizens, violating their freedoms and their rights and, ultimately, threatening their autonomous existence.

The guidance approach recognizes a *multiplicity* of power centers, *but* holds that power is distributed very *unequally*. Although the guidance perspective views the actions of government as reflecting, in large measure, the distributions of wealth, authority, and social honor within society, it does credit the government with a significant capacity for autonomous action. It sees this measure of autonomous power as deriving not from police and economic might alone, but from the principles of legitimation responsible for replacing sheer force with an authority that can command the loyalty and willing compliance of those subject to it. If only to maintain its legitimacy (aside from a need to serve a *variety* of groups, not just the most powerful), the government must attempt to deal with social problems of the many, not just the elite few, or, ultimately, collapse.

Measuring the Government's Impact

One way to understand the independent impact of the government is to look at the resources it takes away from various social groups (via *differentiated* tax rates) and compare them to the resources (including services) it provides various social groups. Do the rich pay more taxes and the poor get more services? This would be an application of government power on the side of more quality. Or, do the rich take advantage of so many tax loopholes that they pay, proportionally, less than the poor? In this case the state would be magnifying the exploitation of the poor by the ruling class. Does the government in effect follow the intrasocietal distribution of power, or is there a measure of reallocation? If reallocation does take place, is it merely token or more significant—and in what direction?

For a person who has never studied these matters, seemingly obvious answers come quickly to mind. Sample: Because the most prominent American tax is the progressive federal income tax, the richer a person is the more he or she is taxed. Some critics say just the opposite: Because of lower tax rates on capital gains than on salaries, tax shelters, tax-exempt bonds, and various other deductions, the tax structure favors the affluent; the rich get richer and the poor have children. It will come as little surprise, if we recall our excursion into societal knowledge, that the answer is much less clear than these flat statements suggest. We shall introduce but a few of these complexities before we advance a tentative conclusion.

One of the best established facts is that the *before*-tax income distribution of Americans is highly unequal *and* has changed little over the past 25 years. As can be seen from Table 1, which shows the distribution of income by population fifths, the highest income fifth of the American population received 43 percent of the total income in 1947 and only 1.4 percent less in 1971, while the share of the lowest fifth increased by only 0.5 percent (from 5.0 percent to 5.5 percent).[3] Changes among the other fifths were similarly small.

Moreover, these figures measure primarily earnings, leaving out most income from capital and physical assets. Ownership of capital is highly unequal: The richest 19 percent of families own 76 percent of all privately held assets, and the poorest 25 percent have no net assets.[4] An illustration of the difference between the *earned* income distribution and the *total* distribution of all family income (adjusted to include capital gains) is provided by a 1966 study. The percent of all money income received by the richest fifth of all families in 1966 was 47.9 per-

Table 1 Percent of Aggregate Income Received by Each Fifth of Families and Individuals: 1947, 1960, 1971

ITEM AND INCOME RANK	1947	1960	1971
Families	100.0%	100.0%	100.0%
Lowest fifth	5.0	4.9	5.5
Second fifth	11.8	12.0	11.9
Middle fifth	17.0	17.6	17.4
Fourth fifth	23.1	23.6	23.7
Highest fifth	43.0	42.0	41.6

3. *Statistical Abstracts of the United States, 1973*, p. 330.

4. Lester C. Thurow, "More Are Going to be Poor," *The New Republic*, 171:18 (November 2, 1974), 26.

cent (versus 42.6 percent if only earned income is measured); the total share of the top 5 percent was 22.1 percent (versus 16.0 percent). The share going to the lowest fifth was 3.7 percent (versus 4.3 percent).[5]

The preceding data suggest that over the period from 1947 to 1971, government interventions, which might be thought to affect before-tax income (for example, through minimum-wage laws), have not brought about a change in the overall income distribution. But how do taxes affect the distribution of net income, that is, what people actually have to spend? A detailed study of the question (including the effects of progressive income tax, the regressive sales tax, tax deductions that favor some over others, and so on) concludes that a *range* of possible effects has to be allowed for, although the range is not very large.[6] Keeping this in mind, the study found that:

1. For those earning more than $2,000 but less than $30,000, which was roughly 87 percent of all American families in 1966, the total tax effect was either proportional (that is, taxes took the same proportion from the poor and those with moderately high incomes, thus leaving the shape of the income distribution unchanged) or *slightly* progressive (that is, taxes created a somewhat more egalitarian income distribution).

2. The burden was *slightly* greater on the very poor (below $2,000 a year) primarily because of the sales tax, and *slightly* greater on the rich (above $30,000 a year), because of the progressive federal income tax.

3. In sum, the *after*-tax distribution of income was slightly (at most 5 percent, perhaps as little as 0.25 percent) more egalitarian than the before tax distribution.[7]

If we were to stop here, examining only the reallocative effects of what the government takes from the people, the government impact would have to be considered quite small. But let's add outflow—the services rendered—to the picture, before we draw a conclusion. This turns out to be even more difficult; so difficult that several authors declared the task impossible. They point out that many of the services the government produces are "public goods" whose proportional benefits to various segments of the population cannot be assessed. The main item on this list is national defense, which still consumes one-third of the federal budget, though this represents a decrease from the 49 percent of 1960. Similarly, it is said, cleaner air and water, *de*-pollution, benefits all. Other services are "disputive": Even if two individuals get the same amount of service, it may mean different things to them.

5. Joseph A. Pechman and Benjamin A. Okner, *Who Bears the Tax Burden?* (Washington, D.C.: The Brookings Institution, 1974), pp. 45–46.

6. Ibid., p. 6.

7. Ibid., pp. 1–10.

Fair enough. Keeping these significant reservations in mind, we still can ask: Of those government outflows whose prime beneficiaries can be determined, which segments of the population get more? Whose problems get more treatment? The answer is that a disproportionately higher share of these funds go to the aged and the ill, to families headed by women, and to other economically weak categories, as compared to other segments of the population. For example, in the period from 1950 to 1972, federal grants to state and local governments for public health and welfare assistance rose from about $1.15 billion a year to about $14.1 billion.[8] More specifically, federal expenditures for retirement and disability rose from $4.7 billion in 1950 to $76.9 billion in 1974; old-age, survivors and disability benefits, from $0.7 to $53.5 billion; unemployment benefits, from $2.0 to $5.2 billion; and Aid to Families with Dependent Children, $0.2 to $4.3 billion in the same period.[9]

To be sure, not all these funds go to the economically disadvantaged. Social Security benefits go to all eligible persons over 65, which includes aged millionaires. Moreover, the size of the Social Security check is geared to previous income, though the formula in use favors the very poor. Veterans' benefits constitute a significant chunk of government pay-outs available to those eligible regardless of income. And several specific programs benefit the middle and upper classes more than the poor. Support for housing is a prime example.[10] Still, despite these exceptions, the federal government's services, when all considered together, favor the weaker groups, because most benefits are given either to all groups or only to the weak.

State and local government services seem to be less progressively distributed than the federal ones, though it is again difficult to determine how equally services are being distributed and who is benefiting most from a particular service. Most low-income metropolitan areas are reported to receive less frequent and generally inadequate garbage pickups, less police protection, as well as fewer parks and other recreational facilities.[11] Lower per-pupil educational expenditures are alloted for children of low-income parents; similarly, the education allocations disfavor

8. *Statistical Abstract of the United States, 1973*, p. 288.

9. Edward R. Fried et al., *Setting National Priorities: The 1974 Budget* (Washington, D.C.: The Brookings Institution, 1973), p. 69. Figures for 1974 are the expected fiscal 1974 figures.

10. See Alvin L. Schorr, "National Community and Housing Policy," *Social Science Review*, 39 (1965), pp. 433–443.

11. S. M. Miller and Pamela Roby, *The Future of Inequality* (New York: Basic Books, 1970), pp. 84 ff. See also S. M. Miller and Martin Rein, "Can Income Redistribution Work?" *Social Policy*, Vol. 6 (1975), pp. 3–18.

minority children and rural areas.[12] On the other hand, state and city governments pay a share of the costs of many social assistance programs, such as Medicaid and welfare.

If it is true, as we suggest, that jointly, all levels of the government spend more on the economically weak and thus, on *average*, transfer funds to them from the taxes of those better off, why do measures of the distribution of income among the various groups show little change decade after decade? One reason is technical: Some benefits, for instance, some supplements to the poor, chiefly Medicaid payments, are not generally counted as income when national income distribution is measured. On the other hand, direct cash transfer payments such as Social Security, welfare, disability, and veteran's allowances are counted as income. So, in toto, it would still seem that there ought to be an allocative effect. The answer is that *without the estimated $86 billion a year in income transfers by the government, the national income distribution would have grown more unequal each year.*[13] Thus, the use of government power does *not* serve to reduce inequality, but to prevent it from growing significantly year by year.

Table 2 shows the interaction of taxes and "transfer payments" in a specific year. As can be seen, the lowest income category received far more in transfer payments than it paid in taxes. Correspondingly, the highest income group paid out fairly high taxes, but got back relatively

Table 2   Taxes and Transfers as Percent of Income, 1965[a]

	TAXES				
INCOME CLASSES	Federal	State and Local	Total	TRANSFER PAYMENTS	TAXES LESS TRANSFERS
Under $2,000	19%	25%	44%	126%	−83%[b]
$ 2,000–4,000	16	11	27	11	16
4,000–6,000	17	10	27	5	21
6,000–8,000	17	9	26	3	23
8,000–10,000	18	9	27	2	25
10,000–15,000	19	9	27	2	25
15,000 and over	32	7	38	1	37
Total	22	9	31	14	24

[a]Income excludes transfer payments, but includes realized capital gains in full and undistributed corporate profits.
[b]The minus sign indicates that the families and individuals received more from federal, state, and local governments than they, as a group, paid to these governments in taxes.
Source: Joseph Pechman, "The Rich, the Poor and the Taxes They Pay," *The Public Interest*, 17 (Fall 1969), 33, based on *Economic Report of the President*, 1969.

12. James S. Coleman et al., *Equality of Educational Opportunity* (Washington, D.C.: U.S. Department of Health, Education, and Welfare, 1966).

13. Fried et al., *Setting National Priorities: The 1974 Budget*, p. 68. Data are projected for 1974.

little in transfers. The five categories from $2,000 to $15,000, however, paid roughly the same percentage in taxes and got back roughly the same percentage in transfers. With nearly all the net aid from transfers going to the lowest income group, it is not hard to see how the distribution of tax revenues and services helped to keep the heads of the very poor above water, rather than to realign the total income distribution.

In sum, it would appear that the government does reflect a *relatively* more egalitarian thrust than the socioeconomic power base would lead us to expect. Yet it is strong enough only to prevent an increase in inequality, rather than to advance equality of income and resolution of related social problems.

One Citizen, One Vote?

If each adult citizen has one vote, why are governmental expenditures and regulations not much more geared toward promoting an egalitarian society? Firstly, even as a formal requirement, the ideal of "one man, one vote" has been gradually approximated but never entirely achieved. Whereas in 1860 only 17 percent of the population was eligible to vote, by 1960 the percentage had risen to 60 percent. Historically, the first barrier to fall was the requirement that voters own property. After the Civil War, black men were enfranchised. During the twentieth century, the literacy tests and poll taxes that curbed participation of blacks in the South were made illegal; the franchise was extended to women; the age qualification was lowered from 21 to 18; and, most recently, residency requirements for voter registration have been greatly eased.[14] Still, rural votes continue to outweigh urban ones. Based on votes cast in the 1952 election, Robert Dahl computed an index of advantage for votes cast in particular areas of the country. With 1 being the value of the index, if actual and proportional representation were equal, Nevada scored 14.8 while New York scored 0.17.[15] This means that it takes 87 votes to achieve the same effects in New York as 1 vote does in Nevada. Although the series of Supreme Court rulings in 1962–1964, requiring reapportionment of election districts so as to approximate "one man, one vote" has to an extent redressed the rural-urban imbalance in the House, nevertheless, a fundamental prorural bias still persists in that all states, populous and sparsely settled alike, elect two senators each. And the Senate is more powerful in making public law and policy than is the

14. Murray Gendell and Hans L. Zetterberg, eds., *A Sociological Almanac for the United States* 2nd ed. (New York: Scribner, 1964), p. 54. Figures originally assembled by R. E. Lane, *Political Life: Why People Get Involved in Politics* (Glencoe, Ill.: Free Press, 1959), but supplemented for the later years.

15. Dahl, *A Preface to Democratic Theory*, p. 114.

House. No wonder farmers get their way more often than do workers, not to mention urban consumers.

Aside from the fact that each citizen does not have one equally weighted vote in formal constitutional terms, the government responds significantly more readily to some social groups than to others, because such groups can deliver the votes. Groups differ greatly in their ability to mobilize voters according to their level of cohesion and mobilization (what percentage of the relevant category of persons they have succeeded in organizing), the amount of resources they have at their disposal (such as money for campaign financing and the number of volunteer campaign workers they can deploy) as well as the degree of persuasive power they have with their members (that is, their ability to influence their members' voting preferences).

Over the years there has been a long series of attempts to limit the ability of interest groups to influence elections, particularly through limiting their campaign contributions. In an effort to restrain spending by big business on behalf of its favorite candidates, Theodore Roosevelt proposed a ban on corporate campaign contributions, and such a law was passed by Congress in 1907. Later, the Taft-Hartley Act extended this prohibition to labor unions as well. However, these restrictions were very laxly enforced, and the laws did not ban voluntary contributions by corporate executives or members of labor unions. As a result, many avenues remained for circumventing the intent of the law. Corporations, for example, have often given their executives bonuses or expense accounts with which they as individuals could make campaign gifts. Unions spend dues money on voter registration and get-out-the-vote drives, as well as on union newspapers and other communications that influence members' views on political issues. During the course of the Watergate scandal, it was revealed that a number of corporations had made illegal campaign contributions.

A factor that enhances the power of interest groups is the increasing cost of financing an election campaign. Between 1960 and 1968 the amount spent on presidential-year campaigns doubled, rising from $27,202,155 to $56,397,261. (These are official figures; experts estimate that far more was actually spent.)[16] Low-budget campaigns have great difficulty getting their message to the voters, although there is no one-to-one correspondence between out-spending and out-voting one's rival. Thus, very roughly speaking, each person may have one vote, but the forces that try to sway persons to vote for one person or another are heavily stacked in favor of the champions of the approaches to social problems that attract the support of interest groups, not the public at large.

16. Robert A. Diamond, ed., *Politics in America* (Washington, D.C.: Congressional Quarterly, 1971), edition IV, pp. 80–81.

Finally, much government business takes place out of the reach of voters through lobbying, and not via the legislatures but directly in executive agencies. Often agencies end up "representing" particular interests (for example, the Department of Commerce caters to the interests of business, the Department of Labor, those of the unions) and may negotiate with one another on behalf of these respective clients, to the exclusion of all others, especially the citizens at large.[17] The American Medical Association for many years had the ear of the surgeon general, although its influence has declined in recent years. The head of the Office of Education is usually chosen after careful consultation with the educational establishment; the head of the National Science Foundation, with the natural scientists; the secretary of agriculture, with the Farm Bureau and other major farm lobbies, and so on.

Partial correctives to the power of interest groups have been found by increasing the professionalism of the civil service, the body of government agencies, as distinct from their political heads. Thus, the offices of prison wardens and postmasters are today more often occupied by competent civil servants, rather than by persons who in the past had received such an office as a token of indebtedness to lobbies. Also, by giving weak groups their "own" agencies—Office of Economic Opportunity to the poor, office of civil rights to minorities and women—new counterlobbies are created. However, compared to agencies that are closer to the main interest groups, these agencies are relatively weak. That is, the government impact does not merely reflect the societal power profile, but it also rarely sways far from it. Thus, the government may try to attain rights for minorities, more product safety, more pollution controls, stronger gun control, and so on, than the lobbies favor, but rarely are the lobbies ignored, especially for longer periods. Most social problems are much more likely to gain due attention after concerned individuals form effective public interest groups of their own.

SOCIAL POWER

Alternative Views

All societies are stratified. Social positions, and the people who occupy them, are arranged in layers that differ in the assets they possess, including wealth, prestige, and power. Those in the higher strata not only tend to be better off economically and enjoy higher social status, but they also command more of the means and know-how needed to get their way when their viewpoints or interests clash with those of others.

17. David Olson, "Studies in American Legislative Process," *Public Administration Review*, 28 (1968), 280–286.

We already have seen that they get their way more easily with the government than do weaker groups. In addition, the advantaged have many direct avenues for making their power felt within society.

The ways in which the foundations use their funds is a case in point. Foundations choose which social problems deserve their attention, which programs to favor, and which individuals are worthy of their grants. Who makes the policies of these foundations? Waldemar Nielsen studied the thirty-three major foundations (each with over $100 million in assets).[18] He found that while the foundations are subject to a minimum of government regulation designed primarily to prevent them from acting in self-serving ways on behalf of individual or corporate interests, they are barely publicly accountable in any other sense. A founding donor —the super-rich or a corporation—is free to choose virtually anyone he or she wishes to serve on the board of trustees, and the trustees in turn set the criteria of eligibility for future board members and take an active role in choosing their own immediate successors. Because these people tend to choose others like themselves, the result is that the vast majority of foundation trustees are old, white, males, alumni of Ivy League schools, Protestants, of British or Northern European origin, residents of the eastern United States, and Republican. Occupationally, the biggest single group is businessmen, followed by lawyers, and then by a smattering of other professions.

These trustees, Nielsen found, often kept the foundations' investments closely tied to companies they were associated with, even when this has resulted in substantially diminished benefits to charity.[19] In addition, foundations closely linked to the automotive, chemical, and petroleum industries have proved reluctant to finance research and experimentation on safety and antipollution devices associated with these industries or studies of questions related to tax equity and the oil-depletion allowance. Also, they tended to channel funds toward those institutions (hospitals, universities, and colleges) with which a trustee is also affiliated. As a result of the close financial ties between the business community and the foundations studied, Nielsen finds that for a large number of foundations, "The boards ... are currently ridden with conflicts of interest incompatible with their objective and exclusive devotion to philanthropic purposes and the public interest."[20]

Another example of how the privileged exercise greater control over policy-making institutions than other people is the composition of the

18. Waldemar A. Nielsen, *The Big Foundations* (New York: Columbia University Press, 1972), p. 21.

19. Ibid., pp. 309–322.

20. Ibid., p. 317.

Medicare-Medicaid Advisory Council, a part of the Department of Health, Education, and Welfare.

> The Medical Assistance Advisory Council was established under the Social Security Amendments of 1967. . . . [According to the statute authorizing the creation of this council] . . . members shall include representatives of State and local agencies and nongovernmental organizations and groups concerned with health and consumers of health services, and a majority of the membership of the advisory council shall consist of representatives of consumers of health services. . . . [However] . . . of the 21 members only four might possibly be characterized as "representatives of consumers of health services."[21]

Furthermore,

> An analysis of these questionnaires indicates that only 15 percent of the members of Advisory Committees represent consumers. Actual Medicaid patients constitute only 4 percent of total membership. On the other hand, provider representatives—physicians, nurses, pharmacists, hospital administrators, for example—account for approximately 70 percent of all members of Medical Care Advisory Committees.[22]

In short, although one cannot necessarily assume that the privileged (in terms of their position in the higher layers of the stratification structure of society) automatically or exclusively control the direction of social programs, they tend to have a disproportionately large control of the way social problems are defined and approached. This seems to be true throughout the gamut of social institutions, from hospitals to voluntary welfare agencies, from birth-control clinics to Better Business Bureaus.

Whereas many social scientists would agree with the preceding observation, they would be less in agreement as to the more precise degree to which social power is concentrated in the hands of a few elites and as to the consequences of such concentration for societal guidance. The alienation approach asserts that power is concentrated almost entirely in one class, property owners, while the other classes are virtually powerless. This class contains or controls those at the top of various power pyramids, especially the corporation magnates, the military chiefs, and their allies in the ideology-maintaining machines (churches, Madison Avenue).[23] Alienation theorists differ as to how united they believe the

21. *Medicare and Medicaid Problems, Issues, and Alternatives*, U. S. Senate Committee on Finance (Washington, D.C.: Government Printing Office, 1970), p. 134.

22. *Medicare and Medicaid Guide* (Chicago: Commerce Clearinghouse Publications, 1972), p. 6759.

23. C. Wright Mills, *The Power Elite* (New York: Oxford University Press, 1956).

ruling classes are. Some refer to the various elites as if they were one integrated, tightly coordinated ruling class; others see various divisions among them (for example, big business versus small business, farm owners versus industrialists), but hold that these differences are not basic, because vis-à-vis the propertyless, they share the same basic outlook and vested interests. Above all, they all belong to, and act on behalf of, the same class: Those who get most of the privileges, the wealthy, who are committed to the status quo (from which they benefit) and hence opposed to all fundamental correctives.

The propertyless, powerless, classes, or masses, are viewed as excluded from power now, although—here views differ—they may be perceived as waiting, in various degrees of readiness, to rise up, overcome the ruling class, and introduce an egalitarian society, free of conflict, and capable of facing its problems effectively. Until this occurs, it is said, the ruling class both sustains the problem-causing social structure and blocks all but insignificant correctives.

The political arm of the consensus approach, which reaches far into political science to include scholars such as David Truman, Gabriel Almond, and Sidney Verba, and is represented within sociology by David Riesman,[24] espouses a fundamentally different viewpoint. It sees a plurality of power centers or power groups, none dominant, each seeking to pull the society's public policies toward its interests and ends. Groups include the manufacturers, farmers, military, labor unions, churches, social workers, teachers, black organizations, and many others. All classes and collectivities are potential power bases. Unaffiliated individuals, the public at large, fall largely in the crevices between groupings. Most significantly, there is a tug-of-war among the various groups. No single group is powerful enough to dictate the definition or handling of social problems. The course followed is the result of an averaging effect of the relative tugging and pulling of these many diverse groups, which quite often results in a stalemate, or a policy zigzag (following for a time a course which pleases some, then one that favors others). For some this is the essence of democratic politics: "Everybody's" viewpoints and needs have some leverage. "No one group or class is decisively favored over others by the cumulated decision on public issues."[25]

The neoconservative approach has seldom dealt so explicitly with the power question and is less of one mind about it. Generally, neo-

---

24. David Riesman, *The Lonely Crowd* (New York: Doubleday, 1953), p. 191 ff.

25. Truman, *The Governmental Process*, pp. 14 ff; William Kornhauser, " 'Power Elite' or 'Veto Groups'?" in *Culture and Social Character*, ed. Seymour M. Lipset and Leo Lowenthal (New York: Free Press, 1961), pp. 252–267; Charles O. Jones, *Introduction to the Study of Public Policy* (Belmont, Calif.: Duxbury Press, 1970), pp. 28 ff.

conservatives see "natural" societal power relations, based either on legitimate authority or created by the market mechanism, as more wholesome than the exercise of government power. Such power, they say, may be arbitrary and illegitimate, as is indicated by the abuses uncovered during the Watergate era. To the extent that the privileged classes are getting their way, this is depicted as a reward for extra effort, talent, or responsibility. If the rich can afford to set up a foundation, why should they not be allowed to determine if its funds are used to fight mental retardation or, say, pollution? If the rich have the time to serve on hospital boards, "naturally" they should have more say as to what the hospital focuses on, and so on. Elites, leadership, and expertise are all seen as essential, whereas mass participation endangers societal qualities ·from aesthetic attributes to entrepreneurship, to rational management (see pp. 21–22, 26).

Finally, *weak* government (that is, strong socially based elites) secures the individual's freedom and provides the strength of character, family, and community required to solve their own problems, ranging from overcoming alcoholism to dealing with delinquent children, from "climbing out" of poverty to refraining from drug abuse.

The Guidance Perspective

A Skewed Power Distribution: The guidance approach sees an unequal power distribution among a plurality of social groups. There is no one ruling class or one power elite that monopolizes the power, rendering all the rest into powerless classes or masses. At the same time, the social groups differ significantly in the amount of power they command. Thus, in the United States, both labor unions and the manufacturers wield power, but the labor unions have less power than the manufacturers. Both the AMA and the nurses associations affect health policy, but the AMA much more so. Both teachers' and parents' associations affect educational policy, but teachers' associations are more potent, and so on.

Any Social Status Can Be a Power Base: To form a power base, individuals must form a cohesive group; a mere aggregate of individuals is rarely effective. While theoretically any combination of individuals may form a social group, bus drivers, skid row winos, and suburbanites rarely join to form one. Groups usually coalesce among persons who have a similar social status. Karl Marx held that economic status was *the* basis for the formation of a social group (a cohesive class). Since Marx's time it has been often established that other kinds of status can serve as a source of coalescing, including race, ethnicity, age groups ("the youth"), education attainment ("college educated"), and sex (women, homosexuals). Various attempts have been made to reduce these various social categories to economic ones—for example, to see blacks as the dispossessed and the whites as the property owners, or to see a *class* struggle of the sexes.

As I see it, while economic differences often exist among such social groupings, they do not constitute the sole basis, or frequently even the main basis, on which these groups are formed. Thus women are as concerned with being treated as inferior persons as they are with being paid less. Jews tend to unite around religion, culture, and concern for Israel rather than on the basis of economic interest, and so on. In fact, the membership of such social groups often cuts across economic lines. Thus, black groups have middle-class as well as working-class and lower-class members; members of women's groups are found throughout the social structure, and so forth. Indeed, poor blacks feel closer to nonpoor blacks than to poor whites, and poor whites tend to see greater affinity with middle-class whites than with lower-class blacks. Similarly, members of women's groups feel more aligned with other women, whatever their class, than with men.[26] This is the reason Karl Marx believed the workers would have had a much higher revolutionary potential than would peasants. The peasants were dispersed all over the land and were rather individualistic. Through their jobs, the workers were brought "under one roof" and had many opportunities for interaction. To be socially connected, the members of groups require occasions to interact (such as social clubs, voluntary associations), must have a positive feeling about their group, and subscribe to at least some of its *sub*culture norms, traditions, dialect. Thus, the history of groups coming into their own—workers, blacks, women—invariably reveals reduced interaction with members of other groups and increased interaction with group members as well as increased identification with group symbols.

The coalescing process by which an aggregate of individuals becomes a cohesive social group, able, *in principle*, to act in unison, takes many forms. Often it entails developing symbols of identification that allow members to register their dedication to the group. These may range from an item of clothing, such as the *dashiki*, to a form of hairdo, such as the Afro or long hair for the "youth" counterculture movement. Included also are participation in group institutions such as private schools, adult education classes, and social clubs, and subscription to the group publications, such as *Ebony* and *Ms.*

Note that no coalesced social group ever included all or even most of those who have the same status. Many women do not belong to women's groups, many blacks do not belong to black groups, many homo-

26. For a study of the relative power of ethnic versus economic factors, see Andrew Greeley, "Political Participation Among Ethnic Groups in the United States: A Preliminary Reconnaissance," in *American Journal of Sociology*, 80 (1974), 170–204.

sexuals do not belong to gay groups, and so forth. The significance of those who join is that they are more likely than nonjoiners to maintain similar views as to what the social problems are and what is to be done. Because they are tied to each other on social issues, as well as a similar status position, those bound into a cohesive group are more likely to act on behalf of their interests or needs, than those who do not belong to such a group.

Mobilization: The actual power base is never the statistical aggregate of status holders (for example, all workers) *or* a social group (all members of a workers' bowling club), but the segments of it mobilized by specific action organizations (for instance, a labor union local). It is a common mistake, one that is generated by the way most data are available for social observers and social analysts, to use statistical aggregates to assess the power of a status category. Women provide a good example of how a group's mere statistical size can be a misleading measure of its power. Women constitute a majority of the population. However, in 1973, only 13 of the 535 members of Congress were women, and none of them were senators. In contrast, blacks, who constitute a much smaller statistical percentage of the American population as a whole, had 15 representatives and 1 senator.[27]

The significance of a status-category's numerical size for its ability to affect the course both of nongovernment programs and of the government itself is determined by the extent to which the members of such a category are available, or "mobilizable," for action on specific issues or, generally, for support of the group's approach to deliberate, guided, societal change. A group that can activate more of its members to vote or demonstrate or contribute funds or otherwise support what it is after will more often get its way (all other things being equal) than a group similar in size but less mobilized. And, over time, the same group, with little change in its size, may grow much more, or much less, politically effective. Thus, the black community did not grow much in percent of the total U.S. population from the late 1950s to the late 1960s, but it did grow much more effective politically. Registration of black voters climbed from 1.4 million in 1960 to 3.3 million in 1970 in the eleven southern states, and by 1974, 1,307 blacks were holding political office in the South, more than five times as many as in 1968.[28]

In the mid and late 1960s much was made of a new political group, the American youth. The "alienated youth" was seen as a major factor in the civil rights movement, the movement against the war in Vietnam, and in the 1968 election campaigns in which early successes of the youth's

27. *Statistical Abstract of the United States, 1973,* p. 375.

28. *U.S. News and World Report,* February 25, 1974, pp. 56–59.

hero, Eugene McCarthy, induced President Lyndon B. Johnson to refuse to run for reelection. In reality, only a few thousand young Americans actively participated in any of these movements, while hundreds of thousands lent them occasional support, such as participation in weekend demonstrations. Even these amounted to no more than 10 percent at most of the 26 million Americans between the ages of 18 and 24.[29] Moreover, youth was divided on important issues. For example, 47 percent of a sample of youth agreed with the statement, "Fighting the war in Vietnam is damaging to our national honor or pride," while 51 percent disagreed. On a question concerning suggested solutions to crime and violence 34 percent of youth stressed harsher penalties and enforcement of laws, 15.5 percent stressed changes in the police and courts, and 13 percent stressed attacking root problems.[30] The youth *was* a very significant factor in those years, only it was not "the" youth but only a small mobilized segment of youth. As public life is shaped by small mobilized segments of all the politically relevant groupings, a change in the mobilization of any particular group is much more significant than the statistical size of its population base.

Organizations mobilize collectivities for action in general or with respect to specific issues. Thus, farmers, Indians, Protestants, welfare recipients or even liberals per se do not act for or against social interventions or exercise power; rather the groups to which they belong are activated by specific organizations such as the Farm Bureau, the American Indian Movement (AIM), the National Council of Churches, the National Welfare Rights Organization, and the Americans for Democratic Action. In an attempt to guide their constituencies, these organizations engage in such activities as giving advice on which candidates to support, sponsoring demonstrations, and organizing volunteer campaign workers. Note that even applications of power that are individualistic—for instance voting or writing letters to one's congressman—are, at least in part, organized. Indeed, one organization seems to have been so effective that it got its members to flood a TV network with protesting letters about a program that had not yet been aired.[31]

A major reason why these organizational factors must be understood is that these activating agents, which "turn on" social groups to act on social problems, are scarcely neutral; they have a "slant" that affects the final power outcome. Mobilizing organizations tend either to radic-

29. On the size of cohort, see *Statistical Abstract of the United States*, 1973, p. 31, Preliminary (1972 figures).

30. Jerald G. Bachman and Elizabeth Van Duinen, *Youth Look at National Problems* (Ann Arbor: University of Michigan, 1971), pp. 14, 49.

31. "NBC Gun Program, Never Shown, Attracts Letters," *The New York Times*, April 26, 1975.

alize *or* moderate their members; they almost never simply reflect members' incoming, "innocent" positions. Studies of labor unions tend to stress the conservative effect of these organizations. For instance, Robert Michel's often cited study shows that as unions grow older, union leaders tend to stress protection of the organization's viability, which means softening its radical goals.[32] On the other hand, a study of the AFL-CIO, the National Association for the Advancement of Colored People (NAACP), and the National Council of Churches found that as the size of their staffs grew, these organizations became more liberal and reformist.[33] Similarly, a well-known study by Samuel Stouffer revealed that leaders of voluntary associations were more likely to be tolerant (as the democratic rules of the game prescribe) toward dissidents such as Communists, socialists, and atheists than were the rank-and-file constituencies. For example, 84 percent of community leaders but only 61 percent of a cross section of the population studied would allow a socialist to speak in their community in favor of government ownership of railroads. Similarly, 64 percent of the leaders but only 39 percent of the ordinary citizens would allow an atheist to give a speech; 51 percent of the leaders but only 39 percent of the citizens would allow an admitted Communist to speak.[34]

The extent to which organizations do or do not authentically express the wishes of their social base as well as the direction they give to their members' energy are pivotal factors in determining to what extent the power exercised will be intrainstitutional or extrainstitutional. (Another factor that influences the same result is the extent to which the system is responsive or rigid.)[35] Thus, if the hierarchy of a labor union is much more conservative than its members, wildcat strikes, in which members act on their own, without authorization from the leadership, may be on the rise. Radical organizations may foment protests and uprisings that would not have occurred spontaneously. In any event, if one seeks to understand why people lie in front of bulldozers to stop urban renewal schemes rather than demonstrate peacefully or sign petitions or

32. Robert Michels, *Political Parties* (New York: Free Press, 1958).

33. Henry J. Pratt, "Bureaucracy and Group Behavior: A Study of Three National Organizations" (paper delivered to the American Political Science Association, 1972), cited in James Q. Wilson, *Political Organizations* (New York: Basic Books, 1973, pp. 226, 233n; for a discussion of the use of violence in achieving political goals, see William A. Gamson, "The Meek Don't Make It," *Psychology Today*, 8 (July 1974), 35–42.

34. Samuel Stouffer, *Communism, Conformity, and Civil Liberties* (New York: Wiley & Sons, 1967), pp. 28–41.

35. For additional discussion, see Amitai Etzioni, *The Active Society* (New York: Free Press, 1968).

shift their votes to obtain the same goal, one must understand, aside from general system considerations and whether the authorities are relatively responsive or not to the members' basic needs and demands, the nature of the mobilizing organizations.

This is not to suggest that the public at large, people without affiliation or organizational membership, play no role. But, their role is much smaller than has been often suggested, while that of organized groups is much greater proportionally than their size would indicate. Moreover, while the public at large is likely to offer passive and disorganized resistance to alienating conditions or to policies they oppose, organized groups typically initiate coordinated activity in support of specific proposals and offer more effective opposition.

Coalition Building: Most important, the direction of public policy and intervention against social problems is indicative not merely of the relative power of the various social groups and their mobilizing organizations, but of their own coalition formation, as well as that of the opposed groups, the countermobilized forces. As the decision point approaches, numerous groups tend to coalesce into a few camps in favor of or against a policy. A winning or blocking coalition may not be made up of the powerful groups, but contain a wide collection of weak groups or some weak groups working with a powerful one. As a rule, only minor concessions can be won when the weak face the powerful, squarely united.

An analysis of how the shifting alliances of organizations representing various constituencies affected the fate of federal aid to education from 1918 to 1965, when such a bill was finally enacted, provides an example. Three issues polarized the relevant interest groups, in turn: racial segregation, fear of federal domination of local school systems, and government aid to parochial schools. Until these issues were resolved through compromise, a coalition sufficiently wide to bring about passage of a federal-aid-to-education act could not be achieved. The NAACP, originally favorable, grew progressively more militant against segregated schools and joined the opposition in the early 1950s, remaining there until the mid-1960s when aggressive Justice Department action to enforce court-ordered school desegregation had ensured that federal aid to education would not be used to buttress the dual school systems in the South. Conservative groups such as the Daughters of the American Revolution, the Chamber of Commerce, and the Farm Bureau remained in opposition to the bill, but lost in power over the years. The Parent Teachers Associations, educators, organized labor, and womens' and Jewish groups consistently favored federal aid to education, although educators opposed a 1961 bill limited to school construction. Protestant groups also supported the bills as long as the proposals did not weaken the separation of church and state by granting aid to Catholic parochial schools; Catholics meanwhile refused to back any bill that did not allow their schools to share in the funds.

Until 1965 the various alliances were roughly evenly matched and stalemate resulted. The 1965 Act succeeded in effecting a workable compromise by focusing federal allocations on underprivileged children. Funds were made available for much broader uses than merely school construction, and so the educators were content; furthermore, in the climate of the antipoverty drive the conservative camp was not aroused to its usual defense of local autonomy. In addition, the Protestant National Council of Churches had by this time relented somewhat in its opposition to aid to parochial schools, and the bill was able to allow for funds for books for parochial schools and use of supplementary educational support, thereby gaining Catholic support.[36]

As the preceding illustration suggests, struggles among interest groups over whether and how to take action on a social problem usually divide according to far more complex cleavages than "haves" versus "have nots," weak versus strong, and public versus private interests. The elites of business, government, labor, and other blocs are often divided among themselves over whether to favor or oppose particular interventions. Some may favor a course of action for reasons of expediency (for example, a small concession now may obviate the need for larger ones at a later date), others may favor it out of guilt (for example, some liberal whites may support the cause of blacks), and still others out of self-interest (for example, they too have to breath the polluted air). Similarly, elites may oppose a course of action for any one or more of a number of complex, selfish or selfless, extraneous or relevant reasons. At the same time, persons in the lower reaches of power, whose apparent self-interest may be directly affected by a proposed strategy, may be scarcely activated at all. This inaction may be the result of apathy or distrust of politics, preoccupation with the struggle for survival, or sheer disorganization.

AN EXAMPLE: ORGANIZING
THE FARM WORKERS

Structurally, migrant farm workers are nearly at the bottom of the American stratification system. Farm workers' wages are low, and the living conditions on the farms are among the worst in the nation. That the perennially "hopeless plight" of the farm worker has begun to change for the better over the past dozen years illustrates the difference between mobilization and its absence.

36. Our discussion draws on Frank Munger, "Changing Politics of Aid to Education," *Transaction*, 5 (June 1967), 11–16.

Until quite recently, the farm workers had proved impervious to unionization efforts, and even today successful organization is still largely confined to California. A major reason was that the migrant workers are a heterogeneous group. They include Mexican-American families and single, male, transient Filipinos, Japanese, native Mexicans, and American whites. Throughout the history of union organizing efforts, the Mexican *braceros*, or seasonally imported laborers and illegal aliens have provided a ready pool of strikebreakers, making the strike a far less effective tool for farm workers than it has been for other categories of workers. Not surprisingly, this situation has also promoted ethnic division and distrust among the farm workers. Moreover, large numbers of farm workers have looked on their occupation as only a temporary one. Many of the Mexican Americans and some other farm workers (like the Okies) are upwardly mobile, at least in their ambitions. In contrast, many other white farm workers are typically downwardly mobile; many are alcoholics, bums, or in other ways dropouts from white society. In short, although similar in economic status, cultural and ethnic differences made the farm workers a rather uncohesive and difficult-to-mobilize group.

In the early 1900s, the International Workers of the World (Wobblies) attempted to organize the farm workers. However, the Wobblies (mostly white males) largely appealed to, and focused on, the transient, single, white male workers, who were then as now only a small minority of the California labor force. This contributed to the Wobblies' inability to establish a wide power base, and so their organizing efforts were short-lived. In addition their radical demand to abolish the wage system repelled most workers who just wanted a fair wage for their day's work.

The U.S. Communist party in the 1930s attempted to include a variety of ethnic groups in their union-organizing efforts and in fact achieved some success. Thirty-seven strikes were organized over a 3-year period. Modest wage increases were obtained, but not union recognition, and when the top leaders of the Communist farm workers union were arrested in 1934, under a law banning advocacy of violent political change, the fledgling movement was broken.[37]

Numerous other organization drives by committees backed by the AFL-CIO through the 1950s and 1960s were without much success. The Agricultural Workers Organizing Committee (again made up of white males) concentrated their efforts on organizing the skid-row workers, mostly men without families or community ties. Again the organizers were unable to form a power base.[38]

37. Joan London and Henry Anderson, *So Shall Ye Reap* (New York: Crowell, 1971), pp. 29–32.

38. Ibid., pp. 46–77.

Throughout this period, federal, state, and local officials often intervened actively against unionizing efforts or were neutral on the side of the growers. Labor legislation covering wages and standards was either not extended to agricultural workers or not enforced. During strikes, county sheriffs and deputies were called out by the growers to protect the strikebreakers and to prevent the picketers from handing out strike literature or talking to those working in the fields.

The weakness and disorganization of the California farm workers began to be overcome when in 1962 Cesar Chavez, a Chicano and former farm worker, began a union organization effort among the grape pickers of Delano, California. Unlike the "bread-and-butter" unions of the AFL-CIO, Chavez's union was in large measure a charismatic movement whose goals went far beyond the typical union demands for better wages, shorter hours, and more fringe benefits. The UFWA (United Farm Workers of America) has fought for provisions protecting field workers from dangerous pesticides and sought to operate clinics, build retirement villages and open credit unions. Also, the UFWA wants to reform the work relationships that have characterized agricultural labor, replacing the farm contractor with the union hiring hall.[39]

Because of its identification with the civil rights movement and its religious overtones, the UFWA developed close ties with student activists as well as with church groups.[40] Over the years this coalition has proved to be one of the UFWA's greatest strengths. Not only do the students and church groups supply much needed funds, but their capacity to appeal to consumers made available to the UFWA a technique that put pressure on the growers in ways the field strike alone had never succeeded in accomplishing, mainly because growers could so easily hire strikebreakers. This technique was the boycott.[41]

The growers appealed to their political allies in Sacramento and Washington to help them break the boycott. Thus, the Republican governor of California, Ronald Reagan, announced in 1967 that he was eating more grapes than ever.[42] Similarly, President Nixon in 1969 branded the boycott illegal under the Taft-Hartley Act. The growers' greatest coup was to convince the Department of Defense to ship 2,167,000 pounds of grapes to Vietnam in 1969, but this was not sufficient to relieve

39. Peter Barnes, "Chavez Against the Wall," *New Republic*, December 7, 1974, pp. 13–16.

40. John Gregory Dunne, *Delano* (New York: Farrar, Strauss & Giroux, 1971), pp. 82–84.

41. London and Anderson, *So Shall Ye Reap*, p. 160.

42. Mark Day, *Forty Acres* (New York: Praeger, 1971), pp. 88–97, 140–168.

the economic pressure of the consumer boycott.[43] By 1970, through a combination of strikes, boycotts and threats of boycotts, the UFWA had obtained contracts with most major wineries, the lettuce-growing subsidiary of United Brands, the citrus-growing subsidiary of Coca-Cola, and the large table-grape growers.[44] In the following years, as the UFWA weakened as the result of internal disputes and poor administration, the growers, resigned to deal with a union but seeking one more easy to deal with, turned to the Teamsters. Thus, change was largely tied to the level of mobilization of the workers.

By 1975, the Teamsters were organizing ten times more farm workers than Chavez's UFWA. The conflict between the two, though, was one reason both together organized no more than a fraction of the workers.[45] Divided mobilizers mainly help the counter mobilization forces.

IN CONCLUSION

Power—the ability to make one's definition of what is problematic and what is to be done about it "stick"—is invested both within the government and in mobilized social groups—that is, cohesive aggregates of individuals acting in unison. The government power to a considerable extent reflects the relative power of the various social groups; however, in the process of converting social power into government power, the power's impact tends to become somewhat more considerate of the weaker groups.

The ability of a specific social group to affect the government's course, or that of the numerous institutions that affect social problems, as well as to block or alter the course of action favored by other social groups, is largely determined by four factors: (1) the group's place in the stratification (or status) structure; (2) its degree of cohesion; (3) its level of mobilization; and (4) the allies with which it forms coalitions as compared with the opponents that coalesce against it.

Much of the discussion in this chapter deals with public aspects of social problems, specifically, government and institutional policy; note however that the same factors work on the personal aspect of social problems. Thus, if some groups can impose an economic policy that requires

43. London and Anderson, So Shall Ye Reap, pp. 160–161.

44. Day, Forty Acres, pp. 88–97 and pp. 140–168. For a recent account, see Ronald B. Taylor Chavez and the Farm Workers (Boston: Beacon Press, 1975).

45. The New York Times, Aug. 31, 1975.

high labor-force mobility, competition, efficiency, and productivity as prime values, this will affect not just, say, the level of pollution but also the level of intrapersonal tension, opportunities to work out one's problems in stable, affectionate relationships, and so forth. In short, all aspects of social problems, collective and personal, are affected by the societal distribution of power and its use.

CHAPTER 7
CONSENSUS

CONSENSUS VERSUS POWER

During the 1960s and early 1970s the term "consensus" fell into disrepute, acquiring Machiavellian connotations of cynicism and manipulation for many Americans. First, President Johnson urged Americans to "reason together," though in fact, he often meant to get them to see things his way. Then, President Nixon spoke of "bringing us back together," while he ended up ignoring values most Americans hold dear. Within social science, "consensus theory" is a label the adherents of the alienation school affix on works they see as underestimating the role of power in creating social problems and in blocking responses to them, works that also fail to perceive the manipulated nature of consensus.

The idea of consensus, however, is too valuable to consign to the realm of the disingenuous or naïve. It is not mere idealism to aspire to *genuine* agreement with one another on basic values and specific policies or at least on procedures for settling differences. Whenever such authentic consensus is reached, it proves itself a better basis for dealing with social problems than either coercion (for example, sending in the National Guard to quell ghetto riots, to suppress campus protests, or to enforce school desegregation) or economic sanctions (for example, gaining equal employment opportunity for female and minority teachers by withdrawing federal aid from noncomplying colleges).[1]

1. For elaboration of this thesis see Amitai Etzioni, *The Active Society* (New York: Free Press, 1968), pp. 432–502.

A case in point is the confrontation between the New York City administration and Forest Hills residents in the early 1970s. It was one of many clashes in major cities around the country in which residents of middle- and lower-middle-class white ethnic neighborhoods protested attempts to locate in their midst low-income housing that was intended primarily for members of other racial and ethnic groups. In Forest Hills, residents feared that the sites of such housing would become centers of crime and drugs. The city administration countered that its plan to build comparatively low density housing—as opposed to the enormous high-rise projects of the past—in several widely scattered sites would minimize these anticipated ill effects. After the city's initial failure to consult with residents and area leaders to obtain their consent to this plan (as well as its subsequent modified version), the bitterness and belligerence of the Forest Hills residents escalated. Ultimately, the city agreed to build a much smaller number of apartments, primarily for the low-income aged rather than for welfare mothers and their children, the group it had initially intended to house in the area. Although the city might conceivably have succeeded in forcing through its original plan, it was widely recognized that the victory might have been a hollow one, because the alienated Forest Hills residents would likely have vented their hostility on the low-income families moving into the housing. When people have not been genuinely convinced, a policy is difficult to enforce.

It might be argued that if the city had consulted the people in the neighborhood beforehand, it would only have discovered much earlier that residents' prejudices, vested interests, or values would lead them to object to the plan. Experience, nevertheless, shows that when people are not consulted, that in itself can be the *main* source of their opposition; even when the main source lies elsewhere, failure to consult tends to add vehemence to the opposition. But most significantly, our thesis is *not* that consultation inevitably or even usually leads to consensus, only that lack of consensus tends to create serious difficulties in implementing social interventions. Thus, *if* a consensual solution can be achieved, it is the preferred course. Proceeding without it requires a value judgment that means favoring one group over another.

The *extent* to which a society can rely on consensus rather than on power depends, in part, on how skewed its power structure is. The more egalitarian the power distribution, the less the government need rely on its power to promote policies and the more it can (indeed must) rely on consensus among the citizens in shaping its programs. Conversely, the more power is concentrated, the less consensus will be sought or will be possible. Thus, the leaders of a kibbutz or commune, with no police and little economic power at their command, *must* rely on an existing consensus, work to develop one, or concede stalemate. On the other hand, well-entrenched local elites often ignore it. Societies lie somewhere between these two extremes, and their consensus pattern changes over time (e.g., there was much greater consensus concerning the U.S. role in World War II than there was concerning its role in Vietnam). Attention to the extent to which action is based on power or on consensus is essential in understanding the general background as well as specifics of deliberate social change, the handling of social problems.

FACTORS IN DETERMINING
THE LEVEL OF CONSENSUS

The extent to which values are shared significantly affects the level and quality of consensus. If most of us desire a "quality-of-life" society more than one dedicated to the pursuit of economic growth, policy making is much easier than if half of us wish to follow one course, while the other half favor the opposite.

How do we know what Americans think about a given course of action or a general value? Over the past 40 years social scientists, politicians, journalists, and the public at large have turned increasingly to public opinion polls to answer these questions. In assessing where the American people stand on various issues, it is wise not to rely on any single poll taken at one point in time or on a few percentage points of difference between two camps. However, if several polls (or surveys) are employed, and if each uses different wordings of questions, is conducted at different points in time (and hence is likely to capture varying moods), and shows sizable point differences, relatively clear preferences and trends will become discernible. For instance, between 1964 and 1974, most Americans became much more concerned with domestic "intrasocial" problems than with international affairs. When people were asked to list their concerns and worries in 1964, international problems such as avoiding war, combatting Communism, keeping a strong military, and maintaining respect for the United States in other countries were the four most often mentioned concerns, with domestic concerns running fifth.[2] By 1974, however, several polls showed that concern over international problems was at its lowest since the 1930s, while inflation, lack of trust in government, concern over political corruption, the energy crisis, crime, and moral and religious decline were all mentioned more often; in fact, only 3 percent of respondents mentioned any international problem.[3]

2. Poll cited in Ben J. Wattenberg, *The Real America* (Garden City, N.Y.: Doubleday, 1974), pp. 204–205.

3. Gallup poll, May 31–June 3, 1974, *Current Opinion*, vol. 2, issue 8 (August 1974), 85.

Differences in Consensus Formation

The shift in focus from concern with the world in the 1950s to concern with the society's internal problems in the late 1960s and early 1970s seems responsible, in part, for the difficulty of securing consensus during the past decade. The reason is that domestic strategy creates differences of opinion as to which social problems should be dealt with first and as to what the role of government should be in formulating and implementing correctives. In this sense, the great divisiveness created by the war in Vietnam was an exception. As far as polls teach us the U.S. role in World War II, the war in Korea, and, in general, the conduct of U.S. foreign policy was much more widely "consensuated" than was the average domestic policy in the same period. As one observer has pointed out:

> The United States has one President but it has two Presidencies; one Presidency is for domestic affairs and the other is concerned with defense and foreign policy. Since World War II, Presidents have had much greater success in controlling the nation's defense and foreign policies than in dominating its domestic policies. . . . The general public is much more dependent on Presidents in foreign affairs than in domestic matters. While many people know the impact of social security and Medicare, few know about politics in Malawi. So it is not surprising that people expect the President to act in foreign affairs and reward him with their confidence. Gallup Polls consistently show that Presidential popularity rises after he takes action in a crisis—whether the action is disastrous as in the Bay of Pigs or successful as in the Cuban missile crises. . . .[4]

On specific domestic policies, rarely has so great a degree of consensus been attained as that among the 96 percent of Americans (including 83 percent of the blacks) who in 1974 opposed the quota system as a means of reducing discrimination against minorities and women in hiring or advancement.[5] With respect to health care, only two out of ten Americans favor retention of the existing system; the other eight favor an entirely government-supported system or some mixture of private and government funding to ensure adequate care for all Americans.[6] A somewhat less widely supported position, but one on which there is un-

---

4. Aaron Wildavsky, "The Two Presidencies," Ch. 17, *Revolt Against the Masses and Other Essays on Politics and Public Policy* (New York: Basic Books, 1971), pp. 323–330.

5. William Watts and Lloyd A. Free, *State of the Nation, 1974*, (Washington, D.C.: Potomac Associates, 1974), p. 111.

6. Ibid., pp. 294–295.

usually high consensus is population control, favored in 1974 by 71 percent, and opposed by 20 percent.[7]

On most domestic policy issues, the public is much more sharply divided, with about one-third to one-half supporting one course and the rest another. Thus, in 1974, 48 percent favored, while 44 percent opposed, a plan to move welfare families, at government expense, from ghettoes to areas where living conditions and job opportunities are better.[8] Another 1974 poll found that 47 percent of Americans favored, while 44 percent opposed, the Supreme Court's ruling that a woman has the right to obtain an abortion during the first 3 months of pregnancy; the division of opinion on this issue was almost identical to that of a 1972 poll, taken before the Court's decision, which showed 46 percent in favor, 45 percent opposed.[9]

Is there any way to predict whether the American people will tend to favor or oppose a particular way of dealing with a social problem? By and large, the more favored policies are those that are, or seem to be, responsive to the needs of most if not all Americans *and* have been thoroughly explained *and* experienced. A prime example is Social Security. Social Security benefits go to all Americans in the sense that all of us can expect eventually to grow old and become its beneficiary; even if we die before we can collect benefits, our spouses and children will be supported. Experience with the program helped. In September 1936, just prior to its passage, Social Security was favored by 68 percent of Americans; by 1937, 77 percent approved of it, by 1938, 89 percent, and by 1943, 94 percent.[10]

The campaign against environmental pollution has similarly gained a widened consensus over the years. Pollution is a health hazard that potentially threatens the hearts, lungs, and other living tissues of all Americans as well as the wildlife many Americans cherish. And as public awareness of the matter expanded, so did the proportion of the nation viewing air pollution as a serious issue—28 percent took this view in 1965, 69 percent in 1970, and 83 percent in 1972. However, the percentage viewing pollution as a serious problem fell somewhat when the concern

---

7. Ibid., p. 178.

8. Gallup poll, June 2–24, 1974, *Current Opinion*, vol. 2, issue 10 (October 1974), 118.

9. Gallup poll, March 1974 (Field Enterprises), *Current Opinion*, vol. 2, issue 5 (May 1974), 51.

10. Amitai Etzioni and Carolyn Atkinson, "Sociological Implications of Alternative Income Transfer Systems," Bureau of Social Science Research (September 1969), p. 61; Harris Poll, February 14–17, 1973, *Current Opinion*, vol. 1, issue 5 (May 1973), 46.

with scarcities of resources came to be viewed as conflicting with environmental values in 1973–1974.[11]

In contrast, policies aimed at problems that directly affect, or seem to directly affect, only one or a few social groups and are "controversial" (that is, are incompatible with the values, conceptions, or misconceptions of some segments of society) are much less widely endorsed. In 1974, increased support for the aged (the parents of all classes) was favored by 84 percent of Americans, while only 26 percent favored more aid to the poor. Similarly, 76 percent favored increases in aid to young people who could not otherwise afford to go to college, while only 53 percent favored increases in programs to improve the situation of black Americans.[12]

Similarly, the concept of a guaranteed minimum income proposed in the late 1960s had great difficulty gaining public support, though it did make some headway. When the idea of a guaranteed minimum income was first introduced as a way to abolish poverty, few Americans favored it: 19 percent in 1965. Over the years, as the concept was endorsed by a widening circle of liberal congressmen and became a policy proposal of the Nixon Administration, it gained in support, with 28 percent favoring it in 1967, and 32 percent in 1969. But because the plan was seen as benefiting only a minority, *and* because it conflicted with a number of basic values, it never became as popular as other schemes to help the poor in ways that were more compatible with American traditions—for example, through work or charity. Thus, at the high point of support for a "negative income tax" in 1968, 58 percent of Americans polled still opposed it.[13] However, 79 percent favored a proposal that each family with an employable wage earner would be guaranteed enough work to earn $3,000 a year.

This is not to say, however, that Americans never change their attitudes and favor policies that stand to benefit primarily a small segment of the population. Nor should the impression be gained that their motives in favoring or disfavoring policies are entirely self-serving. Thus, just as the values of the work ethic as well as opposition to "big" government have stood in the way of some interventions designed to abolish poverty, so allegiance to democratic values, such as "equal justice under the law," has been invoked to bring about attitude change in spite of deeply ingrained emotional and self-interested resistance. A case in point

---

11. Wattenberg, *The Real America*, p. 226; Watts and Free, *State of the Nation, 1974,* p. 168.

12. Watts and Free, *State of the Nation, 1974,* pp. 275–283.

13. American Institute of Public Opinion, June 1968.

is the change in white Americans' attitudes toward black Americans. In major opinion shifts such as this, many factors are at work, including the spread of college education, which supports sensitivity to libertarian values; the efforts of social movement organizations, such as the National Association for the Advancement of Colored People (NAACP), the Congress of Racial Equality (CORE), and the Southern Christian Leadership Conference (SCLC), which increased Americans' awareness of prejudice against blacks; the improved "images" of blacks on TV and in widely read books and magazines; and specific incidents through which whites became more sympathetic to the cause of civil rights (for example, seeing Commissioner Bull Connor's dogs attack marchers in Birmingham, Alabama, in 1963). The change that took place is indicated by two national polls. In 1944, a nationwide sample was asked whether blacks should have as good a chance as whites to get any kind of job *or* whether whites should have the first chance; 52 percent favored discrimination, 42 percent opposed it. When the same question was asked again in 1963 (just a year before the passage of the first major Civil Rights Act), 80 percent opposed discrimination.[14]

Symbolic versus Reallocative Issues

Like the problem of racial discrimination, most social problems touch both on the perceived self-interest of various segments of the population and on values—religious, moral, political, and so forth—that have deep emotional resonance for those who hold them. The two are not necessarily related. Far from serving merely as pretty costuming to hide a naked self-interest, values can be in conflict with self-interest and can serve as an impetus for behavior in their own right. We use the term "reallocative" to describe those issues that deal *primarily* with social groups' self-interests in gaining and maintaining wealth and power. These tend to be issues that to some extent involve taking wealth and power from those who presently have comparatively greater amounts of these goods and redistributing them in a more egalitarian fashion, so those who currently have little will in effect have a net gain. We use the term "symbolic" to refer to issues that involve *primarily* attitudes, values, sentiments, and knowledge, because the confrontation centers around items that in themselves are trivial (such as mode of dress, color of skin, length of hair) but that are used to stand for, or symbolize, deeper issues. Thus, the civil rights movement was greatly angered at black Americans being called "colored" or "Niggers," while the prejudiced whites persisted —not because it matters what a person is called, but because such terms come to stand for a definition of inferiority, stigma, and discrimination.

14. National Opinion Research Council, *Public Opinion Quarterly*, 32 (1968), 139, 145.

Coming to accept, or at least to tolerate, items that have been invested with such symbolic meanings means occasionally that the symbol has changed (for example, long hair no longer signifies rebellious youth), but more often that a measure of acceptance of the values involved has been reached. For example, calling blacks "blacks," rather than "Niggers," or women "women" rather than "girls," "chicks," or "broads," indicates at least a measure of acceptance of the values involved. That, in turn, means that action on their behalf has a wider consensual base.

Whereas most social problems and the policy interventions proposed to resolve them have both reallocative and symbolic elements, a relatively clear line of demarcation can usually be drawn between them. Indeed, some problems involved primarily issues of one or the other kind. Thus, how society is to respond to homosexuality is almost exclusively a symbolic issue. Its status as a social problem is rooted in public attitudes and not in objective factors such as the lack of resources that characterize poverty as a primarily reallocative issue.

Some segments of the public think of homosexuality as sinful, or morally decadent. Persons who feel this way typically view the gay rights movement of recent years in terms of the decline and fall of Rome; in other words, as signifying a loss of values, decay of the social fabric, a threat to the family. Historically, this view of homosexuality is responsible for state and local laws designating it a crime. Another segment of the public perceives homosexuality as a form of mental illness that, unlike other mental illnesses, is seen as potentially contagious, especially to impressionable children and thus poses special problems. This group generally sees psychiatric treatment for homosexuals as the desired remedy.

In recent years, however, the proportion of the public that has come to view homosexuality as a tolerable phenomenon or even as a perfectly normal "sexual option" has grown. A little over one-third of the women interviewed in the 1940s by Kinsey in his famous study of sexual behavior disapproved of homosexual behavior, whereas over half had no opinion and less than 10 percent were tolerant.[15] A 1973 replication of the Kinsey study by Morton Hunt found roughly the same percentage disapproving, but the tolerant and noncommittal percentages reversed, with half the sample expressing tolerance and only 10 percent expressing no opinion.[16] Whereas 60 percent of Kinsey's sample said they would remain friendly with a person they learned was a homosexual, 68 percent of Hunt's sample said they would do so. Over half of all women and close to half of all men surveyed by Hunt disagreed with the statement

15. Cited by Morton Hunt, *Sexual Behavior in the 1970's* (Chicago: Playboy Press, 1974), p. 304.

16. Ibid.

that "homosexuality is wrong." Asked whether homosexuality should be legal, nearly half thought it should be while about 40 percent thought it should not. Among those under age 35, 60 percent thought it should be legal, 30 percent opposed making it legal and 10 percent had no opinion. Close to 25 percent of the males and over 25 percent of the females agreed with the statement that "being homosexual is just as natural as being heterosexual."[17]

A three-way debate among those who view homosexuality as immoral, as a mental illness, or as a normal sexual state continues. Knowledge (for example, about the "danger" to young children or about possible hormonal differences between gays and straights) figures in this debate, but there are no definitive findings on these questions. Efforts to settle homosexuality's social status center around the law and public attitudes as they are influenced by the pronouncements of psychiatry and the churches. Many social scientists argue publicly that homosexuality is a typical "crime without victim,"[18] one of those crimes that cannot be repressed anyway, such as gambling and prostitution. Thus, as is typical in the case of symbolic social problems, at issue here again are concepts of "right" versus "wrong" and the question of what is the proper public viewpoint: acceptance, tolerance, or rejection.

Reallocative issues, in contrast, involve the distribution of properties, income, jobs, judgeships, congressional seats, and memberships on decision-making boards. Here the dynamics are quite different. When such coveted possessions are to be allotted in greater measure to one group, often the allotments of some other groups must be cut. At the very least, the share of new wealth, new jobs, and new positions that goes to already advantaged groups must be less than what it could have been. (For example increased hiring of women and minorities means fewer jobs, at least fewer *new* jobs, for men and whites.) Thus, while resolution of symbolic issues exacts from individuals a change of heart and mind, reallocation requires concessions, such as giving up control over resources or command positions.

The consensus-building procedures for the two types of issues are different. In the first case, education, persuasion, agitation, and psychodrama (for example, "consciousness raising" and symbolic gestures such as draft-card burning or gay demonstrations) play central roles. Above all, many millions of hours of arguments go into changing the attitudes of whites toward blacks, of men toward women, of Vietnam "hawks" toward "doves." Quite different procedures are available for reallocation,

17. Ibid.

18. Edwin Schur *Crimes Without Victims* (Englewood Cliffs, N.J.: Prentice-Hall, 1974).

including enlarging the total pie, a procedure that is most conducive to reallocation because all sides can increase the absolute size of their share and do not have to clash over changing proportions. If there is to be a reallocation of existing resources, it is often necessary to come to some agreement on a method for staggering the changes (for example, a goal to achieve equal numbers of women in all ranks of a faculty, but only over an agreed upon period, often a quite long one). Finally, third-party subsidies are often part of the process. Thus, when railroad workers and management could not agree to a cut in the locomotive crews and a major strike resulted, the deadlock was quickly resolved when the federal government offered, in effect, to pick up the tab, by allowing the railroad companies to get tax benefits that made up for their concessions to the unions.

Factors in Consensus Building

When we explore the formation of consensus for dealing with social problems, we face a variety of social groups that have conflicting (or potentially conflicting) values and interests, which they nevertheless manage to submerge, at least in part, beneath a sense of shared concern; the groups take the view that what is in "the public interest" or "fair" can therefore be accepted.

The initial positions individuals bring to the process are affected by the basic values they acquire as they grow up.[19] Because families tend to transmit above all the values of the particular regional, class, ethnic, religious, and other subcultures they belong to, societies typically require nationwide consensus-building mechanisms to balance the resulting heterogeneity. Often this is accomplished through a uniform public school curriculum prescribed at the national level. However, unlike such countries as Israel and France, which do have such a national curriculum, most of the real decisions on educational policy in the United States are made by local school boards and individual school principals, teachers, and parents. And, of course, there are private and religious schools that are outside the framework of public education. As a result, the local schools tend to reinforce the particular subculture rather than transmit an integrated set of national values.

19. A complex issue we do not explore here is whether people's values are simply whatever they pick up from their society and subculture or instead reflect a combination of inputs from these sources *and* their basic human needs. According to the first position, people can be made to believe in virtually anything, can be made to be loving or hostile, hedonistic or uptight; see for instance Ruth Benedict, *Patterns of Culture* (New York: Penguin, 1946). According to the second position, if the values society promotes are "dissonant" with people's basic needs, alienation will result, and this, in turn, will cause personal and social problems. For further discussion, see Etzioni, *The Active Society*, Chap. 21.

Universal military conscription or national civic service is another device for inculcation of shared national values, but such programs do not exist in the United States. Service in the present voluntary army is an experience most young Americans do *not* share. The same must be said about volunteer services such as VISTA and the Peace Corps.

The major sources of homogeneity of values for Americans are the media, in particular television. Television is indeed our lowest common denominator, and the values it carries may well be increasingly shared by Americans (for example, the search for quick happiness, glorification of consumer products, violence, a certain lip service to values). However, such a consensus may be neither appropriate nor sufficiently profound to support the needed antidotes to social problems.

Although many social scientists agree that in the United States, the media, especially television, play more of a role in consensus formation than do the schools or military service, there is much less agreement on the nature of the media's effect. Rather than attempt to settle this matter here, we briefly mention the relevant features of the debate. One controversy concerns the media's influence. Some hold that it can mold basic viewpoints and values; others maintain that it is most effective where it is least needed, that it can reinforce views people already have but can rarely modify them.

A second controversy concerns the direction of media's effects. The alienation school and the neoconservatives tend to suggest that the effects are uniform but in opposite directions. The alienation school sees the media as a major force promoting *false* consciousness and an unauthentic consensus. Both are *a*political in nature (the modern equivalent of providing circuses when bread is short) and deflect attention away from basic structural features of society to consumer products, Hollywood glamor, daytime games, escapist soap operas. Neoconservatives see television as loaded with liberal biases, propagandizing a slanted and unrealistic consensus. The pluralistic consensus school stresses the openness of the media, which allows a variety of viewpoints to gain a national hearing—and a national following.

How one judges these contrasting positions depends, in part, on what one uses as criteria for comparison. If one contrasts the era of radio and television with earlier eras, there is probably now a greater ability to reach a nationwide audience and to mobilize a wide range of socioeconomic groups. At the same time, if one compares the American media with the Soviet system, American mass communication is surely much less encompassing, thus more pluralistic, though possibly more subtle and more effective.

All said and done, the American consensus is relatively narrow, shallow, and apolitical. It encompasses matters of taste, products, movie heroes, but not the foundations of social policy. Moreover, whereas consensus on abstract values may often appear quite high, when it comes to specifics, the population is often evenly divided on details that fit *opposing values*. Thus, in one study, 89 percent of respondents endorsed "free speech for all no matter what their views might be" yet at the same time 50 percent favored censorship of books containing "wrong political views."[20] Another study reported that over 95 percent polled agreed that "Democracy is the best form of government," that "Public officials should be chosen by majority vote," and that "The minority should be free to criticize majority decisions." However, 21 percent favored restricting the franchise to taxpayers, and 49 percent wanted to restrict voting to the well informed.[21]

American consensus tends to be weak also because it is often more "anti" than "pro." Thus, in the 1940s and 1950s, anti-Communism, the "cold war mentality," and fear of "subversives" provided a kind of consensus that was mainly negative in nature. When Samuel Stouffer asked a national cross section of Americans in 1954 if an admitted Communist should be allowed to make a speech in their community, only 27 percent said yes; 66 percent favored removing books by an admitted Communist from the public library; 91 percent felt that a high school teacher who is an admitted Communist should be fired.[22] It might be said that on these matters it was easier for potentially conflicting subgroups to agree what to be against than what to be for. With the demise of this orientation, lack of consensus seems to have grown more widespread or at least has become more visible in particular among various age and ethnic groups.

It might therefore be fair to conclude that when all the societal consensus-building mechanisms are taken together, they prove to be relatively weak. They leave the citizens underprepared for unified action and put heavier emphasis on the last stage of the process—the give and take *within* political institutions.

Consensus Building: Institutionalized Politics

At least since the onset of the New Deal era, the scope of social problems for which the government has taken on responsibility has continually broadened. In addition, the circle of people whose consensus

20. Herbert McCloskey, "Consensus and Ideology in American Politics," in Joseph R. Fiszman, *The American Political Arena*, 2nd ed. (Boston: Little, Brown, 1966), p. 46.

21. James W. Prothro and Charles M. Grigg, "Fundamental Principles of Democracy: Bases of Agreement and Disagreement," *Journal of Politics* 22 (Spring 1960), 284, 285.

22. Samuel Stouffer, *Communism, Conformity, and Civil Liberties* (New York: John Wiley & Sons, Inc., 1967), pp. 40, 41.

must be won has expanded to include most members of society, while the number and scope of shared values about what ought to be done and how has narrowed. At the same time, as we have seen, several of the consensus-building mechanisms relied on in other countries to bridge such differences are comparatively weak. The result has been an ever increasing burden on the institutionalized politics, the structure of representation, and it has shown the strain. This may be one of the deeper reasons why the American guidance system is relatively unable to cope with the high volume of demands put on it; it is able to "settle" only slowly on which course to follow, taking a few issues at a time. Accelerating environmental challenges and accumulating internal demands, both calling for collective action, have "overloaded" the system. We should say a few words about the system itself before further exploring its weakness.

Ideas for social policy come from many parts of the social structure: intellectuals, clergy, social movements, political leaders, citizens. A number of correctives that eventually became government policy were originally proposed by extremist groups or social movements—the advocacy of social security by the Townsend Movement is a case in point. In 1934–1935, in the midst of the Great Depression, Dr. Frances E. Townsend, a retired California physician, launched a campaign for "Old-Age Revolving Pensions." Townsend's proposal called for paying every person over age 60 a pension of $200 per month on the condition that they give up all gainful employment and spend the money within 30 days. In addition to providing for the needs of the elderly, the idea was to open up jobs to the unemployed young and to stimulate the economy through greater purchasing power. Critics countered that the plan would cost $24 billion a year to implement, an amount that was then half the national income. But when the idea proved immensely popular, especially among the elderly, Townsend Clubs sprang up across the country and the circulation of the Movement's weekly newspaper soon reached 200,000;[23] a considerably more moderate version of the plan became the Social Security Act of 1935.

Closer to our own time, concepts of civil rights that eventually became the core of the Kennedy-Johnson legislation and administrative programs were first popularized by Martin Luther King, Jr., as well as by other black leaders and organizations and by thousands of black and white activists, especially students, who went on freedom marches, staged sit-ins, and took part in protest demonstrations. The ideas of revenue sharing and negative income tax, now official policy, started as eggheads' concoctions. (Although first advanced by the Nixon Administration in

23. John A. Garraty, *The American Nation*, Vol. II, 3rd ed. (New York: Harper & Row, 1975), p. 728.

1969, a revenue-sharing proposal had previously been prepared by Walter Heller, economic advisor to President Johnson, and Joseph Pechman of the Brookings Institution conducted a major feasibility study of it.)[24]

The long-standing ability of the Democrats and Republicans to co-opt concepts and ideas popularized by social movements and third parties, thereby absorbing their momentum, has been a major reason why American political consensus building has remained so firmly institutionalized in the two-party system. Policy proposals that gain a following are picked up and championed by politicians in different factions of the two major parties, first, as a rule, in speeches, then in local primaries, which in increasing measure over recent years have served as testing grounds to assess the popular base for new positions. Policies (and their champions) that survive these trial runs go on to do battle at national party conventions. At this juncture, the various positions are typically reduced to no more than two packages: the Democratic and Republican "platforms," which contain positions on most social problems from poverty to housing, from drug abuse to mental health.

These, in turn, are often summarized, for the convenience of the public, in terms of *gestalts*, or generalized contexts, representing overall party ideology such as a more activist federal approach versus greater reliance on self-help and the marketplace, and so on. The national election then tests which package can attract the greater following. Without going into it more fully here, this multilevel consensus-building process —as distinct from a single-level one (in which national issues are put directly to a national referendum or plebiscite)—is, *in principle*, an effective procedure.[25] The advantages of such an approach can be demonstrated in a classroom. First try to reach a negotiated agreement via a class-wide discussion on, for example, when the class should meet for an extra session; then try to arrive at the decision by dividing the class into subgroups and asking them to send a representative, with suggestions for a preferred time, to a meeting of representatives. (In the process, it is necessary not to bind the representatives to specific details but to grant them some latitude.)

Although the *direct* method may give a greater sense of individual participation, as in "Navaho" democracy, where all, not just a majority, must reach agreement if serious issues are at stake, it can require many hours, if not many days, to reach a resolution. This limits the amount of collective decisions that can be made using this procedure. It also

24. Walter W. Heller, *New Dimensions of Political Economy* (Cambridge, Mass.: Harvard University Press, 1966), Chap. 3.

25. For additional discussion, see Etzioni, *The Active Society*, pp. 477–480.

allows leaders, who address directly the whole group, to have more impact than is the case in the representative democratic structure.

As we noted in the chapter on power, however, the American representative system does not guarantee an equal voice to all. This is because through control of more resources and greater cohesion and higher mobilization, various social groups can more effectively promote their preferences than can weaker groups and certainly the unorganized citizenry at large (see Chapter 5, pp. 117–118). Various suggestions to curb these forces have been made, including the equal-time rule on television and radio, attempts to set limits on campaign contributions and expenditures, and proposals for government-financed campaigns to take the edge away from wealthy candidates. Most of these proposed schemes are poorly implemented, and those that have been effectively introduced did little to make the electoral process anywhere near egalitarian and open.[26] The result is the adoption of policies that many people, often the majority in fact, do not truly support, yet voted for, either because they wanted to vote down a still worse alternative and only two were given, or because they were temporarily swayed, only to find after the election that the policies being followed are not truly responsive to their preferences. Hence the high proportion of Americans who feel alienated, who believe nobody cares about their views (49 percent in 1972).[27] Thus, people's perceptions about social problems are not effectively expressed and taken into account, *and* the lack of support for the policies pursued becomes in itself a main source of social problems—namely, the sense of alienation that in turn expresses itself in a multitude of personal and collective problems.

Although this distortion caused by powerful interest groups is often noted and its significance questioned,[28] much less attention has been paid to the problem of "overload," that is, the incapacity of existing consensus-building structures to generate sufficient consensus on many unresolved issues with the needed speed. Thus, at any given moment there are scores of *major* policy issues, and many more subsidiary ques-

26. See Watts and Free, *State of the Nation*, 1974, p. 70.

27. We use pre-Watergate figures because Watergate distorted the picture by first increasing the alienation to 59 percent before Nixon's resignation and then temporarily pushing it down to 53 percent after the resignation. Harris Poll, *Current Opinion*, vol. 2, issue 8 (August 1974), 87.

28. See William Kornhauser, " 'Power Elite' or 'Veto Groups,' " in *Social Realities: Dynamic Perspectives*, ed. George Ritzer (Boston: Allyn & Bacon, 1974), pp. 391–405; David Riesman, *The Lonely Crowd* (New York: Doubleday, 1953), pp. 257 ff.; C. Wright Mills, *The Power Elite* (New York: Oxford University Press, 1956), pp. 242–268. Also Arnold M. Rose, *The Power Structure: Political Process in American Society* (New York: Oxford University Press, 1967); and Harmon Ziegler, *Interest Groups in American Society* (Englewood Cliffs, N.J.: Prentice-Hall, 1964).

tions, on which there are basic nationwide disagreements. Included are such basic questions as whether the government or the market should have the greater role in dealing with social problems; how much should be done for the poor and the minorities; how crime should be dealt with, and so on.

The weakness of the political institutions—specifically, their inability to respond rapidly, to develop coherent comprehensive policies—is one reason for the sharp rise in *extra*institutional expressions of needs, such as, demonstrations or collective violence, in recent years. Alienation theorists view this as an indication of the control of the existing regime by the powerful; to consensus theorists, it points to deficient institutional machinery; to the neoconservatives, such extrainstitutional expressions represent illegitimate challenges to political authority; the guidance theorists see evidence of disturbed representation and a politically underdeveloped (hence, overloaded) system. But all, at least implicitly, perceive the same phenomenon: less work performed by the system; more challenges to it.

New Mode of Participation

One answer to the problem of lack of consensus, unresponsiveness, and overload deserves special attention because it is being tried so widely and in so many forms. This solution involves increased participation in the handling of social affairs in ways that bypass national, state, or local political mechanisms and that function directly at places where people work and live, via "private governments." Thus, if one is concerned with the way health care is being provided, one can act upon this concern by participating in the governance of the hospital, clinic, or Comprehensive Health Planning Agency; if education is the problem, one can join the school board; if one is bothered by housing problems, one can join the tenants' association, and so forth. It is argued that in this way the various distorting effects that enter into the bigger picture can be avoided, first of all because the citizens know where "the shoe pinches" and, second, because such localized participation permits consensus building to be carried out day in and day out, not merely at infrequent election times.

A 1973 study reviewed fifty-one case studies of citizen participation in governmental "boards" (charged with policy setting and ultimate budgetary authority) or "committees" (with limited authority or of strictly advisory character). The study showed that 69 percent of the governing boards but only 52 percent of the committees were judged as having implemented citizens' ideas to a significant degree.[29] In 1970, Edward J.

29. Robert K. Yin, William A. Luca, Peter Azanta, J. Andrew Spindler, "Citizen Organizations, Increasing Client Control over Services," prepared for the Department of Health, Education, and Welfare, R1196–HEW (April 1973).

O'Donnell and Otto Reid mailed questionnaires to a probability sample of local welfare agencies asking administrators whether or not boards and committees had a "noticeable effect" on the day-to-day services provided by the agency. In 458 replies, 68 percent of the boards were cited as having had a noticeable effect as compared to 48 percent of the committees.[30]

These data are of course not definitive proof that citizen representation makes the organizations involved more responsive to consumers, and there are other studies whose findings are much less reassuring than the ones just cited.[31] Note also the main counterargument, namely, that citizen or consumer participation reduces efficiency and undermines professionalism of the staff or is incompatible with unionization (which cuts across the facilities and hence makes it difficult to deal differently with each board). Our purpose here is not to review the complex literature about the effects of such direct democracy but to introduce it as a mode of building more consensus than is possible otherwise.

A quite different approach in seeking a responsive social policy involves, not an attempt to gain a say in existing institutions, such as schools or hospitals, but rather the formation of "alternative" institutions in which the basic pattern of ownership and control is meant to secure participation—such a pattern is found in parent-run day-care centers and patient-run health clinics. These movements hope to serve as bridges to a more participatory and decentralized society of the future; in the meantime, they hope to lead at least to more responsive life-styles.[32] This is not the place to try to assess those efforts; it is sufficient to point out that while millions of people have experimented with them, thus far, most people seem to pass through these alternative institutions, rather than stay with them (with some significant exceptions).[33] Opponents point to this rapid turnover as an indication that the high demands participation puts on the citizens are not compatible with the citizens' preferences. The proponents argue that, given a different societal context—for instance, a less demanding work day and less "brainwashing" by television, as well as larger opportunities to get used to the new freedoms and responsibilities—people will be able and willing to adhere to highly participatory institutions and communities.

30.   Ibid., pp. 28 ff.

31.   See, for instance, Citizens Board of Inquiry into Health Services for Americans, *Heal Yourself* (Washington, D.C.: American Public Health Association, 1972).

32.   Christopher Lasch, "Can the Left Rise Again?" *New York Review of Books*, Vol. 17, No. 6 (October 21, 1971), 36–48.

33.   Robert Houriet, *Getting Back Together* (New York: Coward, McCann, and Geoghegan, 1971); and John Fischer, *Vital Signs, U.S.A.* (New York: Harper & Row, 1975).

AN EXAMPLE: CONSENSUS AND
PROGRESS IN CIVIL RIGHTS

In 1963 a broad coalition of groups and individuals, both black and white, banded together under the charisma of Dr. Martin Luther King, Jr., and staged a march on Washington calling for enactment of a federal law banning racial segregation and discrimination. This demonstration, marking the high point of the civil rights movement's strength and unity, culminated nearly a decade of dramatic events: the Supreme Court's 1954 decision in *Brown* v. *Board of Education of Topeka, Kansas;* the Montgomery, Alabama bus boycotts of 1955–1956 out of which Dr. King's leadership had emerged; the turmoil in Little Rock, Arkansas, where federal troops were called in to assist in integrating the schools in 1957; the Greensboro, North Carolina, black sit-ins at segregated lunch counters in 1960; the 1961 freedom rides to desegregate interstate buses; James Meredith's registration at the University of Mississippi under National Guard protection in 1962; and the confrontation between civil rights demonstrators and Commissioner Bull Connor and his police dogs in Birmingham, Alabama, in early 1963.

Some 200,000 people took part in the Washington march, and by the end of the year smaller-scale demonstrations and boycotts had taken place in 800 cities and towns across the country. According to a Harris poll taken that year the sentiment of the American public was by then largely behind the demonstrators: 62 percent of Americans approved of the Supreme Court's decision to desegregate the schools; 91 percent favored federal action on black voting rights; 86 percent favored federal action on job rights; 68 percent supported federal action on public accommodations; 68 percent favored mixed lunch counters; and 52 percent supported federal action for integrated housing.[34]

The movement's efforts were now focused on achieving congressional passage of a major piece of civil rights legislation. To this end, seventy-nine civic groups participated in an intensive lobbying effort that included, in its final stages, monitoring the attendance and voting behavior of each congressman at the crucial junctures of the bill's career. The number and variety of groups that took part illustrate the broad consensus that had evolved around the passage of this legislation; they included civil rights groups such as the moderate National Association for the Advancement of Colored People (NAACP), the more militant Congress On Racial Equality (CORE), and the still more militant Student

34. Harris Poll, August 15, 1963.

Nonviolent Coordinating Committee (SNCC), the Negro American Labor Council, the Urban League, and the Southern Christian Leadership Conference (SCLC), which was led by Dr. King; religious groups such as the National Council of Churches, the National Catholic Conference for Interracial Justice, and the Anti-Defamation League of B'nai Brith; and other groups including the Americans for Democratic Action (ADA), the American Veterans Committee, the National Bar Association, the National Newspaper Publishers Association, the American Civil Liberties Union (ACLU), and many labor unions. The Leadership Conference on Civil Rights (which was first formed in 1949, with a membership of twenty groups), served to pull together the efforts of this broad coalition pushing for civil rights legislation.[35]

These efforts were rewarded the following summer when Congress passed the 1964 Civil Rights Act, whose aim was to bring an end to discrimination in employment and public accommodations, by threatening to cut off federal funds to states and local governments that failed to enforce the laws' provisions. It was not the first civil rights act, but it was both the most advanced one by a long shot and the first with any real teeth in it.

The attention of the civil rights movement shifted next to voting rights. A march was held in March 1965 in Selma, Alabama, to dramatize the obstacles to black voter registration. A few months later the Voting Rights Act was passed. This act authorized the U.S. attorney general to appoint federal examiners in areas where discrimination was prevalent and strengthened penalties for interference with voter rights.

Already, however, the tide was beginning to turn. In the summer of 1965, a riot broke out in Watts, the black section of Los Angeles. It was the first of a series of riots that by 1968 had touched virtually all major cities in the North. The riots were led by blacks who bolted the nonviolent coalition and consensus because they felt progress was too slow. At the same time, court decisions and legislation passed had convinced many whites that blacks had made or been given great gains, though these gains were largely symbolic. Whereas only 34 percent of whites felt blacks were pushing too fast in 1964, 49 percent held this view in 1965, and 85 percent thought the pace was too swift in 1966.[36] A reaction had set in. More and more whites, especially of lower-class, working-class, and traditional middle-class background ("hard hats"), felt that blacks were getting better breaks in jobs and in education than they themselves were

35. *Civil Rights Report, Congressional Quarterly* (Washington, D.C., 1970), pp. 3 ff.

36. Hazel Erskine, "The Polls: Speed of Racial Integration," *Public Opinion Quarterly*, 32 (1968), pp. 513 ff.; see also "After the Riots: A Survey," *Newsweek* August 21, 1967, pp. 18–28.

getting.[37] Finally, many whites who had favored or at least were not strongly opposed to integration in public accommodations (for example, buses, lunch counters, hotels) and in schools felt that a line should be drawn at housing. In a 1966 poll, roughly 50 percent opposed it.[38]

At the same time a split began to develop among blacks over whether to continue to stress nonviolent tactics and racial integration or to begin to push for economic, political, and social power for blacks. In the summer of 1966, Stokeley Carmichael, the newly elected chairman of SNCC, launched the "black power" movement. The new militancy was symptomatic of the widening gap between black and white perceptions of the progress being made and of growing black impatience. Although polls continued to show a majority of blacks committed to nonviolent tactics and the goal of integration rather than black power, a 1966 survey found that only 20 percent of blacks felt the riots were hurting the black cause, whereas 34 percent felt they helped. In contrast, white feeling, not merely against riots, but against all demonstrations, was continually rising. In 1963, 51 percent believed demonstrations helped rather than hurt the black cause, but this figure had dropped to 31 percent by June 1966. By October 1966, 85 percent felt that the civil rights movement was hurt by demonstrations,[39] though a majority of whites still favored aiding the poor (many of whom were black), giving jobs to the unemployed (65 percent), and rebuilding the ghettoes (63 percent).[40]

The growing lack of consensus was soon reflected in the Congress by weakened support for antidiscrimination measures and other reforms particularly favorable to blacks. The coalition between blacks and whites that had prodded Congress began to crumble as white members were expelled from SNCC and then from several other major civil rights organizations as they shifted closer to the black power position. Within the Congress, the coalition of northern Democratic and Republican members that had halted southern filibusters and secured the passage of previous civil rights bills fell apart over the open-housing provision of a new bill proposed in 1966; the bill was defeated as a result.

As long as Lyndon Johnson remained president, the administration continued to press for action on civil rights despite the coolness of Congress and the growing resentment on the part of the white majority. In 1968, a fair-housing law was finally passed, though, as evidence of the

37. Angus Campbell, *White Attitudes Toward Black People* (Ann Arbor, Mich.: Institute for Social Research, 1971), pp. 1–20.

38. "Black and White," *Newsweek*, August 22, 1966, p. 26.

39. Harris Poll, October 10, 1966.

40. Ibid.

changing situation, there was highly organized lobbying against the bill by the National Association of Real Estate Boards.

The strong backlash vote for George Wallace in the 1968 primaries, the defeat of the Democratic presidential candidate, and the election of Richard Nixon reversed the role played by the two previous presidents in promoting desegregation and the ending of racial discrimination. Keeping true to his "southern strategy" of attracting the votes of the once "solid South" with the understanding that he would slow the momentum of government action on civil rights, Nixon brought the White House closer in line with the changing white majority and Congress. Upon coming into office, the Nixon Administration decided to refrain from cutting off federal funds to school districts which failed to adopt approved desegregation plans.[41] In addition, the administration went on record as in favor of neighborhood schools (and thus opposed to busing) and, in general, against doing anything about *de facto* school segregation.[42] Daniel Patrick Moynihan, the president's chief domestic counselor, urged a policy of "benign neglect" of blacks' needs.

In Congress, the old civil rights coalition grew ever more strained as whites who had previously supported civil rights increasingly perceived black demands as "reallocative." Antagonism between blacks and organized labor grew in 1969, for example, when labor supported a congressional attempt to defeat the Philadelphia plan, a proposal to provide jobs for blacks on federal construction projects, and to weaken the Equal Opportunity Commission enforcement powers. At the same time opposition to efforts to combat *de facto* school segregation intensified in the North. A 1971 Gallup poll found 76 percent of Americans opposed to busing.[43]

By 1973, according to Gallup, virtually no one supported busing any longer. Asked which if any of several ways listed would be best to achieve racial integration, only 4 percent of whites (and 9 percent of blacks) cited busing. While only 19 percent of whites and 9 percent of blacks were opposed to integration as an abstract value, the support for specific measures was thin. Only 22 percent of whites favored more housing for low-income families in middle-class neighborhoods; only 27 percent favored changing school district boundaries to achieve integration.[44] Efforts to involve blacks directly in the control of institutions in

41. *Civil Rights Progress Report 1970* (Washington, D.C.: Congressional Quarterly, 1971), p. 50.

42. Ibid., p. 51.

43. Gallup poll cited in Wattenberg, *The Real America*, p. 252.

44. "Gallup Finds Few Favor Busing for Integration," *The New York Times*, September 9, 1973.

the ghettoes continued, though no data on their scope and effectiveness are available.

In summary, there was a close correlation between the scope of the consensus to reform and congressional and White House reforming efforts. It is irrelevant here to establish whose "fault" it was that the consensus divided; the main point is that as it subsided, so did public efforts.

IN CONCLUSION

The ability to deal with social problems and their underlying conditions depends in part on effective consensus on what is to be done. The more groundwork for consensus is laid by educational institutions, the less is the role of the media and the political institutions. At the same time, the more rapid the environmental, social, and moral change, the greater the need rapidly to generate consensus on new issues. National politics, local politics, participation in "private" governments, and formation of alternative institutions all play a role. Currently, all taken together, they do not seem to generate the consensus and expeditious agreement on policy that its implementation requires. Thus, considerable disagreement exists on most aspects of most social problems; this, in turn, is reflected in frequent policy changes, and in the inadequate support for the policies tried. Where consensus is richer and deeper, all other things being equal, more progress is achieved, as illustrated by the 1964–1965 successes of the civil rights coalition.

It is here that guidance theory finds its democratic base, not in the formalistic, civics text formula of "one man, one vote," the majority ruling, but in the deeper sociopolitical sense. A policy that does not have the support of a public consensus, for whatever reason, is expected to be ultimately ineffectively implemented and in itself a source of social problems. And without sufficient capacity to generate authentic consensus, some problems may gain attention, yet remain unresolved; others may be treated with antidotes that the public will not tolerate; and still others remain the intensive concern of minorities fated with an indifferent majority.

POSTSCRIPT

FOR SOME ECLECTICISM

Society's response (or failure to respond) to its problems depends upon the combined action of the five sets of factors we have explored in Chapters 3 through 7. Although it is true that specific problems may be relatively more affected by one factor than the others, especially over a limited period of time, all are operative all the time. Thus, although a lack of basic knowledge about biological processes may well be the chief obstacle to a cure for cancer, other factors may be at work, including: the poor administrative design of the War against Cancer, lack of power to penalize severely those manufacturers who make use of carcinogen (cancer-causing agents) in foods and drinks and absence of consensus on banning smoking.

The reminder that all five guidance factors are at work simultaneously amounts to more than a warning to social science chemists not to forget an essential ingredient in concocting their analytic brew. It stresses our divergence from single-factor approaches as well as the diversity of the intellectual sources we draw upon. Thus, our theoretical concern with the role of knowledge and goal setting—when *combined* with other factors—recognizes that the wiser we are, the better our society may be, but rejects the Enlightenment conception of knowledge and willpower as *the* movers of societal mountains. Similarly, our interest in values and consensus reflects our indebtedness to Durkheim, Weber, and many other social scientists who have pointed to the importance of nonrational preferences and bonds. However, such indebtedness does not mean that we must embrace the view of some sociologists that societies are consensual entities. In the same vein, our attention to power and status-tied resources reflects our indebtedness to *Realpolitik* and Marxist analysis, though again we do not subscribe to the thesis that these factors are more "basic" than the others. A combination of enlightenment, voluntarism, and concern with value and an analysis of power, exercises, resource distribution, and redistribution thus is the cornerstone of our approach to the understanding of the process that underlies the ways in which societies and their members approach social problems.

GUIDANCE FOR WHAT?

We have established the multiple characteristics of an effective guidance mechanism. We ask now what purposes does it serve? The answer to this question points toward a conception of a future that society is committed to bring about or, to adapt a term fashioned by the existentialists, toward the society's central project. For Western societies, in times of peace, the central project has been, for many decades, the pursuit of ever greater affluence. This has meant a continual quest for more easily produced and plentiful products to be quickly devoured, chiefly by individuals seeking to upgrade their personal "standard of living." Of all activities, production has been the most rewarded, and consumption of material objects has been the reward. Thus, the logic of manufacturing and the marketplace took priority over that of the family and community, both of which were redesigned to suit the needs of the productive society.[1]

Indeed, many of the problems troubling contemporary Western societies, when they are not directly traceable to this emphasis on economic rationality, are stubbornly resistant to our efforts to eradicate them, at least in part because their resolution conflicts with industrial efficiency and economic growth. Thus, the hiring of women and minorities may or may not lead to less efficient production (because some have lower skills as the result of past discrimination), but this is of prime concern only if social justice is considered secondary to productivity. Similarly, environmental protection, product safety, and workers' safety —all of which may cut into profits *and* efficiency—are viewed either as barely tolerable or as "high priority," depending on the core project. In a different vein, our belief that many noneconomic activities should be conducted in an economically productive and profit-making way has

---

1. For a recent discussion, see Richard A. Peterson, *The Industrial Order and Social Policy* (Englewood Cliffs, N.J.: Prentice-Hall, 1973).

often led to blatant neglect of ostensible goals and sometimes to serious abuses. (For example, proprietary nursing homes have been frequent abusers of the aged and disabled.)[2] Proposed interventions are judged not only in terms of relative efficiency but according to whether they buttress or undercut the core assumptions of materialism. For example, most Americans feel a "right-to-work" relief program is a better way of coping with poverty than is a program providing a guaranteed minimum income, which, it is often alleged, destroys work motivation.

The question now is will the materialistic project dominate our future as it has our recent past? In the late 1960s and early 1970s many Americans began to try on a colorful wardrobe of "alternative life-styles." How much of this was fad and how much was forecast is not yet knowable. Many of the more bizarre variations are already nearly extinct (for example, nude encounter groups and nomadic flower children), but more moderate adaptations are being adopted by an increasing number of people. These new life-styles *might* become the basis of a new central project (most societies have one).

One of the strongest candidates for such a new project appears to be the exploration of *"inner space,"* that is, the search for greater insight into self and better relations with others. Such an exploration is evidenced by the therapy boom, the wide audience for pop psychology, and the growing interest of men in the "emotional area" once relegated almost entirely to women. Other contenders include the *literati* society, which in contemporary terms would probably involve a further heightening of the current interest in college education, adult education, and various cultural activities—from home weaving to ceramics—aimed at self-expression rather than at a particular market. Still another is the *activist* project, which might encompass renewed political activism on the local and national level, an extension of voluntary service activities, and increased participation in such "private governments" as tenant associations, parent-teacher's groups, hospital boards and advisory councils, and the like. All such future projects would not replace production, but would downgrade it to the level of a secondary activity, just as "inner space," education, culture, and politics have been given lesser emphasis in the materialistic society.

Still, it may be that the materialistic project is not on its way out, that it is merely winded and will soon catch its breath and be off and running again. Some observers predict that resource shortages and economic crisis will resurrect the success ethic of early industrialism, though a shift to a nonmaterialistic project would also entail an adaptation to these conditions, as they are all less economically demanding. (In-

2. Mary Adelaide Mendelson, *Tender Loving Greed* (New York: Knopf, 1974).

terpersonal encounters, reading, and participation in public affairs are much less "capital intensive," less energy consuming, and less polluting than is conspicuous consumption.)

The net effects of improved societal guidance on current social problems is contingent on the emergence of a new core project, rather than the continuation of the present one. Will the future be responsive, at best, to the "lowest" layer of basic human needs,[3] those for material comfort and security, or will it attend as well to the "higher" ones that affect self-esteem and self-actualization? Will the societal project respond to the needs of all society's members or will it serve the desires of the few to the detriment of the many?

The answer, as I see it, depends in part on historical forces beyond our personal and possibly collective control. As for what we can accomplish, our capacity for societal guidance depends on how much of ourselves we are willing to invest in understanding the societal system and its guidance mechanisms and to what extent we can organize ourselves to act on this understanding. Only when the average citizen becomes less locked into materialism and turns instead to a socially active project can the energy needed for "proper" and effective societal guidance be generated. *"Proper"* here has a double meaning. On the one hand, we refer to a guidance mechanism rich in knowledge, wise in goal setting, effectively administered, and based on authentic consensus with minimal application of power; on the other hand, we refer to a mechanism geared to a societal project that is responsive to all the needs of all the members of society. Social scientists who are not allied with any partisan group cannot but gear their analysis to a transformed society responsive to all.

3. For a discussion of basic human needs, see Amitai Etzioni, *The Active Society* (New York: Free Press, 1968), Chap. 21. For additional discussion, see Amitai Etzioni, "Creative Adaptations to a World of Rising Shortages," *The Annals of the American Academy of Political and Social Science*, 420 (July, 1975), 98–110.

NAME INDEX

SUBJECT INDEX

A

Action space, 38
Active society, 95–96
Affirmative action, 80–81, 91
AFL-CIO, 141, 144–145
Agricultural Workers Organizing
  Committee, 144
Alcoholics:
  estimated numbers of, 73–74, 137
  public view, 77
  treatment, 76–77, 105, 110
Alcoholics Anonymous, 8, 76–77
Alcoholism, 5, 6, 10, 19, 36, 46–47,
  73, 84
Alienation approach, 3
  alternative to consensus, 9
  dynamics in, 13–15
  human nature, 12–13
  media view, 158
  poverty in, 29–30
  power in, 125–126, 135–136
  societal reality, 11–12
  See also Conflict approach
Alternative institutions, 14, 164
American Association of Manufac-
  turers, 137
American Indian Movement, 140
American Medical Association, 125,
  137
American Soldier studies, 60
Americans for Democratic Action, 140
Anomie, 24
Antabuse, 76
Antipoverty legislation, 61
Applied vs. basic research, 50–51, 67
Atomic Energy Commission, 68

Authority, 21ff., 68, 97

B

Basic research, 52, 64, 67
  vs. applied, 50–51
Bill of Rights, 69
Bureau of Labor Statistics, 59

C

Cancer, 34–35, 52, 110
Capitalism, 9, 10, 11
Central project, 43
Chicago School, 16
City master plans:
  incrementalist, 98–99
  mixed scanning, 99–100
  rationalistic, 96–98
Civilization, conflict theory, 10
Civil rights, 44, 154, 160, 165ff.
Coercive compliance, 103–104
Coleman Report, 52
Collective conscience, in conflict
  theory, 10
Collective good, 86
Communes, 15
Compliance, 103–105
Comprehensive Health Planning
  Agencies, 121–122
Comprehensive planning, 86
Conference on Economic Progress, 59
Conflict approach, 3, 49–50
  human nature, 12–13
  societal reality, 9–11
  See also Alienation approach